Living for Brecht
The Memoirs of Ruth Berlau

Living
for Brecht

The Memoirs of Ruth Berlau

EDITED BY HANS BUNGE

TRANSLATED BY GEOFFREY SKELTON

Fromm International Publishing Corporation

NEW YORK

Designed by Jacques Chazaud
Printed in the United States of America
First U.S. Edition

Library of Congress Cataloging-in-Publication Data

Berlau, Ruth, 1906–1974
Living for Brecht.

Translation of: Brechts Lai-Tu.
Includes index.
1. Brecht, Bertolt, 1898–1956—Biography.
2. Authors, German—20th century—Biography.
3. Brecht, Bertolt, 1898–1956—Relations with women—
Ruth Berlau. 4. Berlau, Ruth, 1906–1974—Relations
with men. 5. Actresses—Denmark—Biography.
I. Bunge, Hans. II. Title.
PT2603.R397Z562413 1987   832'.912   87-14658
ISBN 0-88064-071-5

Translator's Note

As the editor of this book, Hans Bunge, rightly remarks in his Afterword, "Authors of memoirs must be granted the right to tell their story as it exists in their own memory." He has in consequence refrained from amending factual errors by altering the text or supplying footnotes. I as translator have observed the same principle.

In quotations from Brecht's works I have, wherever possible, made use of the English translations published in Methuen's edition of the plays, poetry, and prose, edited by John Willett and Ralph Manheim. In cases where no English version is yet available in print (notably the "Lai-tu" stories), I have made my own translation.

An ancient Indian philosopher made it a matter of principle to recognize as his pupils only those students who had spent four years listening to him in silence.

I have followed Bertolt Brecht's path for twenty-five years, and been silent just as many. Now I shall try to speak.

—Ruth Berlau

Contents ✺

PART I

Memoirs

1 🪶

Brecht went to bed early and rose even earlier. Everything he did was work, and he never stopped working. He divided up his time, wasting none of it. The effect of this on me was that I could never exercise control over my own time, and consequently had none. There was always something to be done for Brecht. I still have the feeling that in the course of twenty years I never once sat down.

Everyone who worked with Brecht had the same experience. Elisabeth Hauptmann, his collaborator over many years, once described it exactly. During his American exile Brecht, who lived in California, paid a visit to New York, where I was then living. Since Elisabeth Hauptmann was within easy reach, I said to her, "You can write in German, I can't. You can write in English, I can't. Couldn't you spend two hours a week working for Brecht, or better still, two hours twice a week?" She replied, "Two hours for Brecht? Whoever works for Brecht works not less than twenty-four hours a day."

It was quite true. Yet the duties were so interesting that one was glad to take them on voluntarily. Brecht never forced, or even asked, anyone to do anything at all for

3

him. Never. On the contrary, he was always saying, "Now you've been working hard again. You mustn't." But when he would politely ask, "Where are those pictures you took yesterday?" then naturally they had to be ready, otherwise Brecht would not have been able to get on with his work. This usually meant doing them during the night.

Working with Brecht was not always easy. Indeed, it was often quite difficult. But I had the advantage of having joined the Communist Party before I met Brecht.

2 🍃

I do not know what my father's occupation was. He called himself a dealer, but he had no proper office. Perhaps he could best be described as a jack-of-all-trades. To put it more precisely, he earned a lot of money during the First World War. This was nothing unusual in Denmark, for between 1914 and 1918 the country was not directly involved in the war, though getting business from it. We were very rich. As a small child, I remember, I ran around in long furs.

At that time I saw my father as a fine character and a wonderful person. Later my opinion of him changed.

All I wish to say about my mother at this stage is that I love her very dearly. I also have a sister. She is a little older than me, and she was studying law when she became ill. Nobody knew whether it was schizophrenia or another kind of mental illness; in any case, she had to spend eighteen years in an institution. After her release she married, and now she is in the best of health.

I was born in Copenhagen on August 24, 1906. My parents sent me to a convent school in order to learn French. To my very great disadvantage I stayed at school only until my thirteenth year, though I was not a bad pupil and found school quite interesting. When I left, the Mother Superior said to me, "You will regret it later." It is a statement I have never forgotten. If there is anything in my life that I regret, it is my abysmal ignorance. In my firm opinion, there is no way of making up in later life for what one has missed in one's youth.

I had already left school when a disaster occurred in my family. My parents' marriage was not happy, and one day my mother attempted to take her own life. She very nearly succeeded, and it was clear from all the circumstances that it was a genuine attempt.

My sister and I discovered this unhappy event at the very moment we were trying to deal with another. I had become "engaged" at a very early age and now found myself pregnant. At my age this was a punishable offense in Denmark, but (unlike my sister) I did not take it very seriously. I resolved to have an abortion. My sister was against this and urged me to go to my aunt in Hamburg and have the baby there. However, I was not to be persuaded, and one evening we went to see a "baby farmer" to ask whether she would carry out the operation. She consented.

When I and my sister returned home, Mother was not there. Relieved, we sat down to consider how to find the money for the abortion and arrange things so that no one else should know. At some point my sister left the room. Suddenly she came running back, screaming, "Mother is there, lying on the floor!" Our house was very large, and that is why we had not discovered earlier that Mother had gone into a little storeroom, slashed her wrists, and, as an extra precaution, turned on the gas. Luckily we found her just in time.

Thus ended this curious marriage. Before taking Mother off in an ambulance, I wrote a note, "Mother in hospital."

There was no need to say more, since all the floors were covered in blood, smeared around as we dragged her from the room. Anybody could see at once what had happened.

We were waiting outside the operating room in which Mother was being stitched together when our father arrived. He had been to one hospital after another in his search for us. Drunk, he uttered only a single sentence: "Final chapter—scandal." After that, it was two years before I was able to face my father again. I no longer wished to live with him in the same house, and I also did not wish my mother to return to him. She remained in the hospital a long, long time, and she narrowly escaped being transferred to an institution on account of her suicide attempt.

We heard nothing more of our father. Our home was broken up, and I started selling coffee, since we had to earn our living somehow. I also wanted to help my sister pay for her studies.

The coffee business went very well. I had a bicycle, on the carrier of which I stacked my little packets. People bought them willingly, for I was a little cheaper than the shops—and on top of that I was at that time very pretty. I just rang the doorbell and, when someone came to the door, used my powers of persuasion. Gradually I established a regular clientele, which grew and grew. Some people even bought ten pounds at a time. I was earning well, and since Mother was being looked after by the national insurance, there was only myself and my sister Edith to be cared for.

But one day things went wrong. It started to rain, and that did no good to the coffee on the carrier of my bicycle. I remember sitting all evening in front of the stove, drying out my coffee beans, and at the same time wondering how to find something safer. I began to study the newspaper advertisements.

A very elegant dentist in a very elegant neighborhood was seeking an assistant. I introduced myself, and he hired me. I thoroughly enjoyed running around in a white cap and apron, but I did not take my work very seriously. Required to clean the drills, I either threw them away or simply put them back where they belonged. I opened the door when the bell rang but otherwise did not bother myself with the practice.

I was not prepared to devote more time and energy to it, since the wages the dentist paid me were insufficient for my needs. Besides, even if I had wanted to, I could not give up my coffee business entirely, for people were stopping me in the street, wanting to buy.

Then I discovered yet another occupation. The dentist had a platinum lancet in his laboratory. I found that by heating it, one could burn thin lines in wood, and I made professional use of this discovery. I could, for example, burn children's names into rulers and then sell them. From then on the dentist's practice stank not only of phenol and lysoform but of burned wood and roasting coffee as well.

But as time went on I found my work at the dentist's less and less convenient. He now began treating patients only by appointment and between each would take an hour off. During these rest periods he would go out to buy chocolate or coffee (not knowing, of course, that there was a supply of coffee in his own laboratory). All this culminated in his becoming determined to marry me. He was in fact a very nice man, but all the same I had no wish to marry him. First, he was too boring, and, second, I found the odors in his surgery more and more revolting.

* * *

I decided to put myself as far as possible beyond my dentist's reach, and so came on the idea of making a bicycle trip to Paris. Since for that I should need money, I went to the newspaper *Extrabladet* and offered to send them reports about my journey. They agreed and promised to pay me at the rate of 25 Öre a line. Later I discovered I had been cheated, the rate for foreign dispatches being much higher. But I was inexperienced then; it was my first journalistic job.

I set off on my bicycle, rucksack and sleeping bag on the carrier. It was a horribly boring journey, but each evening I sat down and invented the things I should like to have happened. At that time I was very romantic, and among the stories I made up was one about people following me in a car through woods and across fields, and my making my escape by shooting up their tires. Each evening I wrote something of that kind and, as I did so, carefully counted the lines, for at 25 Öre a line I had to write a lot in order to make it pay. All the same, I hardly imagined that all of it would find its way into print. Astonishingly, I proved this time to be too pessimistic.

Before I arrived in Paris a reporter picked me up on the road and interviewed me. Next day I read in the French newspapers: "A Danish girl is cycling alone from Copenhagen to Paris in order to buy a lipstick." So I was made very welcome in Paris and passed around from one place to another. It all went wonderfully, and I thoroughly enjoyed myself.

Unfortunately, the return journey was just as boring as the journey out. Nothing happened, nobody followed me, attacked me, or did anything else to me. I had once again to call on my powers of invention.

In my last article before my arrival in Copenhagen, I announced that I would reach the main square at about ten o'clock. I arrived punctually, my object being to collect my money from the newspaper office. But it was quite impossible to get through. The square was full of people, chief among them bakers' boys, milk delivery men, and news vendors. "Let me through, please," I said. "There's not a chance just now," they replied. "What's happening, then?" I asked. "A lot is happening," a small boy answered. "Ruth's arriving this evening!" I was welcomed like a world explorer, received my money, and treated myself to an enormous party.

Shortly after that, I cycled to Moscow for the newspaper *Politiken*.

When I went there, I was not yet a communist, and I stayed with bourgeois families. One evening—I think it was in 1930—I was playing bridge with the editor of *Politiken* and happened to say, "I should rather like to see Russia for myself. I think I'll cycle there." The editor promptly replied, "Start tomorrow morning. We'll pay you a thousand Kronen a day." This really happened! I said, "I shall need a small map, not a detailed one, but just enough to show me where I am." He promised, "It will all be there. Leave tomorrow."

I set out next morning at nine o'clock. The journey is not as difficult as one might think. Russia is not so very far from Denmark.

You don't cycle through Sweden, of course, but just put your bicycle on a train. That gets you to Stockholm quite quickly, and to a room in the very fine Grand Hotel. Although I arrived on a bicycle, I was given a bath and a massage like all the other guests. From there I went by ship to Turku in Finland and then cycled to Helsingfors (now Helsinki). There my difficulties began.

I had no visa, and it was by no means easy to gain entry to Russia. I went to the Soviet Embassy to ask for a visa, and the people there just laughed, saying, "You're just like all those mountain climbers wanting to bring back an edelweiss or at least a label from every peak they scale. What are you after? A hammer and sickle?" I shed a few tears, then said, "No, I want to see what life in the Soviet Union is really like. I've heard that there are no people out of work and that women have equal rights . . ." There was no need to say more. A man seized my passport and stamped the visa in it. That man was Ambassador Maisky himself. He was very nice, but he wanted to get to know me better before I went on my way. He invited me to spend a few days as his guest. I was to accompany his wife to museums and tell her all about myself.

At the Russian border I at long last found myself sitting on my bicycle. I knew only one sentence in Russian: "Please tell me the way to Moscow." I can still remember it now. In Moscow I learned another word: *drug*, which means "friend." The people everywhere were very, very friendly toward me.

A drama festival was in progress in Moscow when I arrived. Every day saw me sitting in the director's box enjoying the performances. As a result, the articles I wrote for *Politiken* were all about the theater. The editor sent me a telegram: "Not interested in what you saw in theater. Write about other things." I knew exactly what he wanted to read—that the Bolsheviks had hacked me into mincemeat and that I had been raped. That would have made a good story for *Politiken*. But after only a few days in Moscow I knew I should write no such story, for—to quote Bertolt Brecht—"conditions are not like that." The newspaper sent the Danish consul to my hotel to tell me to return to Copenhagen, with or without my bicycle, preferably by air, but anyway at once. And so my career as a bourgeois journalist came to an end, with a telegram

11

I addressed to the editor of *Politiken*: "Kiss my arse." It should not have shocked him too much: The phrase can be found in Goethe as well as in Bertolt Brecht.

I stayed three months in Moscow. Then I did indeed return home by air, but they put my by now decrepit bicycle on the plane with me. "You should keep that," my Soviet friends told me, "and put it in a museum." The journey was rather tedious, though I remember we had to make a few forced landings. But at last, miraculously, we reached Copenhagen airport.

From there I cycled straight away to the office of the Communist Party. "I should like to have this little red book," I said to a man there. "That's not so easy," he replied. "First of all, we must see what you can do." "I can do nothing," said I, and he, "Then I'm afraid you can't have the book." I thought awhile. "I was thinking of taking up acting." His answer to that was, "We're busy just now preparing an exhibition of children's drawings. Go and put them in order. If you do it properly, we'll see whether you can have the little red book, as you call it, or not."

The exhibition really was in a mess, and I was at my wit's end what to do. Then I remembered a childhood experience. I was sitting in a hall full of children, and on the stage stood an artist. He drew pictures of lions and tigers that looked as if they were just about to spring on us children. At the very last moment bars were put in front of them. The child who reached the stage quickest would be given the drawing. I rushed forward like a savage each time, and collected quite a few of them. When the man felt he had drawn enough, he began to tell us jokes. At the end I went home with a chin dislocated by too much laughing. A doctor had to be called to put things right, which he did with a hefty blow.

I now decided I must have this artist for my exhibition.

His name was Robert Storm Petersen (he died a few years ago). Though not a party member, he was very close to us in spirit. Brecht was very fond of him—I think he could be called his favorite cartoonist. But Storm Petersen was not just a cartoonist, he was an actor as well. For sixteen years, I believe, he spent every evening on stage. There was one act of his of which Brecht was particularly fond, and he described it at least a hundred times. A man goes to a party, and in order not to forget his hat on leaving— something one always does—he takes along an apparatus for the prevention of forgetting hats. The apparatus Storm Petersen brought on was larger than two cars together, and it filled almost the whole stage. Storm Petersen sounded the horn, the hat flew to and fro, spun upward and downward—but the machine with its multiple arms always managed to catch it.

It was to Storm Petersen that I now cycled and de- manded from him three caricatures of a kind I had seen in the Soviet Union, depicting a general, a clergyman, and a capitalist. Storm P.—as he was always known in Denmark—actually drew them for me. He also helped me with useful advice, so that the exhibition turned out quite well. I was given my party book.

Incidentally, the stern man who had first questioned me was Aksel Larsen, the former party chairman. To- gether with him I later wrote many scenes for my workers' theater, for Larsen knew the current problems better than I did.

Before I founded the workers' theater I was a pupil at the drama school of the Royal Theater in Copenhagen. It is a terrible school in which one learns nothing, though one recites poems and studies roles for two whole years. Only two of the subjects interested me: elocution—though the teaching was not as good as that of Helene Weigel—

and theater history with Professor Torben Krogh. The other lectures were the same as in any other school and were of no interest to me.

After the first year of my studies, an experimental theater offered me the very good role of Anna in a production of Brecht's *Drums in the Night* (*Trommeln in der Nacht*). Our producer was Per Knutzon, who later directed Brecht's *Round Heads and Pointed Heads* (*Die Rundköpfe und die Spitzköpfe*). The only success I ever had as an actress was in the role of Anna.

Following *Drums in the Night* my impulse was to leave the Royal Theater, for other theaters were offering me engagements, and even a salary to go with them. In the Royal Theater I had to pay out money myself: Forty Kronen a month! But Andreas Møller, the director of the Royal Theater, told me, "Better stay here. We'll pay you 75 Kronen, and you can make your debut as Puck in *A Midsummer Night's Dream*."

That is an awful memory. Our director, though very clever and talented, was completely crazy. I would have forgotten all about him if Brecht had not shown an interest in him. Brecht and I in fact wrote some observations on him together.

I fell off a high ladder onto the stage. That was my debut as Puck in *A Midsummer Night's Dream*. It was a nightmare. I could not even remember my lines. The prompter, a kind old man, kept whispering to me, "Out of the oak and up into the fir." Following his directions I hopped around in a tricot, which made me look completely naked. Our talented but crazy director had hair stuck on me in all the places where hair naturally grows.

Storm P. also took part in this production. I got him into the Royal Theater because I needed him; otherwise it was so boring there. The theater people declared he was just a music-hall comedian, but I thought otherwise. Thank goodness, they took him on.

Storm P. was cast as Snug the joiner. During rehearsals my face muscles were sore with laughing, for he kept on making jokes. He never knew his lines. Before the opening night I implored him not to fool about. He gave me his hand and said, "I swear not to say a word outside my part—which I can't remember anyway." Sitting up in my tree as Puck, I saw Storm P. playing the lion below. After he had killed Thisbe, he turned, raised a leg, and made water over the body. I laughed so much that I nearly fell from my tree. But after the performance Storm P. came to me looking quite innocent and declared, "I didn't say a word."

After this fiasco—and it really was a fiasco!—I played only a few small roles. I did my very best to ensure that I should not have to act. When I was offered something, I would always say, "I can't manage that. It's completely out of character for me."

I rejected all roles—or banished them from my memory—with one exception: that of Christine in Strindberg's *A Dream Play*. She is always saying, "I paste, I paste," and later I was often reminded of this line when I was pasting up Brecht's model books (*Modellbücher*). But of course I did not know that then, and it is a role I have always loved. However, my acting seemed to have a somewhat mystifying effect on the critics. "It's a pity about Ruth Berlau," they said. "Whenever she appears, it becomes a different play."

Apparently, after my Puck in *A Midsummer Night's Dream*, I was thought to be very gifted. But all that was quickly forgotten when I became a communist. Or am I imagining things?

However, I did once get a fine part that I enjoyed playing, and it was connected with a very important encounter in my life.

The director turned up with a thick manuscript, and my first terrified thought was: How can I learn all that? I just cannot learn lines. But then I read the play, and had the feeling that, remarkably, the woman who had written it knew something about Karl Marx. I accepted the role and started to rehearse. Both the director and the theater boss told me, "It's horrible what you're doing." I arrived at each rehearsal with a load of new ideas, and they were at a loss what to do with them. By this time I had already met Brecht, and when I visited him he gave me hints for the production.

The theater people threatened me, "The author will be at the dress rehearsal," but I did not allow myself to be frightened off, and her visit was for me a particularly gratifying experience. At the dress rehearsal I saw a tall and striking woman sitting in the front row. I played my role in the way I had worked out with Brecht. For instance, in order to show the woman is wealthy, and the way in which she flaunts her wealth, I carried an enormous beaver fur around with me. It was always somewhere, either round my shoulders or on my arm; I really made use of it. After the rehearsal I was called to the director's office. I was a bit nervous. But as I entered, the author sprang to her feet and embraced me. "My Martha!" she said. "My play has been done in London, in Stockholm, and in Helsingfors, but I've never seen a Martha like yours."

This was my first meeting with Hella Wuolijoki, who later gave shelter to Brecht and his family in Finland, and with whom Brecht wrote *Puntila*. While I was doing Martha in Hella Wuolijoki's play, Bodil Ipsen had the role of my mother-in-law. She was always saying, "Tomorrow is *The Women in the Pissoir* again." We could not get our tongues round the name Niskavuori. Hella Wuolijoki wrote four plays about the women of Niskavuori, following them, so to speak, from the cradle to the grave.

The last time I saw Hella Wuolijoki was in 1954, about a week before she died. The fourth play about the women of Niskavuori happened to be due for performance, and Hella, eager that I should see it, ordered seats for herself and for me. The play was not doing well (none of her plays, incidentally, ever did), but for her sake the management drummed up a few people to occupy the front row. Hella did not even notice that there was nobody else in the theater. The rows behind us were completely empty.

Hella also insisted that I should have an interpreter. The theater director took on the task himself, being unable to afford the expense of engaging one especially for me. But I could not bear watching and listening and having someone whisper in my ear at the same time. The director and I went out. Hella did not notice that either, so rapt was her attention. At the end we returned to clap furiously, and Hella went home happy. In a woman of such great personality, it was a curious aberration. She wanted to write plays, but she couldn't. In this connection she really was a bit dotty.

My final role with the Royal Theater was that of a nun. I have forgotten the play's title, but I do remember a scene in which the nun plays with a mirror in her cell. She is caught in the act and brought before a judicial panel of nuns. She defends herself against the charge: "I was not looking in the mirror, just trying to catch the sun's rays and bring light into my cell." At this point I stole a glance into the stalls. I could see fine gentlemen in their dinner jackets wiping tears from their eyes. I was astonished. I must possess talent after all—anyway, in a theater where tears are shed.

Problems of the kind dealt with in this nun's story truly do not interest me, and it was for this reason that I became involved more and more in the setting up of a workers' theater. Its origin was quite curious. One day the stage doorkeeper in the elegant plush-lined Royal Theater phoned me in my dressing room and said, "There are four odd-looking men down here, asking to speak to you." I told him to send them up. In walked four sailors who had written a play. They asked me to help with the production. I said, "I know nothing of ships and sea voyages." That was not necessary, they assured me, for they knew all about that themselves. "You only need to tell us where to stand and where to go. We'll look after the rest."

The play was eventually staged with my help, and it marked the birth of my workers' theater—incidentally, the first workers' theater in Denmark. It grew, new people joined, and we were invited to take part in the theater festival in Moscow. We named ourselves RT—Revolutionary Theater. We traveled on a Russian ship to Leningrad, and from there by train to Moscow, where we played. When our company went home, I remained in Moscow to study the children's theaters. Here I met the Norwegian writer Nordahl Grieg, to whose play *The Defeat* Brecht provided a sort of counterargument in *The Days of the Commune* (*Die Tage der Commune*). Nordahl Grieg and I worked together often over several years. He was just as interested in workers' theaters as I was.

At that time I was married to Professor Robert Lund, but it turned out to be a mistake on my part. I know he is an eminent scientist. His publications have been translated into several languages. He is a very fine person. He looked—and remarkably enough, still looks—wonderful. I met him at a party in his country house, and it was (as always with me) a case of love at first sight. At about four in the morning, when we were all hopelessly drunk, I saw him walking around his garden. During the party some bottles and glasses had got smashed, and Lund was picking up the pieces: he had four children, and children like to go about barefoot. I must then have shown my adoration of him so clearly that he suggested we get married. I agreed, and on the whole had no cause to regret this decision. I was married to Robert Lund for ten years. The best times were our many journeys abroad. We went off every year, traveling all across Germany, or to Italy—Rome and Venice—or the south of France—Marseilles and Toulon. That was wonderful. In winter we went skiing in Norway, Switzerland, or the Italian Dolomites. He knew a great deal about art, and our journey to Florence remains for me an unforgettable experience.

I was twenty when we married, he forty. The difference in age worried me not at all. Later, perhaps, it might have become a problem, but during my time with him I never thought of things like that. Only the fact that he was not a communist did worry me a little toward the end.

3 🍂

Chance led in the summer of 1933 to my first meeting with Bertolt Brecht. He and Helene Weigel, his wife, were at that time staying in Torelore on the island of Thurø with Karin Michaelis, the Danish writer. Karin and Helene had been close friends in Vienna, and it was Karin's suggestion that she and Brecht should swap expensive Switzerland, where they had first sought refuge, for Denmark, where living was rather cheaper. Though it meant sacrificing their German-language surroundings, both Brecht and Helene found the idea sensible. The Nazi regime would not last long, they believed, and then they could return to Germany.

In fact, they spent only a short time on Karin Michaelis's large estate. Helene soon discovered an old farmhouse, which she was able to buy. They had to be careful with their money, but unlike so many other emigrants, they were not entirely penniless when they arrived. And it was here, in this "house with the thatched roof," as Brecht described it in his Svendborg poems, that the family lived until they were forced to move on further to Sweden. The house is not in Svendborg itself, but in the little village of Skovsbostrand on Svendborg Sound.

However, Brecht was still on Thurø when we first met. At that time I belonged to a students' committee that arranged artistic evenings. Its president was the Danish novelist Hans Kirk. We sat down with him to discuss our next program. They all looked at me. "You must go and see Karin Michaelis. She can give us a talk." To contact her would mean a five hours' drive, and, they pointed out, "You are the only one with a car." Robert Lund was the owner of a fantastic Lincoln, which he allowed me to use whenever I wanted. But in spite of that, I objected. "Karin can talk of nothing but vivisection," I said. Karin, who had achieved world fame with her incredibly bold and courageous autobiographical novel *The Dangerous Age*, was an antivivisectionist, and she made a habit of introducing her views on the subject into every lecture she gave. It was a subject that did not interest me, and I thought it would not interest our students either. Then suddenly I heard someone beside me remark, not directly to me, but more as if in the course of a private conversation with someone else, "Bert Brecht is living on Thurø now." And almost automatically, it seemed—quite without forethought—I said, "All right, then, I'll go tomorrow."

Not long before this I had played Anna in *Drums in the Night*. It had been my first encounter with Brecht's work. Except for *The Threepenny Opera* (*Die Dreigroschenoper*) we in Denmark knew nothing of his. Nobody seemed to have ever read his poems. But *Drums* had kindled an extraordinary flame inside me, and that was what persuaded me to go to Thurø.

So I made the five hours' drive across country, ending with a ride on a small ferry. I took two friends with me, an architect and a student of economics. Whether in taking this architect along, I had something special in mind, or whether it was just chance, I no longer remember. Possibly I knew by then that Helene Weigel was planning to buy and convert a house on Svendborg Sound, and maybe I thought that by bringing her an architect, I should get a chance of talking to Brecht about my workers' theater.

We settled our business with Karin Michaelis, and she invited us to spend the evening with her. Karin loved young people and was always eager to know what was going on. She put us up for the night in her own house, and the following morning I asked her, as casually as I could, where this man Brecht was living. I think subconsciously I was rather disappointed not to have caught sight of him somewhere along the road, though I had no idea what he looked like. Karin told us the way to his house.

So there we were, standing outside his door. We Danes are renowned for our friendliness and hospitality, but the cordiality with which Helene Weigel greeted us was unusual even by our standards. With her tremendous personality she exuded an air of sovereignty that impressed us, but at first also slightly intimidated us. Who expects refugees to show that much self-assurance?

There was no dismal air of uprootedness in this household. I knew many people who had fled to Denmark from the Nazis. None of them bore any resemblance to Helene Weigel, a frail woman of strange, unusual beauty. Possibly her ears were rather large—that is what people say when they wish to disparage her—but those animated lips, that narrow face! And those remarkable small, firm, expressive hands, which fascinated me then, and which, fifteen years later, I discovered anew when I saw her on the stage as Mother Courage, doling out her tots of brandy in the Thirty Years' War. These were the hands that bade us welcome and cooked our meal. There it suddenly stood on the table, as if summoned by a magic wand. I say that because that is really how it always seemed. Helene invariably cooked for her guests, though apparently she employed two cooks as well as a parlormaid. Yet when she sat down at table, she was always fresh and lively. She was also a unique conversationalist. It was a delight to talk to her: She knew instinctively what would interest her guests.

The mood that day was happy and cheerful. It was a lovely house, well furnished. I had no impression of poverty and harsh fate, such as I had experienced in the homes of other refugees. Helene had a talent for letting nothing get her down. She was very happy to have escaped the Nazis. The only thing that saddened her was that, during a short stay in Vienna on their way into exile, she had not managed to persuade her Jewish father to emigrate with them. He gave her a little money, and also some jewelery, to help them establish themselves.

Only Helene, Brecht, and their son Steff were in Denmark to begin with. Their daughter Barbara joined them later, together with Marie, their servant. Marie came from Augsburg and had worked for a long time for Brecht and Helene in Berlin, where she had managed Helene's household and also done some cooking, as well as cleaning Brecht's apartment daily. She rejoined Brecht and Helene at Skovsbostrand in 1933, and there she remained after marrying the local butcher. That was a splendid story, which amused Brecht very much.

Brecht and Helene were by this time installed in their house on Svendborg Sound, and the butcher called regularly in his van to deliver the meat. Gradually love blossomed between the treasured servant and the butcher, who was not the handsomest of men. I visited them recently, and found them very happy.

But back to Thurø, before Marie arrived on the scene. We were having lunch. When the dessert was served, I became acquainted with a funny habit of Brecht's. He took his little bowl of stewed fruit and vanished without saying a word. When he was gone, Helene assured us that the action was not directed at us. "After lunch Brecht lies down and takes a nap." The student of economy went off for a swim, and Helene commandeered the architect to discuss the conversion of the farmhouse in Skovsbostrand. I was left standing with my typewriter in front of the house, wondering whether to jot down some notes.

The first thing that had struck me about Brecht was his eyes: dark, clear, expressive, smiling eyes. And it occurs to me now that throughout the ensuing years we communicated with each other a great deal with our eyes—perhaps because we were so often surrounded by other people, and on parting, for example, could make contact only through our eyes.

At our first meeting he had given me his hand, at the same time taking a step backward. It was a trick of his that few would find easy to copy. Whatever you do, stay off the grass! Keeping your distance applied not only to his production technique, it was demanded in private as well. Once, very much later, I told Brecht of the impression his curious trick had made on me. He replied, "I'd heard that an actress from the Royal Theater had called. That made me wary." But during lunch we in fact established a good relationship, for Brecht was very full of fun, and so was I. I did not then realize that I was already in love with him.

He was wearing a blue boiler suit with a lot of pockets, round his waist a black leather belt. He was very slim, and he had well-shaped shoulders that fitted comfortably, each one, within a hand. I found this out later, when I so much loved clasping those shoulders.

I was still standing with my typewriter before the house, unable to make up my mind, when I heard a soft "Hallo"

24

behind me. This gentle, questioning call became for many women what one might call the central feature of their lives, as I myself was later to experience. They waited for the call, built on it, dreamed of it. I was hearing it then for the first time. (Now I feel I have gone deaf, for it is many years since I last heard it. Whom else in the world is there to listen out for, now he has ceased to call me?)

Brecht had ended his afternoon nap earlier than usual on the day of our first meeting. We went into his small workroom. I had made up my mind to request both material and advice for my workers' theater, and did not doubt for a moment that he would be ready to help. He told me he had made a play of Gorki's novel *The Mother*, and workers had taken part in the production. He mentioned the names of his collaborators, Slatan Dudow and Hanns Eisler, who had written the music for the play. All this was completely new to me. When he advised me to buy a projector, I laughed for joy. Only shortly before I had got one, and we had used it in our agitprop performances. Brecht was much impressed.

Our talk about the projector is all that I have retained of our first conversation—also that Brecht showed me a gray-covered book with the title *Versuche (Attempts)*. It contained the play *The Mother (Die Mutter)* together with a large number of notes. I said, "Lucky that you brought that with you; I can take it home with me at once." (Strangely enough, we used the familiar *Du* right from the start, something that Brecht did not normally do. But, my German not being fluent, I had difficulties with the polite form of *Sie*, and Brecht understood that at once.) As I went to pick up the book, he said he could not let me borrow it. "I wasn't able to bring much with me when I was forced to leave," he said. "I must keep the book here, I can't give it away."

But I had already learned something from Helene. She

had the practical good sense to make use of my architect for the conversion of her house, and I made use of an equally favorable opportunity to steal Brecht's book containing *The Mother*. The moment I arrived back in Copenhagen, I began to translate it. I wrote to Brecht, telling him I had the book. He forgave me my theft and came to the rehearsals when we staged the play.

When I left Brecht after this first meeting, I saw him standing on a green slope in front of his house. I called out to him, "Don't forget my address." He patted the pocket that lay over his heart. "No, no, I've got it here." His eyes and his laughter accompanied me back to Copenhagen, as well as the stolen book. Though afterward we met frequently, it was two years before we exchanged our first kiss.

There is something else I must say about this first meeting with Brecht and Helene Weigel. The thought suddenly came into my mind that Brecht might make a personal contribution to our students' evening, perhaps give a talk about the theater. He declined. "I'm no good at lecturing," he said, "but Helene might do something." I did not understand. "She's an actress," he explained. When his wife came in, I fell on her. "Helli, you must do something for us!" Brecht supported me. She asked whether I could find a pianist to accompany her. "I'll look after that," I said boldly.

I asked Mortensen, one of our best young musicians, whether he would play the accompaniments. Though he knew no more about Helene Weigel than I did, he agreed. The day for the students' meeting arrived. Once more I made the journey to Thurø—five hours there and five hours back—to bring Karin Michaelis, Helene Weigel, and Bertolt Brecht to Copenhagen. I dropped them off at my house, having a dress rehearsal with my workers' group to attend to, as well as all the final arrangements for the students' evening.

What happened in our large, elegant house I was told later by Brecht himself. As Mortensen rehearsed with Helene, Lund, who is very musical, kept interrupting, saying this, that, or the other was not right. A layman giving advice to professionals! But neither Brecht nor Helene was upset. Brecht only asked mildly, "Do you think so?" and accepted the criticism good-humoredly. He liked my husband from the start, and later they often played chess together. In his association with scientists Brecht was something of a snob.

In the evening they all arrived at the meeting in the best of spirits. Karin Michaelis duly delivered her talk. Charming and ardent as by nature she was, one always felt the urge to embrace her, whatever she said. Then it was Helene Weigel's turn. I had not heard the rehearsals and so knew nothing of her voice. Mortensen had asked me to turn the pages for him, and I took my place beside him at the piano. Helene started to sing: "When I gave you birth . . ." Two pages I managed to turn properly, then I forgot all about it and just sat back to listen. That voice up there—could it really be coming from this frail figure? Her glittering eyes transfixed us. Her art, devoid of all sentimentality despite the moving quality of the words, reduced us all to tears. "When I carried you in my body . . ." "I gave you birth . . ." "My son, whatever you do or try to do . . . stay close to your own people . . ." The young people wept openly. Someone in the audience was sobbing loudly. I remember thinking: Someone must have broken down or seen the light. But I was theatrically experienced enough to realize at the same time that artistic sovereignty of this kind, emotion of this depth, cannot be achieved without technique. I felt completely schizophrenic. At such great moments I am always aware of this dual consciousness within myself.

What can one do when three geniuses—Brecht with his words, Hanns Eisler with his music, and Helene Weigel with her voice—appear together all at once in our little Denmark? There is only one answer: Capitulate. This was in 1933, and not one of the people in the hall that evening has ever forgotten it. My one-time students have since become teachers, lawyers, professors, and so on, but when they hear Helene Weigel's name, and I mention the "Lullabies," they always shake their heads in disbelief, and their eyes soften—or harden, according to whether they have remained faithful to the song and its warning message or not. To the credit of my little native land, I must add that everybody who was present on that evening understood and was moved by, absorbed, and digested this great artistic achievement—I among them. It was sheer wonder.

To conclude the evening, my own little group took the stage. One of our sketches showed how little remains in a worker's pay packet after he has paid his rent, light, gas, insurance, and union fee. Admittedly the content was primitive, but it reflected our attitude in the days of agitprop. We took our task very seriously, and it was only years later that I understood why, at a certain point, Brecht almost collapsed with laughter. The main character, played by a carpenter named Gabrielsen, was standing on the stage, purse in hand, fumbling with a few coins and searching, searching for more. It had all been thoroughly rehearsed, but instead of following our instructions, the actor dragged the scene out unmercifully. I thought he had either forgotten his lines or, finding himself alone on the stage, was making the most of his opportunity. I was in despair. At that moment I heard Brecht's ringing laughter that later became so famous—well, famous to me at any rate. He was the only person in the whole hall who found it comic. He raised a finger and pointed to the empty purse. Why laugh, when the purse is empty? Because the main point is to learn why it is empty. Brecht was laughing because the worker did not realize he was being exploited. He was sitting, as he always did, at the back of the hall, and everyone turned indignantly to stare at him. But Brecht did not let that put him off.

After the show it was decided in the office that my workers should receive money and cigarettes. The question of my compensation was also resolved. Putting on shows like this cost me a lot of money, swallowing up all my earnings from the Royal Theater and more. All this business talk culminated in a fierce row, for only the prominent people in the audience were to be invited to the long, elegant table for a supper of sausages and potato salad; my group would be given nothing to eat. The noise I made out in the kitchen must have been audible as far away as the hall. Suddenly Brecht appeared behind me. "What's the matter?" he asked. How he had got into the kitchen I have no idea. "Come and join us," he urged me, "it's boring out there." I replied rudely, "It's sausages and potato salad I'm worrying about now." "But it's all there, isn't it?" he said. "Yes, but not for my people. Half of them are out of work. Are they to be sent home hungry?" By now the entire committee had gathered around us, murmuring their excuses: So many people . . . the tickets hadn't brought in much . . . anyway, one can't be expected to . . . and so on. Thereupon, Brecht led our chief actor, the out-of-work carpenter, to the table where the notables were assembled, sat him down, and began to discuss with him the scene with the empty purse. The elegant guests had to squeeze together, and my whole company got sausages and potato salad to eat. It was all Brecht's doing, and I loved him dearly for it.

Next morning Brecht invited me to his room. He took a manuscript from his pocket and read out to me passages from his "Ballad of the Reichstag Fire." My knowledge of German was not very great at that time, but above all it was the fact that Brecht himself laughed so much as he read that made it difficult for me to understand. His laughter was infectious, however, and soon I was joining in. He sang some of the verses to the "Mackie Messer" melody from *The Threepenny Opera*. While he was singing, Helene Weigel came in and gave me a black look. My conscience being clear, I did not understand the reproach behind it. Years later I understood it only too well. Helene was of course familiar with Brecht's ways, and she knew this was how his affairs always started. I have been told that usually he accompanied his singing with a guitar. In my case the guitar was lacking, but that, I think, was the only deviation from the rule.

Brecht went out of the room when he had finished singing. The manuscript of the ballad was still on the table, and I could now read it at my leisure. If scorn could kill, I thought, Hitler would fall dead on the spot. Brecht had still not returned. Suddenly, without knowing how it came there, I found myself holding a gray silk shirt in my hands. I buried my face in it: It smelled of earth. With beating heart I hid the shirt inside my jacket. But since Brecht stayed away so long, I became aware of what I had done. I put the shirt back in the place from which I had taken it. The smell of earth had made me feel quite dizzy.

The first play of Brecht's that I translated was *The Mother*. The immediate result was not good, for I kept too close to the original. This is certainly the main difficulty for Brecht translators. If they love Brecht—and presumably only those who do translate him—they try to copy the play in their own language. They want it to be as faithful as possible—and then nothing comes of it. I had exactly the same experience with my translation of *Señora Carrar's Rifles* (*Die Gewehre der Frau Carrar*).

While I was revising my translation of *The Mother*, it was of priceless help to me that we were at the same time rehearsing it. The worker-actors reshaped my text in the very act of speaking it. Brecht had already told me this would happen when I telephoned him during rehearsals, before he came along himself. "Leave it," he said, "it'll be all right. When the workers get into their parts and the production begins, they'll adjust the translation." And so it was, then as later, when together with Charles Laughton Brecht translated his *Life of Galileo* (*Leben des Galilei*), and Laughton as actor tried out the text.

In translating *The Mother*, the most difficult part proved to be the songs, for Eisler's music had to be taken into account. I asked Otto Gelsted, the Danish poet, to do these, and in his first attempt he failed to reproduce their biting quality. Helene Weigel, when she came to the rehearsals, helped us greatly. She could not speak Danish, but nevertheless she had a good ear for what did not sound right, and she was able to give Gelsted some tips. It lies in the nature of things that Brecht's poetry is harder to translate than his prose. None of the poems that Hays, Bentley, and others translated in America is quite right; they are either much too hard or much too soft, only their form preserved.

My production of *The Mother* in Copenhagen was based on the Berlin staging—to the extent, that is, that was then within my power. I had not as many photographs of the Berlin production at my disposal as are nowadays available to theaters everywhere in the *Models* (*Modellbücher*), but I had at least two or three of each scene—and together with those, of course, the direct help of Brecht and Helene Weigel.

We also copied Caspar Neher's stage decorations: plain white linen drapes that could be folded. This solution had been arrived at in Berlin to enable the stage, wherever it was, to be swiftly set and swiftly cleared—important, above all, when one had to reckon with police raids. This was something which, at that time, I did not have to bother about; the main advantage for me was that we were able to make the decorations ourselves. (Much later, when I directed *The Mother* in Leipzig—incidentally, its first production in the German Democratic Republic—I decided on this style of decoration yet again, because I love it so much.)

One of our problems was lack of money. Most of the members of my company were out of work, and the box office receipts were minimal, since our audiences consisted mainly of workers and students. Now and again we received a donation, but our means remained scanty. That was why, instead of a hall, I rented a large cellar for our rehearsals.

Once I accompanied Helene and Brecht down the cellar steps to a rehearsal. I was paying no particular attention to them, since for me everything was quite normal. But I suddenly noticed that Helene had tears in her eyes, and Brecht too seemed very moved. I had seldom seen either of them in that state. The reason? In Denmark we were still able to display the red flag quite openly. Helene and Brecht were recalling the time of their own production of *The Mother*. They too had rehearsed in cellars and given their performances in beer halls, but they had always had to keep a wary eye open for the police.

Dagmar Andreasen, who played the mother, was the only one of my workers who could speak German. In rehearsals Brecht had to make copious use of the language of gesture. Nevertheless, the workers understood him very well, and a really fine performance was the result.

We did not play in proper theaters but in factories, and we did not always do the whole play, often just a few scenes, such as "May 1" and "Copper Collection Center." By then I was already aware that in this way one can provide comment on topical political events. *The Mother* in particular provides scenes suitable for this purpose. I was proud of now being able to show off my projector to Brecht, using it as we did to establish relationships between topical events and the scenes we were playing. We projected cuttings and pictures from current newspapers, for example, on a large screen at the back of the stage.

Three actors in my company aroused Brecht's particular interest: Dagmar Andreasen, who headed the cast of *The Mother*—in Brecht's opinion her acting was truly epic; Gabrielsen, the carpenter who had played in the sketch with the empty purse; and a remarkable man whom everyone called the "dead mason." I had never given the matter a thought, but one day Brecht asked me, "Why is he called that?" I asked the company, then translated their answer for Brecht: "Because he has never really worked in his chosen trade." He had always been unemployed and only occasionally did a few small jobs. It was not that he was lazy, just that times were bad for masons in Denmark—then, and not only then. The "dead mason" was for some reason at loggerheads with the rest of the company, but in spite of that Brecht insisted on having him in *The Mother*, and he played the part of a worker.

When I staged *Señora Carrar's Rifles* with my company, I needed the sound of heavy gunfire behind the stage.

33

At that time we had no technical devices such as today's tape recorder, and Brecht advised us to simulate the sound of guns with drums. The "dead mason" performed that task with passionate dedication.

He also wrote poetry, and I translated his poems for Brecht. He responded by translating some of Brecht's poems into Danish. Then he volunteered for service in the Spanish Civil War. Before leaving, he had a final talk with Brecht in Svendborg. Brecht not only begged him to keep clear of the front line, but made him solemnly promise that he would. He should always have a notebook and pencil on him to jot down his impressions and observations. Brecht was convinced that the "dead mason" was a true worker-poet. He died in Spain, and one of his comrades, who had worked beside him in our theater and gone with him to Spain, told us how he died. It was a dreadful story. The fighters contracted a form of diarrhea that was just as infectious as dysentery, and they became increasingly weak. No one could discover a cure for it. Brecht insisted on being told everything in the greatest detail, and he was very moved to hear that shortly before his death, the "dead mason" had asked his comrade to rescue his notebook and take it to Brecht. The notebook got lost on the way, and nobody knows where the "dead mason" is buried. Many Danes who went to Spain never returned.

After *The Mother* I translated *Señora Carrar's Rifles*, which deals with Spain. This translation has been printed and published. The play was put on simultaneously in German and in Danish. In my workers' theater Señora Carrar was played by Dagmar Andreasen, who had had the main role in *The Mother*. She worked on the railway as a cleaner. She spent all day sweeping, wiping, and shifting things, then came in the evening to rehearsals. She was intelligent and very gifted. (Brecht liked her so much that ten years later he mentioned her in an article as the first actress who had based her performance on a model. She did not simply imitate Helene Weigel's interpretation but used it as a basis to build on.) The Danish production of *Carrar* turned out wonderfully, though of course it could not be compared with the production in German, for this had had Helene Weigel—who had already played the part in Paris—and actors who had emigrated from Germany. Helene unselfishly helped us with our production. Brecht himself came along, as so often, only three days before the premiere.

In Denmark I also translated *Fear and Misery of the Third Reich* (*Furcht und Elend des Dritten Reiches*), or at least some scenes from it, and these I staged in the workers' theater, which had grown much larger since I and the four sailors had founded it.

By the time I got to know Brecht, I had already written a number of articles and was in the middle of a book which I intended to call *Videre* (in English, *Further*). It was a novel, a love story (a conventional love story, I'd say today). Brecht was always wanting to be told what was happening in it, and every time I went to Skovsbostrand I had to translate for him what I had written in the meantime.

I came to the part where the two main characters quarreled. I still recall that her name was Katja and his Preben. After the quarrel Preben left in despair. Katja looked for him everywhere, but could not find him. At last she hit on the idea that he might be in the boat house, to which she then sped. There lay Preben in a pool of blood. He had tripped and knocked himself out on an iron spike. When I told Brecht that, he asked, "Why that? Wouldn't it be better for him to be in the boat house playing Skat with the fisherfolk?" I was shattered—but not so shattered that I stopped writing altogether. The novel was completed and published, and in it Preben still lies bleeding in the boat house.

Among the things I heard from Brecht at that time was that there is no room in art for sentimentality. I was very sentimental, and in this regard I cannot be said to have absorbed very much from Brecht. I am very sentimental still.

Videre was not my last novel. There was another one, which I wrote together with Brecht. It is called *Jedes Tier kann es* (*Every Animal Can Do It*). I provided the material, Brecht the wording. This collaboration taught me a great deal.

But now there was little in the way of collaboration. I was able to pay only short visits to Skovsbostrand, having in the evening to return to Copenhagen. The Royal Theater, my workers' theater, party work, and many other things kept me fully occupied. When I did visit Brecht, we played chess, and now and then he would show me what he had been writing.

It was typical of Brecht to ask people who told him something interesting to write down their experiences. I had a great many things to tell, for I knew a lot of people. "Write that down," he would always say to me. He fashioned a little book with black cardboard covers, cut out letters of the alphabet from newspapers, arranged them to form words, and stuck them on the cover to make a title: *Die zu kleinen Inseln* (The Too Small Islands). By that he meant Denmark. In this book Brecht collected and revised my notes, and in the process I learned gradually how to relate things in five or six lines. They were very like his own Keuner stories, splendid little pieces.

Some of the things that interested him especially he noted down himself. During the summer holidays I spent my whole time in Svendborg. Each morning I would bring Brecht my notes, and he would give me what he had written down for me. That was the beginning of our exchange of work.

Brecht once said, "The worst thing about the islands that are too small is that really nothing is lacking. Everything is there, but only in terribly small proportions. There is nothing that can be used as a measuring rod, since the measure is itself too small. There is a hill in Jutland called the Hill of Heaven (Himmelberg): it is two hundred meters high." But is it not astounding how much of his time on the "too small islands" Brecht was later able to put to use?

Brecht most enjoyed going into the sailors' taverns in Nyhavn. They stand one beside the other, most of them in cellars. He did not care for the large restaurants, if only because of the way the waiters would eye him suspiciously from head to foot. With the sailors he could stick to his boiler suit and be warmly welcomed. He was particularly fond of one sailor. One day he found him sitting alone in a corner, and somebody had placed a lampshade on his head. Three months of hard-earned cash had somehow vanished. He greeted Brecht by raising the lampshade as if it were a hat, saying sadly, "This is all I've got left now to give my mother."

The sailors would pass around pornographic pictures and sing sea chanties. Brecht was sympathetic toward prostitutes. "They are large-hearted people," he said. This was after overhearing a conversation: There was a sailor whose money had all been spent, but he was taken on all the same—on credit.

I think that for a time Brecht's best friend in Skovsbostrand was a small and cheerful cigar dealer. Since there was no telephone in his own farmhouse, Brecht would say, "I'm going to the tobacconist's to make a call." There, in the backroom, I heard him speaking Danish—or rather, mangling it. With the cigar dealer he argued

37

over the difference between hand-rolled and machine-rolled cigars. And there was another important question: Which sort of beer should he drink, Tuborg or Carlsberg? Brecht chose Tuborg, and every evening, in undisturbed privacy, he would drink two bottles of Tuborg and indulge in an orgy of Danish cheeses. Before he sat down Helene had to go around with a fly swatter, swatting every fly in sight. He could not bring himself to kill anything. He had a great respect for spiders.

Brecht did not like us to go on chatting after he had retired with his Tuborg. He was incredibly inquisitive and always afraid of missing something when he was not there. I once surprised him looking through a keyhole, dressed in a long nightshirt. He wanted to find out what we did in his absence.

Brecht and I always conversed in German. He understood no spoken Danish (except from the cigar dealer, who knew no German). He could read the newspapers, though with some effort—an effort necessary to keep up with political events. What I had written in Danish I translated for him as I read it out, and he would correct my German. In this way I increased my command over his language. He understood my Danish German very well and was not irritated by my mistakes. Grammatical errors never upset him anyway. What did upset him was slow speaking, and I was never guilty of that.

My father spoke German perfectly, having been born in the neighborhood of Flensburg on the German-Danish border, and my mother was also a good linguist, particularly in German and French. So really I should have had no difficulty in learning German. However, as I managed quite well with my limited knowledge, and could at least make myself understood, I did not go to any great trouble over it. The day came when it was too late, but

all the same I can read German very well. How else could
I have understood what Brecht wrote?

I have already mentioned that we wrote the book *Jedes
Tier kann es* together. In the process Brecht also helped
me a lot in human terms.

My sister fell ill and was sent to a mental home. Her
fate was a great worry to me. She was a beautiful woman
and a good communist. For a while, after completing her
law studies, she ran "Red Aid" in Denmark. Brecht and
I tried to find out what had caused her illness. She had
never slept with a man; then, for the first time, she fell
in love. He was a neurologist and already married. She
thought this of no account, that it was something she
could learn to live with. She was wrong, and the man
himself did nothing to help her. From the notes my sister
had made we came to the conclusion that he had indi-
rectly been responsible for her breakdown. Brecht had
never met my sister, but he wanted me to make a record
of her dilemma. The case interested him enormously,
and today I can understand why. Incidentally, he wrote
about the case himself, in a piece that we called *"Regen"*
("Rain"). Another story, *"Der Vergnügungspark"* ("The
Pleasure Garden"), which I have in German, he also
wrote alone.

Our book consists of seven short tales, for which I supplied the themes. While visiting my sister, I asked several
other women in her ward how they came to be there.
Some had been ill from birth or were the victims of ac-
cidents, but most of the others gave economic grounds.
In second place came matters of love—sexual frustration,
for example. These stories I repeated to Brecht. Needless
to say, our book is not a novel about mad people. Most
of the women suffered from psychoses from which they

subsequently recovered. We investigated the various causes so intensively that for a while I completely lost interest in my acting career. I stayed away from the Royal Theater for two whole years, going instead to medical lectures.

The idea for the framework surrounding the stories came from Brecht. Seven women killed in a streetcar accident are lying in a mortuary. At midnight they get up, make coffee, and tell each other their love stories. One had found her husband too rough, the second too gentle, the third too wise, the fourth too stupid, and so on. The last of them is a prostitute. She says she has had as many men as head colds.

Our collaboration progressed slowly, for it was a long time before I grasped everything. But in the final result it is hardly possible to establish who wrote what.

In America I received an offer of publication in a pornographic series. That I did not dare accept, for to be labeled a pornographer as well as a communist—that would have been too much for America. Unlike some others, Brecht did not consider the book to be pornographic. I myself think it truly classical. Incidentally, I did eventually publish it, under the pseudonym of Maria Sten.

In this connection I am reminded of my good friend Mogens Voltelen, an outstanding architect, for one of the stories in our book came from him. It is called "Three Days—One Carpet" and is very short. Voltelen had told me about a woman who was always coming up with new demands: one day a carpet, then a necklace, another day something different again. If her husband could not afford to buy it, there would be nothing doing in bed—she would say she "just couldn't." It is an attitude I later found among American women: no diamond ring, no orgasm! Brecht thought it a good story and asked me to write it down for him to put into shape.

I often think of Voltelen, because Brecht was very fond of him. I believe he was in fact Brecht's closest friend in Denmark—because he was my closest friend.

However, it was my misfortune never to have any real male friends, for every man I met immediately fell in love with me. That is no exaggeration. I sought protection by asking myself whether I could ever marry the man. Since meeting Brecht, my answer has been clear.

One day I went to Brecht and told him joyfully that I had found a girl for Voltelen. "I think he'll marry her," I said. Brecht replied, "You'll live to see how foolish you've been." He was right, for otherwise Voltelen would now be in Berlin. He was very gifted and intelligent, but in Denmark—and this was why Brecht called them "the too small islands"—he could not become what he would have been in Berlin. There are letters in which Brecht begs Voltelen to come to the Theater am Schiffbauerdamm, for Voltelen was not only an architect but also a lighting expert. He had invented a fantastic lighting panel. Voltelen, however, was not only married, he also had three children by now, and he was unable to come. The only things of his that reached Berlin are the two low leather chairs in Brecht's workroom.

Our work together on *Jedes Tier kann es* was my apprenticeship. It marked the beginning of a working relationship that later developed into a method. While he was working on his adaptation of Lenz's *The Tutor* (*Der Hofmeister*), for instance, I said to him, "Something is missing here, before he castrates himself. One needs to know why he castrates himself. Lenz forgot that." Then I wrote down what I thought needed to be expanded. Brecht liked that; it gave him something to work on. He took every suggestion seriously and thought it through. One could demand things of him. In Switzerland, when I asked him to put bridging verses beneath the pictures in the *Antigone* model book, he did so. As he himself says in his fine "Lao-Tsû" poem, Brecht needed a "customs man" to call for things from him.

This mode of working was not entirely new to me, for I had had a number of good friends and teachers before Brecht, and I have them still. But Brecht's teaching was something special.

The greatest Danish poet of our time, Otto Gelsted, has dedicated one of his books to me, not just in handwriting but in print: "For Ruth Berlau." I had demanded this book from him, since I often recited poems at large workers' meetings, and as time went on it grew increasingly hard to find anything suitable. For a long time I used a translation of some of Johannes R. Becher's early poems. But then I asked Otto Gelsted for a book out of which I could give readings, and he wrote it.

Though Gelsted was not a party member, I have always regarded him as a communist. He is very well known in Denmark for his translation of Homer. He spent some time in Greece and is expert in both Latin and Greek. My knowledge of many of these "higher things" I owe to him. He had introduced me to Hegel long before I met Brecht. Gelsted was my first great teacher, and I respect him deeply. Of course, he writes in a very different style from Brecht. He is a very emotional, lyrical person. In Gelsted there are many descriptions of Nature, for instance, and that was rather forbidden territory for Brecht—at least until he wrote the *Buckow Elegies* (*Buckower Elegien*).

Up to recent times Otto Gelsted suffered the same fate as Mogens Voltelen: He was known only in Denmark. His poems were sold in editions of two hundred copies, and there were no translations into other languages. Now, however, his *Selected Works* have been published in Moscow in an edition of sixty thousand.

When I visited Gelsted in Denmark not long ago, I brought back with me one of his socks, a thick gray woollen one that consists of little more than holes. I am keeping it, as I keep the red flag that was used on the stage in our production of *The Mother*, and an old cap of Brecht's that played a role in our performance of *Señora Carrar*.

Work on *Jedes Tier kann es* was a gain for me, but it was the cause of an agonizing decision: my break with Robert Lund. It was summer, the time at which we always went on our travels. I was in Skovsbostrand with Brecht when Robert came to ask me whether I would not accompany him. I found it very hard to send him away, for I was very, very fond of him. But I did send him away, because I was unwilling to give up my work with Brecht. Robert came at eight o'clock, and at nine I was due to visit Brecht. I was living at that time only a short distance from his house. In the early hours of the morning I had written the chapter that Brecht was now expecting. I took it to him, and we then worked on it together. Robert Lund returned to Copenhagen.

On one occasion Brecht was away from home. I no longer remember where he was—perhaps in London. It was at a time when I was particularly fed up with the Royal Theater. I wanted to get away. As if in answer to my prayers, the director of a provincial theater, Gerda Christoffersen, came along and offered me a role in a rubbishy play. It was called *Peter the Great*, though it had nothing to do with the famous tsar. I went to the director of the Royal Theater and told him I wanted to tour Denmark with this play. He responded by telling me that he wanted me to take on a big role in a play written by a clergyman. I knew this play, and I said, "It's such a bore, it'll only get a single performance." The director flared up. "How can you possibly know?" "I'm convinced of it," I replied. "I can't bear the play. I want now to do a popular piece. Please give me temporary leave." Surprisingly, he consented. The play at the Royal Theater really did manage only a single performance, whereas our rubbishy one did splendidly. Hardly a miracle; we played each night in a different place.

While we were in the neighborhood of Svendborg, Helene Weigel would sometimes travel with us in the theater bus. She found it wonderful to be at last with real theater people again. Though our performances were worse than third-class, Helene nevertheless enjoyed herself hugely.

And truly the tour was not in the least boring. Our director appeared as an actress as well. I was told she could never remember her lines, and that I should whisper to her what to say. I, who couldn't even remember my own lines! But in fact she knew very well what she had to say; I realized that when once I whispered something wrong to her. In the bus the director would sit in a rocking chair that was firmly lashed down during the journey. Helli conversed with her a lot. The elderly director had of course no idea who she was—or did her instinct perhaps tell her? I was the only one with whom Helli was not satisfied, because I took nothing seriously. I well remember how seriously Helene Weigel took her theatrical art.

Brecht never went to the Royal Theater, and hardly ever to the theater at all—or at any rate only very unwillingly. But once, when I was playing a comic role in a play by Kjeld Abell, a talented writer whom Brecht respected, he did come to a performance. When I returned to my dressing room I found him standing beside my makeup table. He looked at me reproachfully. He had left me a note—which I hardly dare admit has now vanished—on which he had written, "Is this supposed to be art?" He was quite right. My makeup materials were all jumbled up together, and everything was smudged red and blue, blue and red. I never took such things seriously. Helene Weigel, on the other hand, took it very seriously indeed. "Have you seen her makeup boxes?" Brecht asked me. "They are always neat and properly arranged. That is a part of art." He even wrote a poem about it. But I had no interest in the art of acting. I just wanted to *make* theater.

I admired Helene Weigel as an actress even before I saw her on a big stage. She knows a very great deal about the theater. For instance, she was very helpful in the selection of costumes for Hella Wuolijoki's play. In such things she is masterly. I don't think she is by nature a play director, though she would probably be better than anyone else we have here in Berlin. But she is at any rate a splendid actress.

During their time in Denmark we rehearsed scenes from *Saint Joan of the Stockyards* (*Die heilige Johanna der Schlachthöfe*). I played Joan, Helene the role of Frau Luckerniddle. Frau Luckerniddle is sitting outside the factory, waiting for her husband to come out. All, except for her, know that he will never come out, because he has fallen into the meat-cutting machine. To prevent her from causing a scandal and to make her go away, somebody offers her food, which she then takes and goes off. The way Helene did that, the way she played a woman waiting—it was fantastic. Or how she demonstrated to Dagmar Andreasen "a person who is hungry"—simply incredible. Later, in *Mother Courage*, we were to see her playing grief, when her son is shot. Fortunately, there are photographs remaining to convey to us something of such art.

The production of the *Saint Joan* scenes came about purely by chance. I was cast as a Salvation Army girl in a play at the Royal Theater, and in order to study my role I went to Nyhavn, the street where the sailors' taverns are. Salvation Army girls were always going there to save the souls of the drunken sailors. I managed to buy the uniform with its curious cap from one of these girls, and since I had the costume, we took the opportunity of rehearsing Brecht's Joan too. Some very good pictures of me in the role still exist.

4

In 1937 Brecht and I took part in the International Writers' Congress for the Defense of Culture. Others there included Martin Andersen Nexö from Denmark, Ernest Hemingway from the United States, and Nordahl Grieg from Norway. The congress opened in Paris, then moved to Madrid. I went to Spain with most of the participants, while Brecht returned to Denmark (he had no great liking for bombs). The political chief of the Soviet fighters in Spain took me there in his airplane. This was Mikhail Koltsov, who was later sent to prison for ten years and then executed, though after Stalin's death he was rehabilitated. He was a splendid comrade.

I remained in Madrid for quite a time. There I got to know Egon Erwin Kisch, who admitted me into his circle of journalistic colleagues and taught me a lot. But I also remember seeing him running around in total confusion, unable to make up his mind what to write about first. The atmosphere was so overpowering that one needed time to collect one's wits. We talked a great deal about this, a discussion in which Nordahl Grieg joined. Then, together with Grieg—and perhaps with some of the other writers, I cannot really remember—I went up to the front line. Since during my previous travels I had often gone hunting, I am quite handy with a gun.

In Madrid I also met Ernst Busch. He sang his unforgettable songs at troop meetings, in hospitals, through loudspeakers at the front, and also in children's homes. His voice put courage into many of the fighters. His contribution in those difficult times was altogether exemplary: Single-handed, he produced phonograph records and song books. He was very friendly with Maria Osten, Koltsov's antifascist German wife. She was the most beautiful woman I have ever seen, and beyond that, she was a well-known writer. She adopted a child with dark, almond-shaped eyes and took it back to Moscow with her. (When we stopped off in Moscow on our way to America, Brecht and I paid her a visit. She and the child were living in one tiny room, and Koltsov was in prison. Brecht was very concerned about her, but there was very little he could do to help her.)

I also remember Bodo Uhse and Erich Weinert. Indeed, I shall never forget the sight of Weinert seated in uniform at his typewriter when a shell stripped off the balcony before his very nose. He looked up indignantly— and went on writing. It was at this time he wrote his poem *"Unsere Heimat ist heute vor Madrid"* ("Our home is now outside Madrid").

One evening—and there is no evening sky to compare with Madrid's—I was present at a large meeting of the International Brigade. A number of the wounded were also there, and I sat between Erich Weinert and Willi Bredel, both of whom made a speech. Weinert sweated profusely as he did so, but his speech was fantastic. Bredel too was wonderful. After that there was singing. In a pause between the songs one of the severely wounded soldiers said in a thin, weak voice, "And because a man is human . . ." When I told Brecht there had been a call for his "United Front Song," he sat for a long while in thoughtful silence. But was that not why they were all there—because a man is human?

My time in Madrid was spent mostly with Soviet comrades. I saw the young pilots returning to their quarters utterly exhausted. They would lie down wherever there was an empty space, rest awhile, drink coffee, eat a little (usually just large Spanish grapes), then after an hour go out again. Many of them are no longer alive. Never since have I seen such strength, such dedication, such bottomless hatred and love. I was deeply moved.

I also visited the fighters at the front. The Red Army soldiers slept beneath their tanks. Among them was a woman whose name I shall not reveal here. She was about to return to Moscow. Before leaving, she went among the soldiers, offering to take letters or verbal greetings home with her. She knew intuitively that very few of them would ever return. During the night she came to me with a request to prepare a hot bath for her. She had not wanted the soldiers to contract syphilis or any other disease from the Spanish whores. To my regret I was unable to provide her with a bath. This was the finest example of understanding for the soldiers that I came across from any woman out there.

I returned to Brecht with stories of this nature, and he was not satisfied. He was hoping for an account of the political background to the Civil War, and all I could talk about was fantastic experiences. I was, of course, much too emotional.

The Spanish Civil War interested Brecht to such an extent that later, during his stay in Sweden, he collected a large group of returned fighters around him for discussions. They comprised people from many countries, among them Germans who had come to Sweden following the defeat. Brecht wanted to know why, in spite of all the available resources, the battle had been lost. Why, he asked, had the anarchists, Trotskyites, and communists not joined together to present a united front? There was no satisfactory answer. At the start the Spanish government had given land and farmhouses to the landworkers—and because of that had received no help from the capitalist countries, who declared Spain to be communistic. So the government took it all back, in the hope that help would come. We needed weapons, and we were relying on Britain and France, among others, to supply them—unfortunately, in vain. Why, on the other hand, did the support for Franco function so efficiently? These were the matters Brecht wanted to discuss. I remember that Margarete Steffin wrote up these talks, which she took down in shorthand. It is to be hoped her records have survived.

In a political sense I was still far too immature for Spain. Though I had seen a lot, Brecht was cross with me for not being able to tell him everything he wanted to know. For the first time ever he shouted at me. It takes time to understand exactly what is going on.

But perhaps there was also another reason for Brecht's anger: my late return to Denmark. I had been meaning to stay only until the Writers' Congress ended, that is, about two weeks in all, and I had even written to Brecht, giving him the name of the ship on which I was booked to return. Instead, I went up to the front line, and from there I sent little news. Then, in Madrid, I met Georg Branting, the Swedish lawyer who was in charge of a committee set up to support the Spanish Republic. It seemed to me more important to help him than to sit idle in peaceful Denmark.

Brecht had viewed my long absence and my silence with suspicion, and—as he always liked to do—he set about teaching and instructing me with the aid of his

"Lai-tu" stories. These stories can now be read in print. Kien-leh, Kin-jeh, and Me-ti are names for Brecht himself; he called me Lai-tu or simply Tu, and I am also the sister and the pupil—once even the favorite pupil.

There are about three dozen "Lai-tu" stories, and they were published after Brecht's death as a supplement to *Me-ti/Buch der Wendungen*. Brecht showed me the book by the Chinese philosopher Me-ti or Mo-di, which (in a German translation) had inspired him. He even allowed me to borrow it when I was in Skovsbostrand. But I was not allowed to take it, or anything else of his, back to Copenhagen. That was my punishment for having stolen *The Mother*.

Brecht's "Me-ti" stories are a collection of philosophical, political, and ethical thoughts about the problems of our own time. When Brecht came on a problem, he would write a little story around it, and he devoted quite a considerable time to this work. I believe his object was to find a literary form for the depiction of dialectic methods. His model was Lenin's essay on "Climbing High Mountains," which he also quotes in his *Buch der Wendungen*. He was much attracted by the Chinese method of describing things by means of parables, and it was all set out as the words of a Chinese sage. Brecht loved Chinese names, which he said sounded like rare blooms, so he thought up Chinese names also for Karl Marx and Friedrich Engels, for Lenin, Stalin, and Plekhanov, as well as for Lion Feuchtwanger and Karl Korsch.

Though the "Lai-tu" stories take the same form as the "Me-ti" ones, their aim is clearly a different one. They are not reflections on the ways of the world but simply and solely attempts to guide my moral behavior. I should never lose sight of the importance of Me-ti—that is to say, of Brecht—to myself, and as his pupil I should model myself on him.

If Brecht had had enough fellow workers, the "Lai-tu" stories—or at least those that deal with Spain—would never have been written. He always needed collaborators and pupils. Because I had stayed so long in Spain and thus put myself out of his reach, he found it harder to work. His lack of collaborators was the reason why he clung so closely to me. When he eventually left Denmark for Sweden, I stayed behind to work in the Danish underground movement. For a time he approved my decision, because I was able in the beginning to visit him now and again in Sweden. But when he fled to Finland, he urged me—indeed, forced me, by reminding me of the demands of my antifascist work—to leave my homeland and follow him. The decisive factor was not primarily personal and private relationships; for him it was above all a question of his work. He had to have somebody to listen to him. I saw clearly from his letters—often no more than short notes—that he needed me.

But back to Denmark. I still remember exactly what gave rise to the first "Lai-tu" story, which was called *"Feuermachen der Lai-tu"* ("Lai-tu Making a Fire"). Because Brecht so disliked living in hotels, hating hall porters as he did, I bought a house in Vallensbäk for our meetings. The small farmhouse was primitively furnished. Basically it contained nothing but two long work tables, a few chairs, and a narrow log stove, though the architect Mogens Voltelen did put in a handsome light pine floor for me. (Brecht later had one exactly like it laid in his summer house in Buckow.)

By the time the house was ready, winter had set in, and since I was no longer living with Robert Lund, I had no car at my disposal. All I had was a motorcycle. At this time of year, with the bitter cold and all the snow, I felt it unwise to drive to the house on my motorcycle, so I rented a hotel room instead. Brecht, however, insisted on going to the house. He seated himself on the motorcycle behind me, and we drove through the snow to Vallens-bäk.

We arrived frozen stiff, and I hastened to light a fire. It was hard work getting the wood to burn. The stove had a small recess for boiling water in a kettle, but when I went to fetch the water, I found the pump frozen solid. I was in utter despair. Finally I scooped up some snow and melted it. All this time Brecht sat watching me, in his mouth the cigar that never seemed to go out, not even on the motorbike. He said not a single word. We stayed there for eight days, writing the play *Alle wissen alles* (*Everyone Knows Everything*). In the process we laughed ourselves silly. Strangely enough, the play seems to have amused no one else.

I shall insert the story here, otherwise it will get lost.

The play was my second collaboration with Brecht, following *Jedes Tier kann es*. The Danish witticisms I recognize as my contribution, but apart from these I find it very difficult, even after rereading, to distinguish what was Brecht's and what was mine, which sentences or twists in the action I had provided to move the story forward.

The main character is a famous Danish burglar whom Brecht regarded with downright admiration. This burglar lived very modestly, spending only 3,000 Kronen a year— the police eventually worked this out after reviewing several unsolved burglaries. Invariably, when the stolen money ran out, another burglary would take place somewhere. On the last occasion 9,000 Kronen had been stolen. The police were able to reckon that the burglar could live for three years on that, and would then have to break in again. Thus, after many years, they finally caught him. It created a sensation, but no one was happy about it, apart from the police. Karin Michaelis, who was then seventy, went to the king and said, "This man must be released from prison and allowed to live with me. I shall stand surety for him. He is a national hero." She owned a large estate with several houses. The king gave his consent at once, as everyone did when Karin wanted something, she squinted so charmingly. The burglar-cum-national-hero went to live on Thurø.

Brecht and I once asked permission to visit his house, to see how he was living, but Karin said, "No, nobody can get in. He's got five locks on his door, and an extra three on his writing desk." Brecht found that priceless, that in the end a burglar comes to look on everyone else as a criminal from whom he must protect himself.

What I have given here is just the main story. The only person who understood the play was Storm Petersen, who did some wonderful drawings for it. When Brecht's pupil Peter Palitzsch eventually read the play, he considered the denouement—for us the comic point of the whole thing—a mistake. That I can't understand. Even Grete Steffin, who had the task of putting my text into proper German, was severely critical, and she introduced into the play a story about a fountain pen, which I find very bad. Grete was of the opinion that for a crime story the play contained too little. Basically what she objected to was that Brecht had spent eight days alone with me at Vallensbäk.

I think there were thirty-five characters in the play. I set about staging it, and produced it as if I were the devil himself. As the opening night approached, the whole of Copenhagen shivered. The critics spread the rumor "Ruth Berlau has written a play! She is producing it herself! And it's even coming out in the Apollo Theater!" To the critics I was like a red rag to a bull. Indeed, they even called me "Red Ruth." But strangely enough, they still seemed to like me. So long as I kept off the stage, they found me easy enough to stomach. All of them were keen to come to the opening performance.

Just then the political economist Fritz Sternberg came to Copenhagen. He was at that time a good friend to Brecht, in whose house I had met him once before. Sternberg came to the dress rehearsal. After it he told me, "You can't put that on tomorrow, it's quite impossible." I no longer recall what was supposed to be impossible or why it was thought to be impossible, but I was stung. "Very well, then," I said, "there'll be no premiere." When one is in a state of exhaustion after weeks of hard work, nothing seems to matter. Suddenly it was no longer important to me to have the play performed. Even the reaction of the critics and all the other people who had bought tickets left me indifferent. But the actors, after all their hard work—that was dreadful. All the same, I canceled the performances.

So, instead of launching a premiere, I went off to Brecht in Skovsbostrand with Fritz Sternberg. I was glad to be out of Copenhagen, where there was of course uproar. In a small town like Copenhagen everyone knows everything within minutes. The well-known Danish critic Schyberg told me he went to my apartment in the poor district of Kattesund, where he saw my milk and breakfast rolls waiting outside the door. He returned home in despair, knowing the premiere was off. The disaster I quickly forgot, but not what I learned from writing and directing the play.

With Brecht, writing and stage directing were always closely linked. It can be said that even when he was writing he was at the same time directing, for he always saw clearly in his mind what would be happening on the stage. The cancellation of a premiere never worried him. In the twenties, for instance, he canceled Arnolt Bronnen's *Vatermord* because he was not satisfied with what came out in rehearsal. With the Berliner Ensemble too he was constantly putting off the first performance, when the production had not reached the standard for which he was aiming. Even when he was told that the theater was booked solid and one firm or another had tickets, he was not to be moved.

I am not claiming to have already shared this attitude in Copenhagen. *Alle wissen alles* was given no further rehearsals, and there has been no attempt to stage it since, but looking back, I feel I was justified, at least to some degree.

I have already written about the house in Vallensbäk, our journey there, my efforts at making a fire, and our work on *Alle wissen alles*. A week later, we returned to Svendborg with the play in our pocket. Helene Weigel was at the railway station to meet us. I can still see that frail little figure advancing on us . . .

I am convinced that I had no alternative but to travel to Svendborg with him, for he needed company. He was not prepared to spend five hours all by himself. On the following day I returned to Copenhagen. Up till then Brecht had not said a word about our journey to Vallensbäk and our arrival there. Two days after I reached Copenhagen I received "Lai-tu Making a Fire" through the post, just as it is, without either letter or greeting. In the story he accused me of being too clumsy, of making heavy weather of the fire-making, and disturbing the peace of the house. That was the last straw! There had I been, fighting against the cold and the ice, anxious to get the house warm and the tea brewing, in despair because nothing was going fast enough—and all my efforts he had seen as "slave labor," aimed at making him feel an "exploiter"! He was making excuses for himself, not for me. I must admit I was not exactly enthusiastic about this first "Lai-tu" story.

Later Brecht wrote another story about "Lai-tu's house for Kin-jeh." In this one Kin-jeh had not visited the house for a whole year and only now and again inquired about it. Lai-tu did not grieve about that, for she had once heard Kin-jeh declare how important this house was to him as a place of refuge, "when once again he wished to write the truth about the oppressors." It would have been convenient for Brecht if I had taken this attitude, but it was not how I felt—neither before nor after he had explained it to me.

Several of the "Lai-tu" stories arose out of our conversations: "Tu, wanting to learn how to fight, learns how to sit still," for example. I should understand that one does not fight for fighting's sake but to achieve something worthwhile. "Me-ti said: If you are not striving for enjoyment, not trying to make the best of things as they exist and not anxious to achieve the best position, why then should you fight?"

When once I found "the small islands" had really become too small for comfort, I thought of going to America. Brecht then gave me "Me-ti's Advice." Me-ti asks how Lai-tu can leave "when the three kingdoms of Deh, Sueh, and Noh are still not united, though they have so powerful a common enemy?" Lai-tu replies that the union of Denmark, Sweden, and Norway does not lie within her power. (I have not achieved it even yet!) But the wise Me-ti says: "The union of the three kingdoms is a distant goal. But even more distant than a distant goal is no goal at all. Your journey has no goal."

I cannot say to what extent this story influenced me. Enough to say that I did not go to America, though I did go to England. Brecht had no objection to that, for he was working at the time in London on a film of

I Pagliacci. I went with him, having obtained from Nordahl Grieg's Norwegian newspaper a commission to write a report on British miners.

From London I went on to Cardiff. I presented my journalist's pass at a colliery, and the mine directors allowed me to accompany the miners down the pit. When I returned—I was staying in a little boarding house owned by an ex-miner—I said to him, "You've been exaggerating. My trip was very pleasant. The tunnel is well built, and there is even electric lighting. Why did you tell me it was so horrible down there?" He asked me how far down I had gone. "To the fifth or sixth level," I replied. "Uhuh," he grunted. I became curious. He fetched his son's kit. "Here, take this overall and this lamp, and tomorrow go right down to the bottom. If anybody asks, give them my name."

At five the following morning I did in fact go down to the twentieth level. I even did some boring, and when I talk about it can still remember the feel of the borer in my hand. By the end of the shift I was exhausted. Just as I was, I went to the director and told him what a disgusting fraud it was to show a journalist only the pleasant side of a job.

Brecht helped me write my article for the newspaper. He was curious about everything, and I was able to tell him things I had seen that left him by no means indifferent. For example, I had stood at the pithead as the coal wagons came up. The last wagon was just as black as the preceding ones, and I thought it also contained coal. Then I saw men get out. They moved a little to the side and began to chop up some dampish wood, which they then bundled up and carried off. I asked, "What are you doing with that?" They replied, "Just for a little fire." (Actually, they described it in more detail; the terse formulation is Brecht's.) It was a good article. For Brecht, poverty was an interesting point politically. All day long miners slaved in the pits, and at the end of it had no coal to heat their own homes.

I was not the only one whom Brecht helped. In London he was working with Sybille Binder, the famous actress, whom he had known in Berlin. Unfortunately, she developed breast cancer and died in exile. Brecht wrote a very beautiful poem for her.

He met a lot of people in London, among them Gerda Goedhart, whose photographs are the best we have of him. She always kept well clear of all the cliques that invariably formed about Brecht. I liked her very much for her integrity and reliability. She was always a good friend, even when things were not going well for me.

In case Hanns Eisler has not told one of the best stories about Brecht in London, I shall tell it myself:

The wealthy English lords, princesses, and whoever else passes there as upper class are sophisticated people. They were curious to meet artists like Eisler—and would tolerate even Brecht—and they showered them with invitations. Eisler and Brecht accepted these, in the hope of prizing money out of them. They were thinking in terms of about five thousand pounds—not, of course, to spend on themselves, but for "good causes." However, they had no success, and departed as poor as they came. All the same, one of these princesses (Elizabeth Princess Bibesco) was particularly interested in Brecht, and she invited him—in all sincerity—to the Savoy, which is the most elegant hotel anywhere in the world. And that was the reason why Brecht was unwilling to go. Eisler and the other comrades urged him on: "You must, Brecht! Now's the chance." They badly needed money for a newspaper, a theatrical production, or something of that kind. So off Brecht went. Now, to get into the Savoy you need a dress suit. Brecht had never possessed such a thing in his whole life. He decided to go in the clothes he always wore. Dressed like that, he got no further than the hall porter. A look from him was enough, and Brecht turned tail. In films of the Wild West people who are not wanted are shot when they enter the saloon; in the Savoy the hall porter only needs to shake his head!

Brecht went to Eisler and said contentedly, "It didn't work, they wouldn't let me in." Eisler had in fact warned him to have a shave beforehand and tidy himself up a bit, though to me he added with a sigh, "We all know what Brecht looks like when he's shaved." They sat down together and wrote out a telegram to Princess Bibesco, who had spent two hours waiting for him.

Eisler later added a rider to this story. He once went into the Hotel Sacher in Vienna with his wife Steffy. Though he was wearing no tie, he sat down and ordered a lavish meal. The waiter took the order and returned shortly afterward with a plate covered by a cloth. Steffy was wondering what was happening when without a word, Eisler took something from the plate, rose, and went out. When he returned, he was wearing a tie, which he of course returned when he left. "You can see from that how corrupt Austria is," Eisler observed to me. "Without a tie, you won't even get inside the Savoy. In the Sacher they lend you a tie as soon as you've ordered an expensive meal."

In 1939 I published the *Svendborg Poems* (*Svendborger Gedichte*). I am very proud of this edition, which I brought out all on my own, and I am annoyed with myself to this day for having, out of pure modesty, allowed Wieland Herzfelde and his Malik publishing house to put their names to it. For Herzfelde later abused me; he called my edition "ugly." I did not follow the style of his edition of the *Collected Works* but modeled myself on the volumes of *Versuche*, which the firm of Kiepenhauer had brought out. It was stupid of me not to have named myself as the publisher. As Brecht once said to me in a letter, "You are the most generous person I have ever met."

Brecht was yearning to see something of his in print again. He had been spoiled, for in Germany everything he wrote had been published immediately. He was even permitted to decide on the format, typeface, and layout himself. My edition of the *Svendborg Poems* was planned while he was still in Denmark, but when he moved to Stockholm I had to carry on by myself. Grete Steffin did, however, help me very unselfishly with advice, for I was completely inexperienced.

When the poems appeared I was anxious to recover a bit of the money I had invested, for I had meanwhile separated from Robert Lund and was no longer well off. Previously I had rehearsed with my workers' theater in our large apartment, but now I needed another large room for rehearsals. I rented an attic in which there was neither lavatory nor heating. Both had to be installed, and for that I badly needed money from the *Svendborg Poems*.

The little book was priced at three Kronen. In order to give a slight boost to the takings, Brecht and I decided that he should sign a hundred numbered copies, which we would then sell for ten Kronen each. A doctor took two copies straight away, and many of our comrades, who had never even met Brecht, also bought signed copies. A lot of money flowed in. But Poul Henningsen, one of our most advanced and wealthiest architects, asked me on the telephone how much the book would cost without Brecht's signature. He decided to buy the cheaper edition. "The poems are just as good without the signature," he said. When I indignantly told Brecht that, he just smiled. "He's a sensible fellow," he said.

Brecht was very pleased with the publication of the *Svendborg Poems*. In the numbered copies he wanted the sentence printed: "Published under the auspices of the Diderot Society." He devoted much time and labor to the establishment of a Diderot Society, but unfortunately it never came to anything. The notice in the *Svendborg Poems* is a fabrication.

In the *Svendborg Poems* the author's name is given as Bertolt Brecht. Years before Brecht had told me, "The Malik Verlag is starting to publish my collected writings. I'm wondering if 'Bert' is right." Everyone always called him that. By now I was used to being confronted with the most curious questions. Was Brecht joking, or did this really mean a lot to him? "Bert or Bertolt? Bertolt Eugen Friedrich? What do you think? Do you like Bert?" With him you had to think swiftly and give a swift answer. The only answer that occurred to me then was "I suppose at the time 'Bill' instead of 'William' wouldn't have been quite right either . . ." Brecht's reply was a grin. So it was in Denmark that Bert changed into Bertolt.

Brecht badly needed money. To help him, I acted as go-between with the publishing firm of Hasselbach for a Danish edition of his *Dreigroschenroman* (*Threepenny Novel*, published in English as *A Penny for the Poor*). I also found a translator, but there is a sad story connected with that. One day Otto Gelsted came in his threadbare little raincoat to visit me and said, "I should like to translate the *Dreigroschenroman*." It had never occurred to me that he would want to translate such a long novel, and anyway he had come far too late.

I told him it would earn him only a thousand Kronen. "Well, all right," he said. He was really in need of money. So I had to tell him the truth. However, I did eventually manage to get him the job of translating the songs in the book, for which he was paid five hundred Kronen. Looked at in terms of working time, that was for him a much better bargain. Unfortunately, the translation as a whole is not really good.

The greater part of the *Dreigroschenroman* was written in hospital, when Brecht was suffering from a kidney complaint. Brecht worked together with Grete Steffin, without whom the book would never have come into being. None of Brecht's manuscripts are written in his own handwriting. The most he ever wrote by hand were brief notes. Everything else he wrote on his typewriter, including drafts and even his poems. He dictated the *Dreigroschenroman* to Grete Steffin.

Before Brecht's arrival a great many German emigrants had already been admitted to Denmark. I looked after a number of them. They came to collect food packages, cigarettes, and when it happened to be payday, a little money as well. Gradually we Danes learned to respect these Germans. We were impressed by their modesty, their industry—they were as busy as ants—and their ability to order their lives, to prepare themselves. "Prepare for what?" I once asked my cook, who tended each time to make the food packages larger and larger. "Hitler will be coming here too," she replied categorically, "and that's what we must prepare for."

Truly it was Brecht's countrymen who gave us Danes our first lessons in acting unlawfully. One day my cook showed me her party book. I had not managed in three years to win her over. The German emigrants, on the other hand, had not only won over my cook, but, it seemed, they had also had a word with the news vendor on the street corner, for suddenly our Danish communist newspaper, which had formerly been concealed beneath the counter, was to be seen hanging above it in a favored position, plain for all to see.

* * *

In 1936, for the first time since he had gone into exile, a play by Brecht was performed in a major theater. This was *Round Heads and Pointed Heads* (*Die Rundköpfe und die Spitzköpfe*), and the director was Per Knutzon, who had already directed *Drums in the Night* at an experimental theater, with myself in the role of Anna. He was a good director and also a good party comrade. Unfortunately, Brecht had difficulties with him, for Knutzon had given the main role to his wife, Lulu Ziegler, who could not come to terms with the epic style. All the same, it was in my opinion an interesting production. But the Catholic church foamed at the mouth, offended by the use of a picture of a Catholic saint to conceal the door of the nuns' safe, and demanded a change in the play. The Zionist organization also protested, accusing Brecht of anti-Semitism. This was ridiculous, for Brecht was neither pro- nor anti-Semitic; the question did not interest him at all. His point was to show that racism was being used to divert attention from the class struggle.

Not one critic understood the play. That made little impression on Brecht. He altered nothing, and he did not remove the picture of the saint. He stuck to his principles, with the result that the production received only a few performances.

In later years Brecht's attitude in such cases became less lofty. I saw an instance of this in 1954, when the Berliner Ensemble gave some guest performances at the Sarah Bernhardt Theater in Paris. After we had stitched Picasso's Dove of Peace on the red plush curtain, the festival management came to demand its removal. We were shaking with indignation. For us to remove the Dove of Peace, our symbol! That was unthinkable. In such circumstances we would rather not play at all. Brecht should decide. But he was not to be found. He was running somewhere around Paris, buying crime stories and visiting a dogs' cemetery in which he was interested. When at last he returned, he said merely, "If that's the way it is, take the dove down."

There was trouble again when, after the performance of *Mother Courage and Her Children*, the audience called repeatedly for Brecht. He did not come on stage, for he had already gone to bed. This certainly did not mean that Brecht was indifferent to the sensational success of the Berliner Ensemble in Paris. He considered it important, not only for himself but for his country, for the German Democratic Republic.

After *Round Heads and Pointed Heads*, Per Knutzon directed *The Threepenny Opera* in Copenhagen. This was another unhappy occasion. Brecht even declared it was the most dreadful experience of his whole time in exile. He fell out so completely with Knutzon that in the end they were no longer speaking to each other. This was terrible for me, since Per and I were very good friends, and now, for better or worse, I had to range myself against him. This time it was neither directing nor casting that caused the trouble; it was money.

The rights in *The Threepenny Opera* belonged to the German publishing firm of Bloch-Erben, whose Danish representative was Carl Strakosch, a Jew. His job was to collect the royalties on behalf of Bloch-Erben. Brecht knew that. He was always very knowledgeable about contractual matters. He told Per Knutzon, "If you can arrange to pay me direct, then do that. If you can't, then pay the royalties into a blocked account in Denmark." Knutzon promised to hand the money over to Brecht. At the railway station before leaving for Skovsbostrand, Brecht once again insisted, "On no account must the money be sent to Hitler Germany. Better not stage the play at all— it is not all that important." Despite this, Knutzon and Strakosch sent the money to Hitler Germany, which meant that it was not Brecht but the Nazis who profited from it. Brecht never got over that.

Strakosch had also been a good friend of mine. I tried to arouse his conscience: "As a Jew, you can't continue to work for Bloch-Erben. Everybody knows that a double-dyed Nazi is now in charge of Bloch-Erben. Within six months at the latest you'll have lost your contract with the firm." When I said that, Strakosch picked up the telephone to ask the police to throw me out of his office.

We thought Per Knutzon's behavior particularly bad, since he was a party comrade. I went to the party's First Secretary, Aksel Larsen, and demanded Knutzon's dismissal. There was a tremendous row, which ended not with Knutzon's dismissal but with an admonishment to me.

Helli Weigel, who was reluctant to get mixed up in all this, was waiting for me in a restaurant close to the party building. We had arranged to go on to Malmö to see *Señora Carrar's Rifles*, which Curt Trepte had staged with Naima Wifstrand in the main role. My interview with the party chiefs had gone on so long that I had to get airplane tickets in order to reach Malmö in time. It was Helli's very first flight. The production pleased her greatly, and she quickly made friends with Naima Wifstrand. Naima was also my Señora Carrar when I later directed the play in Stockholm.

Brecht had little luck with the theater in Denmark. Not even *The Seven Deadly Sins (Die sieben Todsünden)* could change that, though the ballet was choreographed by the famous Harald Lander. Ilona Wieselmann, who later played Yvette in *Mother Courage and Her Children*, took the part of Anna I, and Margot Lander danced Anna II. Otto Gelsted, who had done the translation, and Ilona Wieselmann were constantly visiting Skovsbostrand for Brecht's advice.

66

At the first performance the king sat in his box and declared (this I know for a fact), "No, this is not what the famous Danish Royal Ballet was founded for." The production was taken off after only two performances. The effect on the audience was "off-putting," the ballet was considered "odd." But we enjoyed ourselves tremendously, for really it is a very fine play. What I liked best was the idea that Anna's suitcase was too small, and—because it was too small—she became a prostitute. The things Brecht can come up with!

The ban caused a great scandal. Everyone was indignant, the translator, the director, and the entire company. Only Brecht was content: "Good, so they understood it." He was used to theater scandals. I, at any rate, had the feeling that he would have been rather disappointed if there had not been a scandal. "The Danes are a polite people; no rotten tomatoes, just a royal ban." This was the old king; he had understood the play. The king we now have understands nothing; he is just a car snob. I once went skating with him.

Brecht's deadly sin during the emigration period was to demonstrate his loyalty to Marxism. This was worse than all the "seven deadly sins of the petty bourgeoisie" put together.

After this ballet Otto Gelsted translated *Saint Joan of the Stockyards*. With this he took on more than he could manage, though one must admit that it is next door to impossible to find Danish equivalents for what Brecht himself called his "sloppy" verses. Luckily I managed to sell the play to Andreas Møller, the director of the Royal Theater, before the translation was done. The Royal Theater signed a contract with Bodil Ipsen, at that time Denmark's greatest actress, in which the theater bound itself to give her the role of Joan. The play was never staged in Copenhagen, but Bodil Ipsen was able for a time to live very well, for until she had played Joan, she could not be given notice. This was the only success Brecht's *Saint Joan* achieved in Copenhagen, though I am not suggesting that Bodil Ipsen saw it as a success for herself.

I cannot say definitely when my active collaboration in Brecht's plays began. I had no part in the Danish version of the *Life of Galileo* (*Leben des Galilei*), though I was able to arrange for Brecht to meet Niels Bohr, and I collected material for him. He himself never visited libraries.

To contact Niels Bohr was not difficult for me. I knew him slightly, since he owned a summer house very near to my and Robert Lund's house, and his sons were close friends of my sister Edith. Niels Bohr was interested in everything. He knew at once who Bertolt Brecht was. He did not, of course, conduct Brecht personally around his institute; for that he had his assistants. And it was not as if Brecht had studied atomic physics, though he had read a great deal about it. What he was looking for was a way of presenting problems of physics on the stage in an uncomplicated, easily comprehensible way.

Recently, at a meeting of young scientists in Denmark, I came across one of Bohr's former assistants, and I voiced my regret that Bohr had after all helped produce the Hiroshima bomb. This assistant defended his ex-chief stoutly, but I was not convinced. "Only for peaceful purposes," says Bohr at the outset—then off he goes to America to work on a war bomb. Unfortunately, Einstein and Roosevelt were also in favor of the bomb. I find this curious.

To return to my starting point: I did not contribute a single line to the *Life of Galileo*. At that period I had never even given a thought to the possibility of collaboration. Brecht's collaborator in this play was Margarete Steffin. Maybe my enthusiasm helped slightly to inspire Brecht—that's quite possible. I thought everything he wrote splendid, showed it to other people, then came back to tell him what they had said. But I had no idea then how important such a participation in his work was for Brecht.

Over the years I came to realize that he found it simpler to write a play when he could think of certain actors, at least in the main roles. He could visualize how they would move and speak. In Denmark Brecht had come to know the great actor Poul Reumert, and he saw him in the role of Galileo. While working on the play, Brecht often mentioned him. He needed to see a living being in front of him as he wrote. Whether anything eventually evolved out of this "casting" was less important, and in the case of Poul Reumert nothing did come of it, unfortunately. Later, in Berlin, Brecht adapted George Farquhar's play *The Recruiting Officer* (known to us as *Pauken und Trompeten*) for Regine Lutz. Because she was on hand, he also resumed work on *Turandot*.

Most of his plays Brecht wrote for Helene Weigel. She took no part in the work of writing, but she inspired him as an actress. It must be acknowledged that *Mother Courage and Her Children* owes its existence to the existence of Helene Weigel. The idea of the dumb daughter Kattrin came to him when he realized that his travels would take him and his family to many foreign countries. He took into consideration the fact that Helene would be able to play this role even in countries whose language she did not know. As it turned out, the play was staged in none of the countries to which Brecht was forced to emigrate. I have often wondered how Helene managed to bear it: She was young, wonderful to look at, and the stage was her element. Unfortunately, exactly the opposite of what

Brecht had visualized happened: Helene Weigel did not play even the dumb girl. Instead, she was effectively condemned to remain dumb for fifteen whole years.

Without a doubt, while writing the play Brecht had envisaged that Helene would later play Mother Courage herself. Again and again he declared, "When I get back to Germany, my very first production will be *Mother Courage* with Helene Weigel." And so it was to be.

Many of Mother Courage's ways were reflections of Helene Weigel, though I only became truly aware of this after seeing her play that role on the stage. Brecht had always admired her business talents. Mother Courage is a trader, and all the bargaining scenes owe their inspiration to Helene. I am not suggesting that she was like that in reality, but I do maintain that nobody else can play these scenes as she did. Who could ever equal the way in which Helene Weigel bargained over the chicken in the second scene? Many of the details were worked out together with her during rehearsals: for instance, the bargaining with the recruiting officers over the buckle at the start of the play; the sale of schnapps before and after the death of Tilly; the dispute over the shirts for bandaging the wounded. I don't have room to list all Helene Weigel's great scenes here; I can only say that with all other productions I have seen, and particularly with my own production in Holland, I came to realize what a fantastic actress Brecht had in Helene Weigel as Mother Courage. That collaboration between author, director, and actress is one of the precious moments in theatrical history.

While Brecht was working on *Mother Courage* he would show me his manuscripts or read me passages from them. It was all very strange to me, for at the Royal Theater I was acting in plays that bore not the slightest resemblance to Brecht's. The longer I knew Brecht, the more I came to feel that what we were doing at the Royal Theater was rubbish. Even Shakespeare we had not really understood. And for this reason it was a long time before I could really help Brecht. All I could do was point out what I did not understand. Sometimes Brecht rewrote such passages, and he always accepted my criticisms, amateurish as they were, in a very positive spirit. Perhaps I suggested two or three things of which he was able to make use, but I have no cause to flatter myself. What most impressed me was the atmosphere of playfulness and high spirits in which Brecht worked. It was always fun.

I learned gradually through practice. The scenes for my workers' theater I always wrote myself, the ideas coming mainly from Aksel Larsen, the party chairman. I would ask him, "What's happening? What ought we to write about now?" We produced agitprop as best we could, according to our understanding and above all, our conscience. What I had learnt in the Royal Theater was of no use to me, so I always showed my things to Brecht. He gave me an important tip: True mastery lies in restraint. Into one small sketch I would always tend to put everything: abortion, unemployment, the exorbitant price of coffee, the inadequacy of workers' insurance, and so on. Brecht told me kindly, "I feel you've crammed in a bit too much. In my opinion, one should concentrate on just one thing at a time. Don't you agree?"

This gentle, almost hesitant way of voicing doubts is also something I have learned from Brecht. It neither oppresses nor depresses, because it in no way questions the work itself. The person criticized is allowed the choice of accepting or rejecting the suggestion. Writers are sensitive people. A criticism that at the wrong moment finds fault with trivialities can destroy growth. The aim of criticism should be to aid production.

In Alexander Abusch's book about Schiller I found a sentence by Goethe that applies equally well to Bertolt Brecht. Goethe says in connection with Schiller, "One learns only by loving." This kind of love has nothing at all to do with sex. For Brecht, criticism was effective and useful only when it was made in a spirit of real love. This, I think, I quickly realized. There were times when it would have been wrong to say anything of a negative nature. One had to concentrate on the positive side of things and withhold criticism. Once by myself, I would note down the things I had not understood or would like to see changed and later find an opportunity to bring them up. Had I spoken out at once, Brecht would have stopped writing. A whole day would have been lost, and lost days were unbearable to him.

Work with Brecht was not always easy. He had a tendency, which I had noticed in Denmark with great concern and found impossible to understand, to harbor antipathies. All of a sudden, for no discernible reason, he would be unjust toward someone, rather in the way a dog sometimes takes an instant dislike to a certain person. I found this puzzling and, during rehearsals with my workers' theater, very unpleasant. I spoke to him about it. "When you dislike somebody, you must surely have a reason for it," I said. But he had no reason, as one came to realize when one looked deeper into the matter. Referring to a member of our company, for example, he once said, "He's stupid." "That's not true," I replied, "he's no stupider than so-and-so and so-and-so, and you like them." "Yes, but—" he would then say in his own defense, but nothing came out that one could put a finger on.

In Berlin too I saw evidence of this tendency, and one day I voiced my criticism to him: "You're no longer the wise teacher you once were. You are rude to your people, and you show antipathy toward one or the other without any cause." Brecht's reply was, "I have no pupils, I have employees." Those were difficult times. Brecht was no longer the person he had been in exile. Then he had never shouted at anyone, now he did. Perhaps it was because in Berlin Brecht was having a difficult time himself. He had flung himself body and soul into practical theater work, but the "travails of the plains" were still like trying to cross a log bridge. The situation changed only when Brecht got a theater of his own, the Theater am Schiffbauerdamm.

One of Brecht's poems is called "On Teaching Without Pupils," and in it is the line, "There speaks the man to whom no one is listening." This situation occurred again and again during the years of exile: No people, no people! And Brecht was so dependent on contacts of this kind. It was for this reason that he was continually inviting friends to Skovsbostrand. Among those I came to know were Karl Korsch, Walter Benjamin, Fritz Sternberg, Hermann Duncker, Herbert Ihering, and most important of all of course, Hanns Eisler. They lived, sometimes for quite lengthy periods, close to Brecht's house, and he would show them what he had written and discuss it with them. He seldom spoke of his plans. What he wanted was talk about concrete subjects.

Whenever Benjamin and Brecht came together in Denmark, an atmosphere of comfortable intimacy was the immediate result. I know that Benjamin has written about his talks with Brecht. As far as I am concerned, Benjamin was a great teacher. I was so ashamed of my ignorance that I learned very quickly. I grasped every opportunity to pick up something new, and from Benjamin I picked up a very great deal. Brecht was tremendously fond of Benjamin—in fact, he truly loved him. They seemed to understand each other without the need of speech. They would play chess together in complete silence, and when they rose, they had had a conversation.

The friend Brecht awaited with most impatience was Hanns Eisler. The day at last arrived when he announced his coming, and a small house on the Svendborg Sound was immediately rented for him. The two friends got on splendidly together, but in one respect they were complete opposites. Eisler enjoyed swimming, something Brecht seldom did. When visiting each other's houses, Eisler always came on foot—a walk of about ten minutes—whereas Brecht invariably used his car. Eisler in consequence had to do his swimming and walking by himself.

I remember them when they were working together on *Round Heads and Pointed Heads*. They were listening at the same time to Hitler speaking on the radio, exchanging glances, and shaking their heads in disbelief. They laughed a lot, Brecht even to the point of shedding tears. Eisler paced the room continuously. But both were listening intently. As the cries of *"Sieg heil!"* echoed out over the silent Svendborg Sound, I closed the window, thinking the Danes might misunderstand their reasons for listening to such things. Before the *Horst Wessel Lied* we switched the radio off, and Brecht pronounced the subtitle to his play *Round Heads and Pointed Heads*: "A horror story." Afterward both sat in complete silence and smoked—Eisler one cigarette after another, Brecht, in the rocking chair, cigars that kept going out. Nods and glances passed between them, but neither said a word. Yet at no time did I ever detect in either of them any sign of despondency.

Brecht and Eisler never shook hands or exchanged the customary greetings of "Good morning" or "Goodbye." They took up every conversation at the exact point at which they had left it on their previous meeting. Their friendly communion had something of a Chinese flavor. While Brecht was working in Denmark on *Fear and Misery of the Third Reich* (*Furcht und Elend des Dritten Reiches*), he gave Eisler several scenes to consider. Eisler went out into the garden and read them through at once. "Brecht expects that of me," he said, "so I mustn't be lazy." When he returned to the workroom he said spontaneously, "Great! Splendid!" But then came some suggestions for changes. Brecht noted them down on small scraps of paper, which he then stowed away somewhere. When he came to work on the revisions, he could not find them. Declaring that the lost passage could never be reconstructed, he searched and searched. Brecht felt guilty, but Eisler consoled him, offering to repeat his suggestions. It was no good; Brecht wanted his original notes, and everyone in the house was sent off to search. At last, delving into one of his many pockets, Brecht fished them out. Now he could get down to work again. Once more they could circle around each other and pace up and down, blurting out occasional sentences. Brecht typed some words on his typewriter and read them out. He laughed so much as he did so—his cigar still fixed in his mouth—that I could not understand a single word. But Eisler understood it all.

It is interesting to what extent Brecht's work with his various collaborators differed in kind. Each helped Brecht in his own way, by collecting material, making copies, inserting corrections, and so on. And each of them Brecht put to work in that particular way. Among these assistants—most of them, it must be said, women—Elisabeth Hauptmann stood out as the only exception. She truly collaborated in his plays, above all in the period before his emigration. For example, she discovered John Gay's

The Beggar's Opera, translated it for Brecht from the English, and then joined directly in the writing of *The Threepenny Opera*. The same happened with other plays of this period. There is no doubt in my opinion that her share in Brecht's work is a large one.

Elisabeth Hauptmann has told me the way in which they worked together. She and Brecht lived in Berlin in two neighboring apartments, connected by internal telephone. Thus she could always be reached, day and night. Once the other assistants had departed, he and she would go through what had been discussed and prepare themselves for work the following day. She was always willing to work till she dropped. Once, when Brecht had to make a journey, he left her a pile of "homework." The play *Happy End* was written in this way, Brecht contributing only the lyrics. But *Happy End* gave him the inspiration for *Saint Joan of the Stockyards*. I believe his literary collaboration with Elisabeth Hauptmann was the closest Brecht ever had. She was herself a writer, and she placed her talent at his disposal.

Margarete Steffin—Brecht called her Grete—joined his circle in 1932. She was not a writer herself in the full sense of the word, though she had written a few plays for children and made some good translations. But writing was not her strongest talent. What Brecht most valued about her, however strange it may sound, was the fact that she was a communist with a truly proletarian background. For him this was of more importance than one might think.

Grete had come to him from an amateur theatrical company. She played the housemaid in the 1932 production of *The Mother*, and Brecht got to know her during rehearsals. At the start she worked for him solely as a secretary. I have known many first-class secretaries, but none to match Grete Steffin. No one could take down shorthand so swiftly or with such understanding, when Brecht was dictating or when she was taking part in a discussion, and I have never seen anyone else type so fast.

It was only after a year or two that she began to work with him in a different way. One needed time to get used to Brecht's manner of thinking and the speed and variety of his thoughts. Brecht has named Margarete Steffin as his collaborator in many of his plays. Unlike Elisabeth Hauptmann, she did not join in the writing of them, but she was a relentless critic. She wanted to ensure that even the workers would understand Brecht's poetry. She insisted he rephrase formulations she considered "twisted." Particularly in this regard she was indispensable.

I remember that in Denmark Brecht possessed a little cardboard donkey. It had a movable head, which it shook when one pulled a string. Round its neck was a label on which was written, "I want to understand you too." When I found something unclear, I would pull the string, and the donkey would say, "No!"

Grete Steffin was even stricter than I was. Unlike me, she knew a lot about the forms and rules of versification. She pointed out to Brecht, for example, the bad iambics in *Arturo Ui*. Of course, it was all done with the greatest good humor. When I say "strict," I mean, in relation to Brecht, a light-handed strictness.

I have never met a harder-working person than Margarete Steffin. Since she wished to learn Danish quickly— and she really did succeed—she translated my bad novel, *Videre*, into German. She was then able later to translate Nexö. She had an enormous gift for languages, and in Sweden and Finland too could make herself understood in the native tongue. She spoke and wrote both Russian and English perfectly. She was in fact a linguistic genius.

Grete and I had a fine time together, and that was owing to the fact that Brecht lived so far from Copenhagen. When people came to visit him, he would send me a telegram, "Please pick up." This happened, for instance, when Fritz Sternberg and then Brecht's old school friend, Otto Müllereisert, came to Denmark. One day I received a telegram: "Please pick up collaborator Margarete Steffin." I had no idea who Margarete Steffin was, but I drove to the station in my large Lincoln car to fetch her. I was then still married to Robert Lund and I had a fine apartment, to which I took her. She stayed with me for three months. I offered her a room because I knew emigrants must be careful with their money. In fact, Grete was not poor, but hotels are expensive.

Grete kept in touch with Brecht by letter or by telephone. Although he needed her to work with him, Helene Weigel was unwilling to have her at Skovsbostrand. Grete was tubercular, and Helene feared for her children. On Christmas Eve Grete broke down and told me everything: She was in love with Brecht. Of course. What else? But I still find it puzzling that he kept her waiting so long in Copenhagen before he came to see her. There's no help for it, I must say it some time, despite my love for him: Brecht was a coward. I can imagine that it was a full three months before Brecht could bring himself to tell his wife, "Grete is here too."

At that time I was very close to Helene, and the situation caused me some concern. Helli badly wanted to learn typing and to work as Brecht's secretary. But genius though she was, Helli was not cut out to be a secretary. I found her one day with a plaster bandage around her wrist; she had strained a tendon while typing. Many things she could do—but not that.

Nobody could replace Margarete Steffin as Brecht's secretary. When he had made corrections on a draft, he would, without having to ask, find a clean, freshly typed manuscript on his desk the following morning. And the typescript had the neatness and spotlessness Brecht needed in order to continue his work. He had a preference for fine-grained paper, as thin as that used in making cigarettes. It called for great ingenuity to write on this, particularly when several carbon copies were required, but Grete Steffin managed it. In Finland she typed *Arturo Ui* on airmail paper, so it would not cost too much to send by post.

When Grete did at last move from Copenhagen to Skovsbostrand, Helene prepared a very nice room for her, with furniture of Danish oak, but on account of the children it was situated some way away from her own house. Nor did Grete eat at Helene's table; Brecht would take the meal to her in the little Ford I had bought for him for three hundred Kronen, then drive straight back. The journey to and fro took about four minutes.

Day by day Grete grew weaker. Robert Lund was treating her, and he decided to send her into hospital at the very time *Round Heads and Pointed Heads* was being rehearsed in Copenhagen. Grete wished at all costs to be present, and Brecht told Robert Lund, "It's no use, she can't go to the hospital now, for I need her." Robert Lund replied sharply, "She is going to the hospital this evening." And so it happened.

Once again Helene Weigel came to the rescue and lent a hand with the rehearsals. Brecht sent for her because he always needed another person at his side. But every day after the rehearsal he would get on a streetcar and make the half-hour journey to the hospital, bearing flowers and fruit and whatever else Grete might require. During the time she was there, she wrote a visionary story for Brecht, telling how she had watched a consumptive patient die—through a hole in the wall. She was very much preoccupied with death, but utterly unwilling to die.

There were difficulties later in getting Grete to Sweden and then to Finland. On account of her illness she could not get a visa for permanent residence in America, only a visitor's visa. It was dreadful to see her wasting away. If we could have left Finland earlier, it is possible she might have been cured, the winter in Finland being too severe for consumptives. But the visa arrived too late.

When in Leningrad I had to share a room with Grete, I knew at last for certain just how ill she was. She coughed so violently that I put my own blanket over hers, but that was no help either. Afterward, in Moscow, she acted as Brecht's interpreter and arranged all his meetings and discussions. Up to the end she tried to help him, but one day she suddenly collapsed. Her face was quite gray. She could no longer stand on her feet, and had to be taken off to hospital.

In the hospital everything possible was done for her in the most touching manner. She was given a very nice large room all to herself, and the most experienced specialists looked after her. I am convinced that if he had not had complete confidence in the doctors, Brecht would not have continued his journey. As it was, arrangements were made for her to follow him after her recovery, though before that she was to spend a few months recuperating in a sanatorium on the Crimean peninsula. Brecht left with her a box of manuscripts, consisting mainly of notes written by Grete herself. All he left behind of his own were things of which he possessed duplicates. It is interesting that when Brecht moved from one place to another, he never left behind anything that he might later need for his work. I have myself gone through and sorted out his manuscripts. Grete's notes must all have remained in her possession.

Grete was very calm when the time came for us to leave the country without her. She hid her sorrow as Brecht bade her goodbye. She was a brave person, a true fighter. Probably she knew inside herself what her real condition was. Curiously, although a party comrade, she had once had her hand read, and she had been told she would die at the age of thirty-three. And that, indeed, is exactly what happened! Now and again she would say in a joking way, "When I'm thirty-three, I shall die." But her tone as she said it was no different from what mine would be if, after breaking a mirror, I remarked, "That means seven years' bad luck." Yet I am not at all sure that she did not, after all, believe in the prediction. Grete Steffin died in Moscow.

Our journey to Vladivostok on the Trans-Siberian express took ten days. Every day Brecht received a telegram from his friends, telling him how Grete was getting on. The final telegram gave precise details of her death. Brecht had feared that she might ask for him at the end. But it was not Brecht she asked for, it was the doctor. The comrade who sent the telegram knew what had been worrying Brecht.

For four days no smile appeared on his face. I offered him my single cabin in the sleeping car, for he was sharing one with Helene, Steff, and Barbara. I could have gone somewhere else. But Helene said, "What for? He'll quickly forget." He smiled again for the first time as we got off the train. On the platform were Russian children selling lilies of the valley. They had been Grete's favorite flowers. When I saw her for the last time, I had brought her some.

Eight days after we embarked on the Swedish ship that took us from Vladivostok to the United States, Hitler invaded the Soviet Union. We realized then that we had left Moscow just in time.

5

When Hitler signed a nonaggression pact with Denmark, Brecht packed his trunks. Many friends, and comrades too, said, "There's no need for you to go now. You'll be quite safe in Denmark." Brecht replied, "No. Now I really know I must leave." This was a year before Hitler's troops overran Denmark. As you can read in the *Svendborg Poems*: "The governments make pacts of nonaggression—little man, make your will."

Brecht decided to move to Sweden. He had no idea how difficult that would be. He applied for an entry visa at the Swedish consulate in Copenhagen. But Sweden was not interested in opening its doors to German emigrants, and particularly not to communist ones. It had more than enough already, and Sweden maintained good relations with Nazi Germany. Generally speaking, any German—and even a Nazi—could get a visitor's visa. It was made out in principle for six months, and the main aim of it was to ensure that at the end of this period the visitor could be got rid of without argument. To obtain it, Brecht would have had to produce a Danish residence permit, also valid for six months. However, Denmark issued permits for only three months, after which time they had to be renewed. For Brecht, Sweden's terms were unrealizable in practice—and basically they were a political abomination, being aimed mainly at communists. Social democrats were protected by Denmark's social democratic government, but communists could be deported quite legally—even to Germany—from the country in which they had sought refuge.

I went to see the State Secretary. He told me, "It is an honor to Denmark to have a Gorki here as guest, but nevertheless we can't give him a residence permit for six months." I had borrowed jewelry and an arctic fox fur from my rich lady friends, but in the end it was only my sweet smile that could persuade the secretary to change his mind. As I left, he said, "Next time you'll find I'm free for you only at night." Brecht found that very amusing. I alerted Georg Branting, whom I had met in Madrid. (He was the son of Hjalmar Branting, one of Lenin's intimate associates, and he had conducted the counter-trial in London to the Reichstag trial; at this time he was a member of the Swedish Parliament.) Branting flew down to Copenhagen at once and completed the formalities for Brecht's entry into Sweden.

Visa difficulties remained only for Margarete Steffin, though she was now married to a Dane (only formally, of course, in order to procure a passport). She spoke Danish well (wrote it correctly too—better perhaps than I do), but she had a German accent. And that is what the secret police agents fastened on. They discovered that she had entered Denmark as a German emigrant and was working as Bertolt Brecht's secretary. Again it was due to Georg Branting that, despite this, she was eventually able to go to Sweden. She was happy there. The climate suited her, and she had a pleasant place to live.

At the outset only Brecht, Helene, Steff, Barbara, and I traveled to Sweden. Grete joined us later. Georg Branting was there to meet us. He had found a house on the island of Lidingö to the northeast of Stockholm, which the sculptress Ninnan Santesson was prepared to rent to the Brechts very cheaply. Ninnan Santesson later made a model of Helene's head, but then regrettably destroyed it. I suppose she was not satisfied with it. Brecht took photographs of the work in various stages of its progress, and to accompany it wrote an essay, *"Betrachtung der Kunst oder Kunst der Betrachtung"* ("Observing Art, or The Art of Observing"). The house had a huge studio, in which Brecht set up his workroom. It was even larger than the long workroom he had later in Buckow on the Schermützel lake. Stairs led from the studio to a small, open room, a sort of gallery with a balustrade. Here Brecht installed his bed.

Though in Sweden he was in reasonable safety, Brecht feared the situation might become increasingly worse. He was always greedy for information, and his little radio became his most prized possession. He trailed it with him through all the countries of his exile, and once even wrote about it in a poem: "Mornings I turn it on and hear the victory bulletins of my enemies."

I returned to Denmark, visiting Brecht in Lidingö only when I had no stage commitments or was on holiday. The first thing I did was to translate *Fear and Misery of the Third Reich* and stage it in my workers' theater. We continued performing it even after the Nazis were in Denmark. They invaded Denmark and Norway on April 9, 1940. The Norwegians resisted for sixty days; the Danes gave in without a struggle. Those were cruel times, for I was no longer in contact with Brecht, mail connections having been suspended. My main fear was that the Nazis would occupy Sweden too and that Brecht would not get away in time. There was nothing I could do for him.

I thought I could at least get Nexö out of Copenhagen,

and so I went to see him. I found him in a very happy mood. Outside his front door stood a large car from the Soviet Embassy. He had been offered an escort to the embassy, where he would be safe and where he would be given Soviet citizenship. But the old man turned them down. "I'm a Dane," he said, "but would you be kind enough to drive me to the airport? I'd like to see the swine land." And he did indeed go to the airport to inspect the Nazi planes with their swastikas. Nexö's behavior was magnificent. Though I had not succeeded in getting him away, I felt in some way comforted. I told myself that, if anything happened in Sweden, Soviet diplomats would surely go to Brecht too and offer him asylum in the embassy.

The period before Hitler came to Denmark was a very interesting one for me. Whenever I visited Brecht in Stockholm, we would talk about the situation in Sweden. Though a neutral state, Sweden was still exporting iron ore to Germany and thus giving aid to the Nazi arms industry, as well as earning a lot of money. In order to show the effects of supporting the Nazis, we wrote the play *What's the Price of Iron?* (*Was kostet das Eisen?*). That is to say, I began working with some members of a Swedish social democratic workers' theater, and Brecht then joined in to help us. In his hands our agitprop play turned into something nearer a knockabout comedy. To round it off, Brecht insisted that the hair of the actor playing the iron merchant should be made to stand on end like a clown's. We managed that with the aid of a wig.

Brecht did not attend the rehearsals. He found constant travel between Lidingö and Stockholm too irksome. Instead, he spurred me on with praise: "You're doing it brilliantly." He was satisfied with my production, which meant that over the past six years I had progressed a bit and learned a great deal. Since I had acting engagements in Copenhagen at the time of the dress rehearsal and opening performance, Brecht had photographs taken. He stuck them in a small leather album, on the cover of which he wrote with his own hand: *Was kostet das Eisen?*

The painter Hans Tombrock has made a drawing of Brecht's workroom during a discussion with former fighters in Spain, most of them Germans. They are shown sitting around Brecht in a semicircle. Tombrock knows their full names, I only their first names. Later, in the G.D.R., I occasionally came across people who asked me whether I did not remember them, mentioning names which were completely strange to me. Now I know that among those who had visited Brecht in Sweden were Anton Plenikowski, Paul Verner, and Herbert Warnke. There they had been called Walter or Peter. As illegal emigrants they had to conceal their true identities.

So tragic were the stories the emigrants brought back from Spain that Brecht decided to write a prologue and epilogue for his play *Señora Carrar's Rifles*. The Spanish Civil War has ended, and the fighters find themselves in a French internment camp. A guard asks one of the prisoners behind the barbed wire, "What exactly made you go there to fight?" The worker from the International Brigade points to Señora Carrar and tells her story. Then comes the play. In the epilogue the point is made: So, after all, the struggle was justified. Even those who had not wanted to become involved had been mobilized. This was the question at the center of Brecht's discussions, since so many people—too many—had lost their lives. The same problem occupied us in *The Days of the Commune (Die Tage der Commune)*. Even a lost battle is not in vain: later generations learn from it.

Hans Tombrock was present at all these discussions. Brecht and he were really close friends. In my opinion,

Ruth Berlau (right) and her sister Edith.
ARCHIV JOHANNES HOFFMANN

Setting out for Moscow, 1930.
ARCHIV JOHANNES HOFFMANN

At the drama festival in Moscow, 1933.
MOGENS VOLTELEN

Ruth Berlau, 1935. MYDTSKOV

Dr. Robert Lund,
Ruth Berlau's husband.
ARCHIV JOHANNES HOFFMANN

Bertolt Brecht and
Ruth Berlau in Denmark,
1933. MOGENS VOLTELEN

Helene Weigel
in Denmark, 1933.
MOGENS VOLTELEN

Bertolt Brecht in Denmark, 1933.
MOGENS VOLTELEN

Ruth Berlau
on her motorcycle
in Denmark, 1937.
ARCHIV BUNGE

Ruth Berlau
as Brecht's St. Joan,
on the roof of
the Royal Theater,
Copenhagen, 1935.
ARCHIV BUNGE

Brecht in
Denmark, 1938.
MOGENS VOLTELEN

Ruth Berlau, 1938.
MOGENS VOLTELEN

Below:
Ruth Berlau in her
Copenhagen
apartment with
Mogens Voltelen, 1937.
MOGENS VOLTELEN

Below right: Brecht
and Karin Michaelis
(seated) in Denmark;
Helene Weigel and
Ruth Berlau (center
back row). RICHSVEJ

Ruth Berlau (right) in *The Women of Niskavuori* at the Royal Theater, Copenhagen, 1938.

Hans Tombrock and Brecht in Finland, 1941.

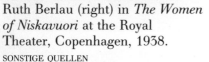

Ruth Berlau (left) as Kristina in Strindberg's *Gustav Vasa* at the Royal Theater, Copenhagen, 1939.

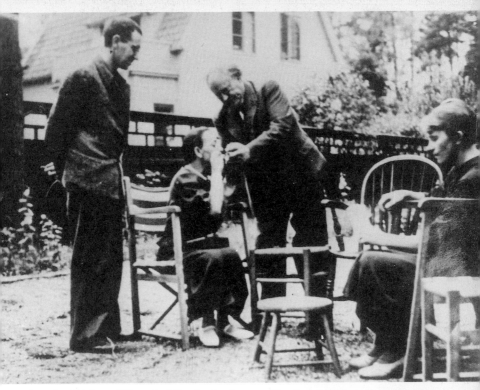

Brecht, Helene Weigel, Martin Andersen Nexö, and Margarete Steffin
in Denmark, 1939. RUTH BERLAU

Martin Andersen Nexö. RUTH BERLAU

Brecht with Margarete Steffin
in Finland, 1941. RUTH BERLAU

Brecht and Lion
Feuchtwanger in
Santa Monica.
RUTH BERLAU

Peter Lorre reading
Brecht's *Svendborg
Poems*, 1943.
RUTH BERLAU

Brecht on the balcony of
Ruth Berlau's New York
apartment. ARCHIV BUNGE

Brecht had only two intimate friends, with whom he also discussed private matters, something he otherwise never did. One was his school friend Otto Müllereisert, and the other was Hans Tombrock.

When I went to Lidingö during the summer I used to live in a tent. Hans Tombrock was the only person who was ever invited to this tent, naturally in Brecht's company. Brecht did not look kindly on anyone visiting me there, but with Tombrock he made an exception.

Herbert Sandberg, the graphic artist, once said to me, "Brecht knew nothing about painting." I asked him how he justified that opinion. Sandberg instanced Brecht's assessment of Tombrock, whom he himself considered "a quite dreadful painter." But in exile Brecht was deprived of Caspar Neher, with whom he could always discuss his plays, and that was a great disadvantage. Tombrock was a substitute for Neher, but he was also more than that: a promoter of ideas as well as a pupil. He made some two dozen engravings for *Galileo*, which Brecht prized highly. Tombrock could identify himself wholly with Brecht's line of thought. They also worked closely together on *Mother Courage*, and Brecht loved his big picture of Mother Courage's camp. Tombrock was self-taught, but in Brecht's opinion very talented. He described himself as a "street artist," because he frequently sold his pictures on the street. But some of them now hang in Swedish art galleries.

Brecht used Tombrock. He could lecture him, something he always liked doing. His essay *"Verfremdungseffekt in den erzählenden Bildern des älteren Breughel"* ("Alienation Effect in the Narrative Pictures of Breughel the Elder") stemmed from lessons he gave to Tombrock. His aim was to introduce Tombrock, who was primarily a landscape artist, to concrete social themes. For a while Tombrock was his sacrificial lamb, but he was a willing victim, quite content with his role, and it was certainly not to his disadvantage. I know of nobody else with whom Brecht had better discussions about art than with Tombrock, the reason being that Brecht could feel himself superior.

Tombrock is writing a book about his friendship with Brecht, in which he recalls their discussions, often word for word. Tombrock was a vagabond by nature. He could never settle anywhere for long. He always reminds me of Ahasuerus, the Wandering Jew.

Brecht thought better when he could speak. In a conversation, thoughts must be clearly expressed, to enable the other person to understand them. Kleist has written a classic essay on this subject. Tombrock is an example of the way in which Brecht used people in order, through discussion, to clarify his own thoughts on various matters. In Sweden he had few people with whom he could talk, and that is why small people like myself and Tombrock were drawn in as an aid to his thinking. Brecht also spent whole evenings conversing with Hermann Greid, an exiled German actor and writer who lived with his Swedish-born Jewish wife in Stockholm. Greid was not a very interesting personality, but there was nobody else around. Brecht had only to telephone him, and Greid would come. The person most deserving of pity was Helene Weigel, who had the job of getting someone to go along each evening.

In Finland this turned into a real problem for Helli. In that dreary neighborhood there was literally nobody far and wide with whom Brecht could talk. When Hella Wuolijoki went off to her estate in Marlebäck, Brecht and Helene were left alone in Helsingfors. The only person then available was a Finnish woman, a writer with whom Brecht had absolutely nothing in common. Helli would ring her, begging her to come round. But neither she nor anyone else was willing. "Why?" they asked. "What's the point?" None of them understood the situation. It was a difficult time for Brecht, who came to regard himself as the voice of one crying in the wilderness.

Hermann Greid had at least picked up something on the theatrical front, though it was not very much. He would come, bringing his manuscripts. Brecht would glance through them, but I do not think he ever read them to the end. However, he could carry on a conversation with Greid, taking a point from one of these manuscripts and then pursuing his own thoughts. I believe Brecht did write something in his working journal about Greid's plays, but mostly his own thoughts about them. If he did ever quote Greid, he must surely have improved on it.

On April 17, 1940, eight days after the Nazis invaded Denmark and Norway, Brecht left Sweden for Finland. Through its policy of neutral trading Sweden had become dependent, and the government was now allowing German troops to move through Sweden in order to attack Norway. Brecht no longer felt comfortable in Stockholm.

I remained in Denmark for quite a while longer. Then Brecht ordered me to leave the country, and the party also advised me to go. One evening, returning from a performance of *Fear and Misery in the Third Reich*, I found my home gone. The window panes had been smashed, the doors torn off their hinges, and everything inside destroyed. This was the work of Danish Nazis. They had long been organized and were a danger particularly to us communists. The Germans themselves did not know who we were; they used the Danish Nazis as secret agents.

When Brecht left Germany, he did not believe the Nazi

regime would last very long, and so he settled down as near to the German border as possible, in order to be able to make a quick return. Of that I am firmly convinced. But when the Nazis spread terror throughout Germany, when political parties and trades unions were banned, when Hitler offered nonaggression pacts while at the same time arming his troops, and when the Danish social democrats proved so irresolute, Brecht's main wish was to get out quickly. I believe he tried to obtain American visas while still in Denmark. However, it was not easy, and it took time. That was why he moved on to Sweden. His next refuge, Finland, was also a temporary solution, owing to the fact that he was still awaiting a visa for America. And in Sweden the ground was crumbling beneath his feet.

He continued to live dangerously in Finland. The idiotic claim that the Soviet Union had robbed Finland of Karelia was inflaming the Finnish people, and Finnish Nazis were running around making open propaganda against the Soviet Union. Their sympathies were with Germany. It was no place for Brecht to settle permanently.

The war between Finland and the Soviet Union had ended by the time Brecht reached Finland. The Soviet ambassador in Stockholm played a major part in the negotiations leading to an armistice between the two warring countries. Unusually, this ambassador was a woman, the famous Alexandra Kollontai, who at that time was nearly seventy years old and almost paralyzed on the left side. Thanks to her efforts, Sweden refrained from joining the war in support of Finland. I have always admired her greatly.

The other great politician who helped to bring about the armistice was Hella Wuolijoki. She was a member of the Finnish Parliament and when there was anything important to be done, she could be found in London with Churchill at 10 Downing Street. Hella was a "very dangerous" communist. Regardless of her own safety, she secretly gave shelter to Soviet patriots on her Marlebäck estate. The Nazis later kept her in prison for four years. Actually, she was condemned to death, but they had not dared carry out the sentence. Shortly before she died Hella said, "I can't understand why the Nazis shut me up. For four years! There was no reason to send me to prison." At that time every table in almost every restaurant was decorated with a swastika pennant, and all the streets were hung with swastika flags. Hella Wuolijoki had been the only person publicly to protest.

Ever since I played Marta in Hella's play *The Women of Niskavuori* we had been deeply attached to one another. Even at that time I had been planning Brecht's refuge on her estate, and I told her, "If anything happens, you must find room for Brecht and his family at once." Hella knew more about Brecht than just *The Threepenny Opera*, something that in those days could not be taken for granted. I was certain that she would take good care of Brecht. She was a very large landowner, tremendously rich—almost a Puntila, in fact.

Before leaving Sweden Brecht wrote me a letter, which reached me by a roundabout route. It was not a proper letter but a scrap of paper on which he had jotted down things that had occurred to him as he was preparing for his journey. He was very cautious, fearing that if war broke out, he would be unable to leave Sweden and would be interned. He was already having difficulties with his residence permit and was being watched more closely than before. Brecht wrote that I also should go to Hella Wuolijoki in Finland, and that from now on he intended to include me in all his travel arrangements. He told me to apply at once for an American visa—an immigration

91

visa if possible, but if that should take too long, a visitor's visa. "For," wrote Brecht, "from now on, wherever I go I shall expect to find you, and I reckon on you always. And it is not for your sake, Ruth, that I am reckoning on your coming, but for my own." He advised me to act calmly, practically, humorously, but also critically. If I needed money, I should borrow it from Georg Branting, to whom he had given a pledge to pay everything back. He was taking the proofs of our book *Jedes Tier kann es* with him, so that we could continue work on it. He gave me addresses in Finland and wrote down Hella Wuolijoki's telephone number. He told me to learn these by heart and then destroy the letter, though I might cut out and keep the last paragraph. This read, "Dear Ruth, come soon. Everything is unchanged, firm and good. J.e.*d*. And that will remain unchanged. However long we are separated. For ten years, even for twenty years. As for Lai-tu: She is instructed to take care of herself and survive all dangers till *our* thing begins, the real thing for which one must preserve oneself. Dear Ruth e. p. e. p. Bertolt."

I will explain the two abbreviations. J.e.d. stands for *Jeg elsker dig*, the Danish words for *I love you*. And e. p. e. p. are the initials of the Latin words *et prope et procul*, which mean *near and far*. I had not the heart to destroy the first part of the letter, as Brecht bade me. I have kept it intact and carried it constantly on me. But I must confess that in more recent years, when things became difficult between Brecht and myself, I sometimes screwed it up and resolved to burn it—naturally on account of that final paragraph. Yet in the end I could not bring myself to do it. Instead, I carefully smoothed it out again. And so it has remained intact.

* * *

At the start of his stay in Finland Brecht lived in Helsinki, not far from the harbor. As always, Helene—it was one of her outstanding qualities—set up a workroom for Brecht. It was not very large, but it gave him enough space to spread out his manuscripts. Besides this workroom, as far as I can remember, the apartment consisted only of a sort of lobby with a glass door and a narrow, though fairly long, kitchen. Helli turned the lobby into a room for the children. By putting up a curtain, she divided the kitchen into two sections, one for cooking and washing, the other as her bedroom. Helli did all this in so natural and self-evident a way that Brecht had no choice but to occupy the only sizable room himself.

When I arrived in Finland, he was working on his play *The Good Person of Szechwan* (*Der gute Mensch von Sezuan*). The first version he had already completed in Denmark, and he dedicated it to Helene Weigel—no later, I think, than 1935. He revised the play once again in Finland, and this is how it was done:

Coffee was in short supply in Finland, not to be seen either in shops or in restaurants. Everything else—meat and eggs, for example—was also rationed. I was living in a small boarding house about eight to ten minutes' walk from Brecht's home. For breakfast we were given something distantly related to coffee; at least, it looked brown. The best thing about it was that it was served in a splendid copper pot. Bearing this copper pot wrapped in newspaper (nobody in the boarding house must see me doing it), I would run punctually at seven o'clock to Brecht's house. Dressed in his leather jacket, he would open the window as soon as he saw me coming down the street, and I would hand him the copper pot. Not a word was said, not even "Good morning" or "Thank you," but it was Brecht's golden hour. Quickly he would pour the stuff into another pot, then sit down at once to work. Each afternoon at about three, after he had eaten and taken his nap, he would read to me what he had written during the morning, and we would discuss it.

In the summer we all moved out to Hella Wuolijoki's estate. There we had a very good time. Brecht and his family, together with Grete Steffin, lived in a blockhouse, six or eight minutes away from the main mansion. It was wonderfully situated in a birch wood right beside the lake. I lived with Hella, with whom I regularly took my meals. There were always mushrooms and talk about mushrooms. I have no idea from whom Brecht took the mushroom conversations in *Puntila*—whether from Hella Wuolijoki or from Helene Weigel, for each strove to outdo the other in their expert knowledge of fungi.

Influential people came to visit Hella in Marlebäck, among them government ministers. They played poker, and it was fantastic to observe how they all tried to bluff each other. The Minister of Finance always came out ahead. Occasionally I was allowed to take part, but no one else was ever invited.

Almost every evening after supper Brecht, Helene, and Grete would come to the mansion. Hella would then serve coffee, which she got from our large neighbor country (Russia), and tell stories about Finland. She was inexhaustible and would keep talking until well into the night. It was all so fascinating that even Brecht kept his mouth shut. Grete Steffin would seat herself behind a palm and take down all these wonderful stories in shorthand. We knew what she was doing, but Hella didn't.

One evening Hella told us about a man she knew. He was the owner of a sawmill, and he became the model for Puntila. If I had not previously known what a true feudal baron was, I should at once have learned it from this story. Hella said she had written a play about this man, but unfortunately no theater had shown any interest. She was thinking of writing a new version of it. She cast a sidelong glance at Brecht, who listened with great amusement as she gave an impromptu account of the play. He knew what she was hinting at. It was the start of their collaboration.

Though Hella was a wonderful storyteller, she was no dramatist. She had no idea how to write plays. Brecht saw that at once, while she was recounting her plot. Starting out from Hella's play and the stories she had told, he wrote his *Mr. Puntila and His Man Matti* (*Herr Puntila und sein Knecht Matti*), bolstering it with observations of his own. For instance, the scene in which Puntila stands on the balcony giving directions to his people was something he had seen in Hella's own house. She had stood on her balcony like a real-life Puntila, scolding her servants, because they had failed to prevent a bull getting to a too-young heifer. One idea was my own contribution: the marriage trial with a slap on the bottom.

There came a time when I fell out with Hella. I left her house and put up a tent in the little birch grove, just a stone's throw away from Brecht's house. I had my typewriter with me. Brecht visited me in the tent, and we would work together. That is where most of the *Flüchtlingsgespräche* (*Refugee Conversations*) were written. Brecht almost killed himself laughing as we wrote them. For him it was not "serious" work, but rather a kind of loosening-up exercise. He did not publish the pieces, but at the time he found his ideas wonderful. I was mad about these stories, and was able to provide a lot of ideas for them—and not for the Danish chapter only.

As summer ended, we returned to Helsinki. Brecht had kept the little apartment in the city, since Marlebäck was habitable only in summer. In Helsinki he wrote his play *The Resistible Rise of Arturo Ui* (*Der aufhaltsame Aufstieg des Arturo Ui*). The first version was done in an incredibly short time, for Brecht was eager to complete the play before leaving Finland.

He was hoping to make some quick money in America with this play. There he could call on Peter Lorre, Oskar Homolka, and all the other great actors he had once worked with in Germany. With them, he thought, it could be staged swiftly. That, unfortunately, was wrong: Nobody in America was interested in the play, and it was neither staged nor filmed.

I remember that in America we met an actor named Donath who had emigrated from Germany. He could imitate Hitler in an uncanny fashion. After we had listened to Hitler's speeches on the radio, Donath would go on speaking in the Hitler style, making up the text as he went along. We would listen, sometimes laughing, but sometimes horrified. He was a good actor who could have played Arturo Ui in America. Unfortunately he was not well known, so nothing came of it.

Brecht knew he could not stay in Finland. He had visas for himself and his family but none for Grete Steffin. He put off our departure for America from one day to the next, waiting for this visa. His reason formerly for not going on to the Writers' Congress in Madrid had been because bombs were falling, yet his decision to remain so long in Finland was no less dangerous. It was just that he could not bring himself to let Grete down. I admired him greatly for that.

Luckily, besides money for the journey, I had enough to keep me in America for about six months, and I also had some jewelry to fall back on in an emergency. But Brecht and Helene had five people to support: themselves, Steff, Barbara, and Grete Steffin.

I applied at the American consulate in Helsinki for my visa and paid the nine-dollar fee. Everything seemed in order, but the consulate decided to send a telegram to Copenhagen to make sure there was no objection to my journey to America. When I returned for the visa, I found the American consul standing there, red in the face, the reply from Denmark in his hand. He read it out to me: "Member of the communist party since 1930, visited the Soviet Union four times . . ." It was a long telegram. Reaching the end, the consul said, "You will never get inside the United States, and it's no use your applying anywhere else for a visa. I shall pass on the information I have received from Copenhagen." He opened the door for me to leave, but did not wish me goodbye. I was by now divorced from Robert Lund, and even if I had wanted to, I could not return to him in Denmark. I had burned all my bridges behind me and had nowhere to go. Despite my own opinion that from a political point of view, I would have done better to remain in Denmark, I had chosen to follow Brecht and was now stuck with my decision.

How I at last managed to prize open the door to America is an amusing story. I went to see the Danish consul in Finland. His name was Baek. I had forgotten him, but he had not forgotten me. He had been consul in Leningrad when I passed through there on my cycle journey to Moscow for the reactionary newspaper *Politiken*.

I can laugh about it now, but it was no laughing matter then. Brecht advised me to say to my Danish consul, "I'm no Dimitrov. Tell him it's all to do with the theater." So in I went and said, "I'm no Dimitrov." But it wasn't that that saved me. The consul merely said, "Go to the American consulate tomorrow, Ruth, but don't tell them you've spoken to me." I went to the consulate the following day and was handed my American visa without any more ado. "It was your ten-dollar smile that did it," Brecht said afterward.

The Danish consul had given the Americans the following message: "This Miss Berlau was married to Professor Robert Lund. She was an actress at the Danish Royal Theater. Though she did join the communist party, she is only a parlor communist. In Copenhagen she used to drive around in a huge Lincoln car, and nobody regarded her as a communist. They just laughed at her." Consul Baek told me this later. As a professional diplomat, he could not of course tell me in advance how he planned to arrange things.

In the meantime we were sitting around on our packed trunks and crates. I witnessed now for the third or fourth time a behavior that was typical of Brecht. He did not treat his manuscripts, books, and papers in the careless manner of Nexö and many others. On the contrary, he went to great trouble to preserve everything he had. He always looked after the transport of his manuscripts himself. So important was this to him that he did no further work at this time. Everything he wished to take with him he laid out on a long table, precisely arranged in order of projects, and checked time and again. When it came to the actual packing, Helene was of course the more practical of the two, but the decision what at all costs to take was made by Brecht himself. When in later years we moved from Switzerland to Berlin, and I left some time after he did, the same practice was followed. The most important things he took with him, the remainder being so arranged that I knew what must be taken and what if necessary could be left behind. Of course he would have preferred me to bring it all along, but that was beyond my physical strength.

It is worth noting that Brecht did not work for immediate effect. The general view is that he wrote about particular situations for a particular time. I do not think that is correct. Often he said to me, "In fifty years I shall be understood—in fifty years." And that is why he took such care of his manuscripts.

We had decided to travel via the Arctic port of Petsamo, that route being the shortest and cheapest. However, by the time we were ready to go, Petsamo was already under Nazi control, so we had to make the long journey through the Soviet Union.

We spent only two or three days in Leningrad. All I remember about that is Grete Steffin's illness, of which I have already written. We went on from there to Moscow, where Brecht was given a great reception. Arrangements for the continuation of our journey had been made even before we arrived. We stayed in a comfortable hotel in the city center, each of us with a room to ourselves.

We spent a week in Moscow. Brecht had been there before: the first time, I believe, with Erwin Piscator, then with Slatan Dudow when the *Kuhle Wampe* film was shown, and then once again with Grete Steffin (I think in 1935). Brecht was no longer the quiet person we were familiar with; in fact, he was very excited to be in Moscow again. He toured the city with us, to see how it had developed and also to study current conditions in the Soviet Union. He was interested in everything that was going on.

We had no financial difficulties in Leningrad and Moscow. Brecht was able to use royalties accumulated from his work with the periodical *Das Wort*, among other things. He bought something for each of us. Helene was given a small brown Persian lamb fur and I a black one. Then as now, I habitually wore black. Brecht liked that.

I had many friends of my own in Moscow, and I visited them. I also had conversations with people from the Writers' Union.

Then came the sad moment when we took Grete Steffin

to the hospital. Six tickets for the Trans-Siberian express had already been bought, including one for Grete. Of course she was unable to travel with us, but we had to leave, otherwise we should have missed the ship in Vladivostok. Brecht left his manuscripts behind with Comrade Mikhail Apletin. Later I was deeply touched when, in his brief speech on receiving the Lenin Peace Prize, Brecht made special mention of Apletin as a good friend for looking after Grete and for keeping an eye on his manuscripts during the war. In Moscow there had been other things to worry about during that time.

We had a comfortable journey to Vladivostok. The train had proper little saloons in which one could play chess or listen to the radio or drink tea from a samovar. One could also collect one's mail at the stations. We spent a few days in Vladivostok. By then Brecht had already recovered to some extent from the terrible blow of losing his best assistant.

We had reserved berths on the Swedish ship *Annie Johnson*. There we were all put into one cabin, I along with the whole family. Dreadful! But there was no other cabin free. Maybe that was because our passage had been booked so late, or because there were too many other emigrants to be accommodated. I immediately made friends with the radio officer. He had a cabin but was obliged to sleep in his workroom so that he could take calls at any time. He said, "You can have my cabin, if you like." I accepted. Naturally, he expected something else in return. After a short while he realized it was his cabin I wanted, not him. Never again in my life have I made so bitter an enemy. Tragically, the *Annie Johnson* was torpedoed on a later voyage and went down with all hands, with the captain and all the other lively people. She was a fine ship, with pleasant saloons and a swimming pool. The food was almost too abundant. We felt in very safe hands. A few days after our departure news came through on the radio that the Nazis had invaded the Soviet Union. Amid our despondency a witticism from Brecht raised our spirits.

On board was a Belgian diplomat. Brecht paid him some attention, feeling that a diplomat should know something about the world. The Belgian, however, was pleased that the Germans were making such good progress, and he predicted that all would be over in ten days' time. Hitler could be dealt with later. He had to say that, since on this ship he did not want to be seen as a Nazi supporter. Brecht never exchanged words with him again. "You can see what an ass he is," he told us. "He's spent his whole life nosing around, and he can't even imagine the Soviets winning."

Brecht was convinced from the very start that Hitler would never defeat the Soviet Union; he was only sad that so much would be destroyed by the war and that such sacrifices would have to be made. He never assumed that Hitler might win. Never! And that is remarkable, for the news bulletins at the beginning were terrible.

The voyage, if I rightly remember, lasted about two months. During this time I came down with mumps. Barbara got it first, then Steff. Since I had had mumps as a child, I had thought I was immune. I was very close to Barbara and Steff at that time, and I disregarded all warnings to keep clear of them. Then suddenly my cheeks began to swell. I with my round face—and now mumps on top of it; it really was a comic sight! The ship's doctor was like Robert Lund: Neither of them could bear sick people at any price. When someone was seasick, the doctor sat in the saloon playing the piano. Once the patient was better, the doctor reappeared on deck. I had a high temperature but was still quite cheerful. The doctor said to me, "Now we'll go and dine together." The other passengers fled when I appeared in the dining saloon. I admit I did not find eating much fun.

We called in at Manila in the Philippines and stayed there two or three days. I was annoyed not to be able to go ashore on account of my mumps. Helli discovered a shop near the harbor where a sale was going on. Brecht went shopping again and presented me with a gorgeous pajama suit in black Chinese silk, embroidered with a dragon. He spent a lot of time in the harbor, watching workers unloading the ship's cargo. They were handsome people but unimaginably thin. Between bouts of work they would eat a tiny helping of rice out of a little green leaf. It made a great impression on Brecht: he never forgot that little leaf with its bit of rice. Our ship put out from the Philippines very shortly before the Japanese occupied the islands. We had always escaped—from Denmark, from Sweden, from Finland, from the Soviet Union—just in time before the Germans arrived. Now it was the Japanese from whom we had to save ourselves. We fully realized how lucky we had been.

Throughout the voyage Brecht was very happy. Every day he went bathing—something he seldom did—dressed in very scanty brown trunks. He was at ease with himself, and he found time for Helli and the children. Brecht never showed much concern for his children, leaving that side of things entirely to Helli. She was the most wonderful mother I have ever met, and I learned a great deal from her.

Robert Lund had four children when I married him, but I had no idea how to treat children. I had only two of them to look after; the other two remained with their mother, though they visited us regularly. Once, on New Year's Eve, I arrived at Brecht's house with all four. Helene and the children had never met before, but all were welcomed with a warm embrace. This was more than I had achieved in ten years.

On one occasion, returning from London, Helene visited me in Copenhagen. She had come to see Grete Steffin, who had just arrived from Moscow and was staying with me. Lund's children enticed Helene out into the park attached to our grounds. There she discovered a little hut in which I had never taken any interest, not knowing what to do with it. But Helene Weigel turned it into a washroom for the children. She was always full of good, practical ideas.

Brecht never treated Steff and Barbara like children but would converse quite seriously with them. As they grew older, he allowed them to take part in his work—Steff in particular. He gave him books to read and asked him for his opinion. Steff was reading Diderot by the time he was eight; he could never have enough of books. Brecht was all in favor of it, even though Helli now and again warned him that Steff must take care of his eyes, which had been weak from a very early age.

At the beginning of their time in exile Brecht wished above all to teach his children how to look after themselves. He wrote in a poem, "One must learn how to come through," and "Take care of your stomach when you are hungry." But one day he told me, "I did that wrong. Now I'm going to tell Steff something else." He gave Steff an example: People are standing on a beach watching a man drown. Some of them are unable to rescue him, since they are too weak. For them it would be senseless to offer help, for they would only go under too. So they must just watch the man drowning. Others are stronger. They accept the risk of drowning themselves and try to save the drowning man. Still others are strong enough to bring the drowning man ashore without difficulty. In that case it is nothing special, for one does not need much courage when one has the will, and above all the strength, to help a fellow being.

Steff, ten years old at most, understood the parable.

During the voyage I was given the task of copying out Brecht's essay "Writing the Truth: Five Difficulties" ("*Fünf Schwierigkeiten beim Schreiben der Wahrheit*"). This essay had not yet been printed, and Brecht urgently needed several copies. I sat in my cabin, sweating over it. For me copying is the hardest thing I know—even harder than learning by heart. Everything must be just so, every letter and every comma in its proper place. The task was never-ending, and I was glad when from the ship we caught sight of the tall drilling towers of San Pedro and steamed into the harbor. Now, for better or worse, I should have to stop my copying.

The questions of the immigration officials dampened our high spirits. Their curiosity is nothing if not thorough. Wherever one lands in America, the drill is gone through, fingerprints taken, questions asked. Each immigrant is examined individually. He sits at a round table, having questions fired at him by four men. The most important question is whether one ever was, or still is, a communist; failing that, whether one has ever had dealings with the communist party. If so, all hope of being allowed into the United States is gone. I must confess to being very nervous at this interview. I was a party member. What should I do if I were sent back? I knew no one in America who could speak on my behalf. Brecht had Lion Feuchtwanger and Peter Lorre and other famous people who already lived in America. I still regard it as a miracle that I got through. Naturally, I could not tell the whole truth.

The immigration committee also wanted to know

whether we had money enough to support our stay in America. One had to be able on arrival to prove possession of a thousand dollars. We had divided our money between us so that each had that amount.

Brecht had been preparing to emigrate since 1932—a fact that he later made known to the Committee on Un-American Activities. At that hearing it was objected that Hitler did not assume power until 1933, but Brecht's answer was that—now, at any rate—it must be clear to everybody that the beginnings of Nazism went back much further. He had long foreseen Hitler's rise to power and had shaped his life accordingly. It was the reason why he had bought a house on the Ammersee, why he and Helene Weigel had got married, and why he had opened a bank account in Switzerland. If he were to be unable to go into hiding in Germany and had to flee abroad, he needed this money to live on. In Germany he had been earning well.

Friends in America had also been collecting money for him. Though for the time being he was not in need, Brecht accepted it. And Alexander Granach had already rented a house for him and his family in Hollywood (Brecht of course would not have said Hollywood but Santa Monica). So financially Brecht was relatively secure when he arrived in San Pedro.

In this connection I am reminded of something Helli once said to me (it must have been around 1935): "I don't know what else I can do; on account of the children I shall now have to accept money from Brecht." They had been in exile for nearly three years, and her small capital had been used up. Only later did I understand the meaning of Helli's words. Her main concern was that Brecht should have the financial freedom to write whatever he considered needful and truthful, without thought of money. Up till 1935 she never made a single claim on his earnings.

Young people in Berlin have sometimes asked me: How could Helene Weigel live with Brecht? For them, Helene Weigel is the embodiment of Mother Courage, the archetypal mother figure. What they wanted to know was: Why did Brecht have other women besides this wonderful woman, and why, despite that, did Helene Weigel remain loyal to him?

I myself do not find that so remarkable. It is a constellation found among many great artists. They are always on the search for people who inspire them. Brecht was inspired by beauty and by youth. I then told these young people of the great artistic companionship that existed between Helene Weigel and Brecht. During the whole period of exile, even in the most difficult circumstances, she had always selflessly seen to it that Brecht could carry on his work with the minimum of disturbance. She had done this unquestioningly, without ever drawing attention to herself. Brecht was able to accept what she offered him without a qualm. But Helene gained something from it too. Today she is in charge of the best, most renowned theater in the world; she is a world-famous actress who can play any role she wants; and she is completely independent. Brecht, for his part, wrote the finest and longest roles in his plays for Helene Weigel. (Incidentally, I have heard that she has promised Brecht to go on playing Mother Courage until she is sixty. That is splendid news.)

Once, when I was disappointed in a person who had not lived up to our expectations, Brecht took a pencil and wrote: "You can expect so much from one person, so much from another, and only so much from a third. You must never feel let down or disappointed if your expectations are not fulfilled. You are then a victim of your own prejudices. If you have *one* person on whom you can rely one hundred percent, then you have much. There are no two such persons." For Brecht this one person was Helene Weigel. Though we never spoke of it, we both knew it was so. Brecht, in fact, was a very lonely person. He had to protect himself, at all times and in all directions. Truly Helene Weigel was the only one on whom he could rely implicitly.

The story of how Brecht and Helene Weigel came together is a nice one. Brecht told it me himself. In the early twenties he was starved, run down, and whore-ridden. He had no work and no idea where to go. At this time Helene Weigel was with the actor Alexander Granach. Brecht and Helene first met after a theater performance in Berlin. He was a full-fledged Bohemian, whereas she was already a member of the communist party. Brecht lied to her, telling her he did not live in Berlin and had intended to return that evening to Munich or Augsburg. Unfortunately, he had missed his train. She offered him a bed for the night in her studio. She made up a bed for him—then went to her own room. A little later there was a knock at the door. Brecht was standing there. "It's very cold here," he said. "It doesn't seem at all cold to me," she responded. "No," he said, "it's warmer in your room." However, he was obliged to return to the cold—on that evening, at any rate: women could not withstand Brecht for long.

Helene Weigel was quite well known in Berlin's artistic circles. Though she had not yet played any major roles, nobody was in any doubt about her talent. When she decided to have a child by Brecht, there was no thought of marriage. She drove around with Fritz Kortner in an advanced state of pregnancy and a seventh heaven of delight. Of all the photographs of Helene Weigel, the loveliest are those taken at that time. Her first child was Stefan; Barbara arrived a few years later.

There is an amusing story about Stefan's fourth birthday. Brecht liked giving presents but disliked doing so for conventional reasons. He almost never gave birthday presents, and there was nothing for Stefan on this occasion. Helene told her son, "Bidi"—this is what the children called him, never any of the usual words for father—"Bidi is today giving you his name." Stefan would rather have had something nice to eat.

Their wedding was not the jolly occasion weddings usually are. Certainly not everybody was pleased. Brecht's great infatuation at the time was Carola Neher. Carola was on tour when she heard that Brecht had gotten married. He went to the railway station to meet her on her return. His old friend Otto Müllereisert, who was a doctor, hurriedly bought some flowers—Brecht himself never thought of things like that—and thrust them into his hands at the last moment. The bouquet was of course meant to pacify Carola, but instead she threw it in his face and walked off.

Brecht had a weakness for peach-colored complexions, and Carola Neher was strikingly beautiful, delicate and full of vitality. She knew that Brecht loved her and admired her great acting talents. He once told me of her powers of mimicry, which must have been extraordinary. When he went into a restaurant with her, she would openly mimic the other people there, a habit which sometimes led to unpleasant scenes. But it was Brecht's opinion that the art of acting stems from an observing eye and a gift for mimicry.

Carola's behavior following Brecht's marriage was stupid. Marriage certificates meant nothing at all to Brecht. Carola was not the only one who was furious, but her fury was particularly virulent. She thirsted for revenge and did not distinguish between personal and professional relationships. When, for instance, she was due to play Saint Joan in *Saint Joan of the Stockyards*, she insisted the play should be directed by the man with whom she was then in love and whom she later married. This was utter madness, of course, since Brecht intended to direct it himself. Maybe this was not the only reason, but anyway the production was abandoned.

Later on, Carola Neher emigrated to the Soviet Union with her husband and worked on the stage in territories where German was understood. She also appeared as a singer; she had a magical singing voice. Then she joined a group that was permitted to tour abroad. Her husband, who was said to be a Trotskyite, allegedly gave her some things to take out of the country. This resulted in a court case, the exact details of which we were never able to discover. Carola was sentenced to ten years imprisonment. Even in prison she was able to continue acting, directing, and singing. Brecht wrote a poem for her on how to help oneself in captivity, how to wash oneself, what one can do to keep oneself fresh and prevent oneself being crushed. I find Brecht's refusal to feel insulted by her behavior quite wonderful. He tried again and again to secure her release from prison. In Copenhagen, for instance, I went with him to the Soviet ambassador, whom I knew well, though Brecht did not. The first thing he did—rather to my embarrassment—was to ask about Carola Neher, whether it was possible to find out where she was.

My aim in telling this story is to show how loyal Brecht always was to his people. In Berlin he took trouble even with those who felt an urge to go over to the West; he did not simply condemn them unheard. Such friendships—all on the basis of working together, for there was no other kind—meant a lot to Brecht, although many of his close associates let him down. Caspar Neher, for instance, has simply vanished as far as we are concerned. Now, after Brecht's death, when he could and should be there to help, he is nowhere to be found. Erich Engel, though old now, is more loyal and of greater use. It is not at all easy to carry on Brecht's work, but Engel is willing to try. That is the spirit of Brecht himself.

6

As we reached America, we saw from the deck of
the ship the people who had come to welcome
Brecht: Lion Feuchtwanger with his wife Marta, Alexander Granach, and others whose names I did not know.
I greeted none of them, not wishing Brecht and Helene
to have to bother about me. I left for Los Angeles with
some comrades I had met on the ship, while Brecht and
his family went to the house Alexander Granach had
rented for them. We had arranged that I should telephone him the following day.

A few days later I got on a bus to visit Brecht. I had
imagined Santa Monica to be a suburb of Los Angeles
that could be quickly reached. The bus driver grew im-
patient when I kept on asking him if it was time to get
out. The journey took nearly two hours. In Copenhagen
no journey lasts more than five minutes. Brecht was waiting at the bus stop. It was obvious that if we wanted to
work together Los Angeles was too far away, so I rented
a room in a house close to Brecht's.

In America one rents furnished apartments. The alternative is to buy an apartment or a house. The house
Granach had taken was furnished with loving care—lit-

erally everything was there—but it was so terribly bourgeois that it made one's hair stand on end. It was an impossible place to work in.

Even at times when we were obliged to live sparingly, Helene had always found a home in which one could live and work. She even made something of the little city apartment in Finland, despite the fact that we went to Marlebäck for the summer. So here too Helene made it her first task to find a reasonable house, and she soon succeeded.

Helene's houses—that would make a chapter in itself! She traded in houses. When you bought a house, you did not need to put down the whole amount at once, but could pay it off in monthly installments. Thus you could live as if you were paying rent until the purchase price was reached. Then you became the outright owner and could do what you liked with the house. In Denmark Helene bought the house on the Svendborg Sound for five thousand Kronen. When they moved to Sweden, she sold it for seven thousand—so not only had she lived there for nothing, she had also earned herself two thousand Kronen.

What Helene bought in Santa Monica was a frame house with a wonderful view over a garden. Brecht, though he supposedly had no feeling for nature, always liked to be surrounded by greenery. Helene arranged it superbly; a large workroom for Brecht was always her first concern. A particularly pleasant feature of this house was that it had two floors. Helene and the children lived upstairs, Brecht on the floor below. I never lived in his family. I needed a home of my own to be able to work.

Our first priority in America was to earn some money. Brecht wrote various film scripts, some of which he managed to sell for a few hundred dollars. As far as I can remember, he was able during the whole of 1941 to write hardly anything of serious concern to him. Our first job was either *Der Schneemann* (*The Snowman*) or *Das Gras sollte nicht darüber wachsen* (*The Grass Must Not Grow Over It*). On these scripts Brecht and I worked closely together. *Gras* was intended as a film for Peter Lorre. Then, for a long time, we spent every afternoon working with an experienced scriptwriter, Robert Thören (an emigrant like ourselves), on a film with a story set in the Bermudas. I still have some drafts written in my curious Danish-English, which is just as comical as my Danish-German. It was a pleasant piece of teamwork that amused even Brecht. Thören was very wealthy. Politically he stood not very far to the left, but at least it was to the left; he was what one might call a bit leftish. He was a sensible man, who later bought himself a chicken farm. He had no desire to continue writing, though he had been successful with his films—unlike ourselves.

Then Brecht got an engagement with a large film company, and he also managed to have me taken on as his secretary so that I could earn some money. He was to write a film for Ingrid Bergman, the famous Swedish actress. I had known her for a long time. She is a very nice person, even more so in private life than in her films. Brecht did not particularly care for her as an actress; he thought her too saccharine, for instance, in the film based on Hemingway's novel about Spain, *For Whom the Bell Tolls*. All the same, that film was an enormous success for Ingrid Bergman. Brecht appreciated that audiences loved her on account of her beauty, but he felt she ought to try and act against her beauty. It was typical of Brecht to call the script he wrote for her *The Gray Goose*.

Brecht also worked on another film script for Ingrid Bergman. Erich Maria Remarque's novel *Arc de Triomphe* had been very successful, and Brecht too was interested in it. It is the story of a German doctor living as a refugee in Paris. He cannot get a work permit and is consequently exploited by French doctors. Once the patients have been anesthetized, the German specialist is allowed to operate on them. But the credit for each successful operation and most of the fee are kept by his French colleagues for themselves. The novel is based on fact. (Incidentally, it is not only in France that such things happen. Brecht tells a similar story in his *Flüchtlingsgespräche*.)

After a number of takes had been assembled and shown, Brecht was summoned to the studio because a problem had arisen. (It was the only occasion, it might be mentioned in passing, that he ever worked directly in the film studio.) In the film Ingrid Bergman is in love with the doctor. The doctor has to leave Paris because the Germans are coming. The girl played by Ingrid Bergman becomes a prostitute. The doctor later manages to smuggle himself into the city and sees that his beloved is living in great luxury; she has since become an expensive prostitute. The film producers declared it was impossible to present Ingrid Bergman in that light: "She makes an unsympathetic impression." Brecht must change it. Brecht had always felt protective toward prostitutes, and so he was at once able to offer suggestions that would make audiences more sympathetic toward Ingrid Bergman. That led the principal French actor to insist that the French people should not be shown in an unsympathetic light either. He became increasingly obstinate. He was totally uninterested in politics—if anything, he was rather against than for us—but the dispute created an interesting political situation. It got to the point where the actor could hardly be coaxed before the camera unless Brecht was also present in the studio.

Brecht's most important film work in America was *Hangmen Also Die*. Brecht's script was a very good one, but the director, Fritz Lang, unfortunately ruined it. In Germany Lang had made the famous film *M* with Peter Lorre, and in Hollywood he was a big man. Brecht would very much have liked to film his *Fear and Misery in the Third Reich* with him, but in Hollywood this was an unmentionable subject: "Nobody's interested in that." So Brecht then suggested a film about the underground movement in Czechoslovakia. He could have written a film script for *Fear and Misery* very quickly, since he had all the material with him. What was happening, or had been happening, in Czechoslovakia, on the other hand, had first to be researched. However, since he was very interested in the subject, he began work with great eagerness. He talked to many German emigrants who had lived for some time in Prague. They knew exactly what had gone on in the Czech underground movement. Brecht's film script was based on fact. It was a black script.

Then suddenly—and I still do not know why—Fritz Lang torpedoed Brecht's work from the rear. This, that, or the other did not satisfy him, and when Brecht made alterations, he found fault with something else. Brecht then did some more work on the script together with John Wexley. Wexley is a great man. He saw at once what Bertolt Brecht was, and both of them took pleasure in their work together. But not even Wexley could save the film.

In it Brecht had written a small part for Helene Weigel. It had hardly any words but was strongly suggestive. She is given a chair to sit on, prepared in advance so that the top bar of the back support keeps falling off. The woman is forced each time to pick the bar up, the aim being to rattle her. It was right that the scene should have very little dialogue, since Helene's German accent sounded horrible in English. My Danish accent is bad too, but I am told it sounds softer and more agreeable than the German one. I believe there are more similarities between the English and Danish languages.

Helene had already been given screen tests, but one day Brecht arrived to find that her role had been cut out. He went home and never allowed himself to be seen in the studio again. He had chosen Helene for this role because he was convinced that no other actress could play it as she would have done. The unspeakable thing was that Brecht had not even been informed about the cut. Such behavior from Lang, who was responsible for the decision, was too brutal. If it had been done by an American, Brecht would simply have laughed and said, "Very well, if they don't want it." But Lang knew exactly who Brecht was.

Nobody in America—with the exception of the police—knew anything about Brecht. Not even the writers and directors who appeared with him before the House Committee on Un-American Activities had any idea of who and what he was, though they put their defense lawyers at the disposal of "this little fellow," as they called him. But in my opinion Lang's behavior was criminal. He drove Brecht out of the studio and destroyed his appetite for work. For Brecht this was one of the major disappointments of his time in America. As a result of it, the film we had planned never came into being. What did emerge Brecht considered horrible; only a fragment of the original story survived.

All of us believed we knew what American film producers were, but when we saw them in the flesh we were amazed at the poverty of our imagination. Producers are in fact stockholders in cheese dairies or coffee plantations who are eager to increase their fortunes with the help of film productions. One day a number of these financial backers came together in Eisler's house. Eisler told them a story. The coffee, cheese, and (for all I know) soap stockholders listened to him, then said, "That won't raise a laugh from anybody." In fact, they themselves had laughed, but they considered film audiences stupid and uneducated. Eisler and Brecht answered them in chorus, "But we are laughing!" Both of them were incapable of thinking or writing beneath their own standards. That was something the film producers in turn found it impossible to understand. Looking on from the sidelines, I found it funny: Here were people with money faced with somebody who could not simply be bought.

Usually, however, it saddened me to see how people treated their fellow beings. For a long time I had been living entirely with people who loved me and were willing to help me. Through Brecht I had come to realize that this happy state is the exception rather than the rule. Nowadays I find it strange to remember how naive I was in my first conversations with Brecht in Skovsbostrand. I was very emotional, and I pestered him with questions such as: What will happen when we have put the world in order, when it has become socialistic or even communistic? How will human relationships develop? Will there still be jealousy, theft, crime? In America, primarily through my work in the film industry, I experienced the depressing realities, among them the fact that Fritz Kortner was not employed on a level consistent with his abilities but was fobbed off with minor roles, while Helene Weigel even had a walk-on part taken away from her. Since then I have long come to understand why, in his *Little Organon (Kleines Organon für das Theater)*, Brecht says that in the theater the first thing to be examined is the relationship of people to one another.

In the first stages of writing *The Visions of Simone Machard (Die Gesichte der Simone Machard)* Brecht worked closely together with me. I believe that our working title for it was *Die Visionen*. Brecht did not originally see it as a stage play; we wrote it as a scenario for a film. Brecht related Simone's daytime activities, and I interpolated her dreams. We made swift progress. I wrote with feverish haste, egged on by the knowledge that I was being allowed to contribute something that Brecht could use.

Later, after I had moved to New York, Brecht and Lion Feuchtwanger wrote the play that has since been published. Several versions were made, each of them typed on paper of a different color. This was Feuchtwanger's normal method. The color series—say, white, green, blue, yellow, pink—was decided at the start and adhered to, so that there was always a chronological picture on hand of the work as it progressed. On the whole, the two men got on splendidly together, but they never managed to agree on Simone's age—not even when the play was staged in Berlin in the fifties. In Brecht's eyes Simone was naive, a mere child, and he kept making her younger and younger. Feuchtwanger saw her as a woman of experience and discernment, and she became increasingly older. Of course, no theater could be found in America for this play either.

That was what Brecht meant by calling Hollywood "a cesspool." However, while Eisler was working on the music for *Simone*, Brecht temporarily forgot the "intellectual stink." I have seldom seen him so happy as he was over this music. "Eisler's presence is a stroke of luck," he wrote in a letter to me. "I hope he will find something here that will enable him to stay on." Again and again, wherever he was living, Brecht set his hopes on Eisler's joining him. Eisler's name crops up in very many of his letters to me in connection with a joint production or the prospect of a joint production.

Since the play had not been accepted, Feuchtwanger

wrote his novel *Simone*, which he then managed to sell to a film company. Just at this time Brecht was in New York. Feuchtwanger wrote a number of letters to Brecht concerning the contract, but he never received a reply. In the end he begged Brecht urgently to let him know that he had at least received the letters. For some inexplicable reason Brecht failed to respond. I then wrote to Feuchtwanger myself, knowing only too well from my own experience how lacerating Brecht's silences could be.

I believe Feuchtwanger's only reason for writing the novel and selling it to a film company was to ensure that Brecht too should receive some money from their work. Feuchtwanger was a good friend. Brecht could depend on him in everything—probably more than the other way round. I recall with warm feelings those hours spent with him and his wife Marta. They lived very luxuriously in a villa in Pacific Palisades, from which there was a magnificent view. The house was tastefully furnished. Feuchtwanger was a booklover of a kind I have never met again. His library was not only immense in size; it also contained some particularly valuable volumes he had collected. Marta Feuchtwanger would now and again come into the workroom with whiskey on the rocks for us—Brecht drank whiskey at that time, though much diluted.

I never saw Brecht drinking vodka or Korn, cognac, or brandy—just (as I have said) whiskey. In London, for instance, he would slip a little silver flask into his hip pocket when we went to the movies. Inside, he would then occasionally take a very small sip from it.

At the end of the writers' conference in Paris, when Brecht was returning to Denmark and I was going on to Madrid, he bought a half-bottle of champagne for a farewell celebration. Arriving in the evening at our hotel, we saw Slatan Dudow, the theater director, who had been waiting for hours to speak to Brecht. Brecht, being tired and in no mood for further discussions, wriggled out of it. We went to his room and drank the half-bottle of champagne. Then he immediately fell asleep. Brecht always became sleepy when he drank anything. In Berlin he would drink two or three bottles of beer each evening to make himself sleep.

Incidentally, wherever he was—here in Berlin too—Brecht would always prepare his own little supper tray. It was quite a ceremony. On the tray lay a breadboard, a very handsome bread knife, a loaf, and something to eat with it, and a tankard with a lid. The beer he took from the icebox.

I observed something akin to this when Brecht visited me in New York and we were living together in one room. A huge orgy of eating would take place every evening—or what Brecht considered an orgy. It consisted of various kinds of bread, coarse salt and radish, which I had already peeled and salted earlier in the day, and three sorts of cheese: a genuine Swiss Emmenthaler with big holes, Camembert, and a wonderful Roquefort, which is still vivid in my memory. Beside him on the table lay a heavy pile of newspapers, which I had collected from my newsvendor on the corner. On evenings like this Brecht would go to bed late. He loved New York and while there was always in a good mood.

In Berlin he would occasionally drink red wine. When the doctors later advised him to cut down as much as possible on alcohol, he sipped a horribly sweet dessert wine with his meals. Besides this he consumed throughout the day fresh lemon juice, with enormous quantities of sugar. He swore that vitamin C saved him from illnesses of any sort. And of course he enjoyed his morning coffee. But when he was told in Berlin that coffee was very expensive and difficult to obtain, he immediately changed over to tea. This impressed me very much.

Only once did I ever see Brecht tipsy. This was in Hella Wuolijoki's house in Finland, at a New Year's Eve party to which the finance minister and other important people had also been invited. The Finns always insist on your drinking along with them; there is no saying no when they raise their glasses to you. Brecht, who surely knew that he was a bit tipsy, tried hard to prevent anyone noticing, but he achieved exactly the opposite. He became unnaturally stiff and, whenever he crossed the room, walked with very rapid, wooden steps. I can still see him.

I also saw Helene Weigel tipsy once. We were in one of the drinking saloons in the harbor district of Copenhagen, where they served a heavy dark ale. Helene really never drank at all, but she did like this sweet black ale. That evening she was for once pleasantly tipsy and observed herself with great amusement.

In Nyhavn I danced with Brecht for the only time in my life, and never since have I seen him dancing. He moved wonderfully, because he was so musical—and he danced very saucily, even saucier than a sailor. In fact, everyone there took him for a sailor, for at that time he was very, very thin and always wore blue workman's trousers. Nobody had the least idea that he was a writer.

Now, I have revealed quite a lot about Brecht's private life. He himself always kept silent about it. However, when one knew him well, one very soon noticed that for Brecht there was no such thing as a private life. For a writer and a man of the theater everything is a part of his work. Brecht kept a constant eye on his surroundings and stored his observations away. In these sailors' saloons, for example, mariners would tell tales of their lengthy voyages. Brecht would listen and watch how the money

121

they had saved over several months would be squandered in a single night. Other people just stared. With a single glance Brecht could take in a prostitute extracting money from a sailor in the course of a conversation. Four or five years later he might say, "Can you remember that redhead down there? She moved her hand like this, not like that." For him outings like this were never a waste of time. I have often noticed how, as a theater director, Brecht made use of things he had observed long before. I have never seen anything else like it. He would suggest to an actor a certain inflection or gesture, and I would suddenly remember: Of course—that is something he saw or heard years ago.

"Small talk" did not exist as far as Brecht was concerned. I never heard it from him at any time. Brecht shunned parties at which people merely chatted, for there was no underlying theme. He either refused to go at all or very soon left. If one told him about something that had happened somewhere, or described something one had seen, he would be silent for a while, then say, "And what of it?" He was waiting for the conclusion, the practical application. One must have had a reason for telling him the story, otherwise it was just idle chat. Being with Brecht could be exhausting, for one was forced to concentrate on the essentials.

He had wonderful conversations with Peter Lorre and with Oskar Homolka. On the other hand, he found it impossible to converse with Erwin Geschonneck, and with Busch it also became difficult in the end. With Alexander Granach I only ever heard him talk about everyday matters, and then only when it was absolutely necessary. Granach, I think, was not the type for discussions. Then, in America, Granach did a very foolish thing. He accepted a role in the Greta Garbo film *Ninotchka*, a propaganda film against the Soviet Union. From that time on

Brecht ceased to mention Granach's name. Previously, when he was writing a film script, Brecht would express the opinion that Granach might play one role or another. But after his political blunder, as far as we were concerned, he was as good as dead. In this respect Brecht was unmerciful. In a similar way he refused Werner Krauss permission to play the role of Galileo bacause Krauss had taken part in the film of *Jud Süss*.

I had been in Santa Monica about a year when in 1942 I left for Washington to attend a women's congress. I had meant to return immediately afterward—that was Brecht's wish too—but I stayed longer than expected.

In Santa Monica I got to know an interesting old Quaker lady who took part in the struggle for the women's vote and for equal rights in general. It was she who invited me to this congress. It had been set up by women who had fought for women's rights in England, the so-called suffragettes, some of whom had even been in prison. The subject of my talk was: What does Nazism mean for women? I told them what Hitler had done for German women: transformed them into a league of housewives.

After the lecture a Danish woman said to me, "But then you're a member of the communist party, aren't you?" I asked what had given her that idea, and she replied that Consul Baek had told her. I went at once to the Danish Embassy in Washington, demanded to speak to the ambassador, and asked him whether a Danish consul was paid to make difficulties in America for his fellow countrymen. Emigrants found it hard enough as it was to get on, I said, and an indiscreet remark of that kind could mean ruin. I showed the ambassador my certificate of divorce from Robert Lund and my contract with the Royal Theater, which was still in force. (However, I did not show him the theater's demand for four thousand Kronen as compensation for breaking my contract. I had told nobody I was leaving, but in any case I was appearing at the time only in Hella Wuolijoki's *Women of Niskavouri*, and that was taken off at once by the Nazis, so the theater lost nothing by my departure.)

The first thing the ambassador said to me was that in view of my divorce certificate, he was in a position to pay out the money that was being paid in for me by Robert Lund in Denmark. From then on I received seventy-five dollars each month, which to me was a lot of money. Incidentally, the divorce settlement had been drawn up by Helene Weigel. I myself had not wanted to take money from Lund, who was not in favor of a divorce. At first we had just separated, and once Brecht left Denmark, Lund thought there was no need for a divorce at all. It went through only after I arrived in Finland. I had asked Lund to give his consent at last, since I had made up my mind to go to America. I wanted him to be in a position to marry again. He needed a home-loving wife for his children, and he did eventually find one. We remained in friendly contact, but at the time Helene felt everything must be put in proper order, and she wrote the alimony clause into the settlement on my behalf.

Once the money matter was settled, the ambassador called Consul Baek into the office and asked him what he had meant by telling people that I was a communist. "You surely know how fatal that is in America," he said. The consul made excuses, saying that all he had meant was a parlor communist. He had not realized that this argument, which had once been useful, was not useful in all circumstances, but on the contrary could cause great harm. I was so angry that the ambassador, in order to calm me down, declared, "We are all communists at heart!" He introduced me to his wife and invited me to stay in his house as his guest, for a few days at least. His intention was to give me moral support and to scotch the "rumor" officially.

I should not have succeeded in waging the battle so sharply and skillfully had I not learned from Brecht how to handle a minister or a consul. Brecht has written a poem, which he dedicated to Lion Feuchtwanger. It begins: "Exalted Vice-Consul, deign to grant your quivering louse the stamp that means happiness," and it ends: "Just bang that little stamp on, your superiors won't eat you up for that." This "didactic poem" is stuffed full of irony. It describes how one should treat people in control of the stamp that will enable one to flee to safety. Brecht, who loathed flattery like the plague, allowed it in such cases—in fact, even recommended it. One should be very friendly and very deferential, but one should also have the audacity to explain to a senior official what his underling has done wrong by assuming in advance that the man in charge will sympathize with the complainant. This is the method I adopted in Washington. It is a typically Brechtian way of looking at things and carrying them out, something that without his example I should not have known. In Copenhagen, when I was pleading with the minister of state for a visa for Brecht's family, I learned from Brecht to enjoy fighting. It is wrong to approach someone in fear and trembling, or in one's thoughts to anticipate the way the negotiations will go. If one is flung into prison, one must immediately demand a typewriter. One must disconcert people by insisting on rights of which they have never before heard.

When the women's congress in Washington came to an end, I began to wonder how I could get to New York. I was keen to see the city, but I did not have the money to pay for the journey. Luck came to my aid. The Danish section of the Office of War Information heard of my

125

lecture in Washington and sent me a telegram asking whether I would care to make a radio broadcast for Denmark. It was not yet a firm engagement, but my journey to New York was assured. The Danish ambassador even wrote me a letter of recommendation, to prevent Consul Baek's indiscreet gossip from spoiling my chances. A communist in the Office of War Information would have been a strange bird indeed.

I wrote to Brecht, telling him I had the chance of a job in New York. Another important consideration was that I wanted to be independent and to earn my own living, and not always to be regarded as one of Brecht's hangers-on. Also, I was not very keen on Hollywood: film writing was carried on in a horrible atmosphere. In addition, I looked forward to being able at last to do some political work.

I wrote my own script for my first broadcast, and also spoke it into the microphone. They were pleased, for my deep voice was particularly suited to shortwave transmissions. I believe my script was also very astute, for I had kept Brecht's "Writing the Truth: Five Difficulties" well in mind. The Office had promised me eight dollars for my first broadcast, but they then gave me twelve dollars and offered me a permanent contract, very well paid. Later I learned that many communists in Denmark had listened to my broadcast and understood what I was saying.

The head of the department was Ida Bachmann. She was not a party member, but she always behaved like a communist. When I first arrived in her office she greeted me very cordially. Somewhat confused, I said, "I hope you don't know who I am?" I considered it an advantage to be completely unknown. But Ida Bachmann knew exactly who I was, and she was delighted to get me for her department. We quickly became close friends.

At the outset I had rented a room with a small closet. It was in a district where, I believe, all the residents except for myself were prostitutes. Once my contract was signed and I was being well paid, Ida Bachmann and I went in search of an apartment to share together. We found it in a very select neighborhood: East Fifty-seventh Street (number 124). The real-estate speculators must have overlooked this small, narrow house when they erected their tall apartment buildings all around it. The rent was cheap, since the house was old and the apartment up on the third floor, with no elevator. Together we paid seventy-five dollars for one large room, a slightly smaller one with a balcony, and a kitchen. The balcony looked out over the famous skyscraper silhouette of New York. Of course—like everywhere in America—we had two bathrooms.

Now that I was able to receive Brecht decently, I felt there was a good chance that he would come. I wrote to him, telling him how I was placed and asking him to plan his journey quickly. He replied that he thought it very nice of me to wish to keep him, but first he had to finish off a few contracts. I had had no thoughts of "keeping" him: I was just glad to have food for us both and a roof over our heads.

It was at least six months before Brecht came. Ida Bachmann very kindly went off to stay with a friend, so Brecht and I had the apartment to ourselves. I gave him the room with the balcony, since it had a fine view and also caught the sun. But it was smaller than mine, and Brecht very soon suggested a swap, though now he had no greenery to look out on, just a boring house.

In New York he was able to work well. He had a lot of discussions and was also able to sign a few contracts. He was in good health. What, on the other hand, he did not like was my daily trips to the Office of War Information. I do not know the reason for his distrust, for despite his allergy toward being "kept" we were dependent on my work for our living. The Office did enable him to make a few broadcasts with Lotte Lenya. After the first one I told him to speak very clearly. That was a big mistake on my part, for his efforts were so exaggerated that the next broadcast was quite awful.

Of course, it was not only to be with me that Brecht came to New York. Nearly all his political friends were living there. With the exception of Hanns Eisler, he had no political friends in Hollywood. Lion Feuchtwanger could not be called a political friend, though he and Brecht were of course always discussing politics. Feuchtwanger, however, was no Marxist. In New York he had, among others, Gerhart Eisler, a professional politician with whom he had some highly interesting political discussions; Eisler's wife Hilde, a very talented journalist; and the political writer and commentator Hermann Budzislawski, who in 1933 started *Die Neue Weltbühne* (*The New World Stage*) and for a time was Dorothy Thompson's secretary and a confidant of Roosevelt, for whom he drafted some election speeches. Others were the elderly Hermann Duncker, formerly head of the Marxist workers' school in Berlin, and the trade unionist Jacob Walcher, a genuine laborer with whom Brecht remained close friends up until his death. Hertha Walcher, a former secretary of Clara Zetkin, was also of interest to Brecht, as was Albert Schreiner, the historian and fighter in Spain. And then there was Karl Korsch.

Karl Korsch was an out-and-out Marxist. Following the 1918 November Revolution he was for a while minister of justice in Thuringia. He was such a relentlessly critical thinker that he unfortunately fell out with his party very soon and was expelled. Brecht respected him— not on that account, but in spite of it. He thought highly of Korsch's analyses and of his judgment. As far as I am in a position to say, the most intensive discussions Brecht had with anyone in New York were with Karl Korsch.

They stimulated each other. I remember with particular clarity one evening, when Brecht was urging Korsch at last to finish his biography of Marx and Korsch was discussing with Brecht the projected versification of the Communist Manifesto. Afterwards I drove Korsch back to his apartment in my car. Returning, I found Brecht tucking in with gusto to his orgy of cheese and newspapers. Suddenly the telephone rang. At the other end of the line was a doctor to whom Elisabeth Bergner had sent me. I thought I was going to have a baby, but I was not yet quite sure. The doctor had taken a blood sample and carried out a test. Now I knew for certain: I was pregnant. I spoke only a few words in reply, then went back to the table. There I saw from the expression in Brecht's eyes that he was very pleased.

Something else that happened that evening remains unforgettable. As we were talking about Korsch, Brecht said, "You should be here more often when we are having discussions like that." At such meetings I was always unwilling to push myself forward, for I had the feeling that Brecht preferred a tête-à-tête, and more came out of it that way. I myself prefer to be alone with my partner for conversations of a special kind. People are sometimes offended when I say, "Do you mind going into the other room?" But that happened often with Brecht. There were times, of course, when he wanted several people around him, but then he was mainly collecting opinions. During discussions with Korsch, however, I considered an audience superfluous, and for that reason I usually withdrew. On this occasion I had failed to find my cue in time, and then the discussion became so interesting that I had no wish to leave.

Korsch was a great man. I say "was" because when I met him later in West Berlin, he was a wreck. At this time the relationship between Brecht and myself was not good, but one evening he came to me and said, "Korsch is here." All I said in reply was, "And so?" Brecht persisted. "Come along, let's go." Strangely enough, he wanted me with him, and we drove off together. We found Korsch on the first floor of a boardinghouse.

On the surface the conversation between Brecht and Korsch gave an impression of humor, but in reality it was not at all gay, and for me—and I think for Brecht as well—it was very sad. Korsch was absent-minded and inwardly at odds with himself. He was at the end of his tether, believing himself watched, betrayed, and persecuted by the whole world. He had—and I say this with all compassion—gone out of his mind. Just to keep the conversation going, Brecht asked him how the world would get along now that Stalin had just died. Korsch looked at him irritably. "As always," he said. Brecht remarked, "There's not much I shall have to cut out, only that one sentence about the 'great harvest-leader' in *'Die Erziehung der Hirse'* ['The Cultivation of the Millet']." Korsch knew nothing whatever about Brecht's "millet" poem. Korsch was, I believe, a writer who could stand by every sentence he ever wrote, and I wondered what those who had so much to cut out were feeling. How happy I should have been had this meeting never taken place!

I continued to live in New York until 1948, when I left America. I traveled to Santa Monica, by land or air, only when I wanted to do some writing with Brecht, just as he traveled to New York only when his stay could be combined with some kind of work.

Our first job in New York was the staging of *Fear and Misery of the Third Reich*. Brecht was hoping to mobilize the Americans against Hitler by showing them conditions as they now were in Germany. The play was to be done in a trade union theater. Erwin Piscator began work, with Brecht supporting him and I enthusiastically assisting Brecht. Then suddenly quarrels broke out, and Piscator left. I can no longer remember what the quarrels were about. I believe Piscator found the whole undertaking unattractive from the start.

In America Piscator ran an acting school for wealthy lunatics. They had no talent, but they could pay. He had married the widow of an electricity millionaire and lived in a huge house. For me the worst thing in his home was the aquarium full of goldfish—and the fact that his wife perpetually ran around wearing a mink cape. Brecht once said, "There you see how the greatest living theater director can be bought with electric light bulbs."

Piscator was a handsome man and very full of wit. I saw him in America for the last time at the New York premiere of *Galileo*. At the end he was quite carried away, and he said, "Now I feel like doing a play again."

Shortly before, I had been at the premiere of Piscator's adaptation of Tolstoy's *War and Peace*. Probably on account of my Danish sense of humor, we had come to like each other a lot. All the same, I could think of nothing to say after the premiere except, "Well, this time everything worked." As all the theater world knows, Piscator's premieres during the twenties in Berlin were pure chaos. Brecht told me that at one of those performances he and Piscator paced up and down outside the theater. "We weren't yet ready for death," he said. Inside, there was an awful racket: a motor was running, the scenery creaked, and not a word could be heard from the stage. At the end the audience hissed and threw apples and tomatoes. But this time, in America, everything worked so well for Piscator that I became mistrustful. He was permitted to

131

work undisturbed in America because he was world famous and his school was run on capitalist lines. Anyone living as elegantly as Piscator could not be suspected of being a communist.

All the same, when Piscator wished to return to Europe after the war, he ran into difficulties. Somebody had discovered in the meantime that he had been a member of the communist party. He had a long time to wait before he was allowed to leave.

Berthold Viertel took over our theater project after Piscator left. The American version of *Fear and Misery of the Third Reich* was given the title *The Private Life of the Master Race*, and for this production Hanns Eisler wrote some very fine music. The performance did not attain the level of the Berliner Ensemble's later production, but it was nevertheless a good ensemble performance with quite a few highlights. I can still clearly remember that outstanding actor Albert Bassermann as Richter, for instance, also Liesel Neumann and Ludwig Roth. Unfortunately, since the play was done in English, Helene Weigel could not be used on account of her strong German accent.

Brecht's English also had a hard sound, but he was more musical than Helli, and in languages that is what matters. Brecht's command of American English was at least sufficient to ensure that when they came to work together, Charles Laughton was not bothered by his accent.

As far as language was concerned, Brecht learned most from the great English poet Wystan Hugh Auden, with whom he wrote an adaptation of Webster's *The Duchess of Malfi* for Elisabeth Bergner. Brecht had difficulty with the iambics of the English original, and that is why he called Auden in. He had a tremendous respect for Auden and would have liked to do much more work with him. What would most have pleased him would have been for Auden to translate at least the lyrics in all his plays. Brecht was despondent when he was forced to look for someone else, Auden either having no time or feeling no urge to do it.

Like me, Auden lived on Fifty-seventh Street, though on the West Side, while my apartment lay close to Park Avenue on the more select East Side. Auden had rented the cheapest room he could find in a plush boarding house. The room was always in darkness, since Auden never pulled the curtains back, nor ever opened the windows. When you entered, it was so full of smoke that you could scarcely see your hand before your eyes. Auden ceaselessly puffed one cigarette after another. His shirt never fitted where it should, and on his feet he wore felt slippers of enormous size. None of this bothered Brecht, who enjoyed going to Auden's room. Brecht was good at adapting himself to other people. The tone in which he and Auden addressed each other was always polite, even respectful.

The *Duchess* manuscript exists only in English, I believe, since it was made for an American production with Elisabeth Bergner. Brecht's aim was to achieve maximum linguistic flexibility, and he worked with such industry that neither I nor Auden could keep up with him. Never, in my experience, was Auden the first to put forward a draft; it was always Brecht who did the preliminary work. He would come in happily, show Auden his manuscript, then make a few corrections. Work was always done in an atmosphere of gaiety. They would spend hours talking of this and that, frequently quite remote things, then suddenly they would discover that some word in the text needed changing, or that sentence A would go better after than before sentence B.

Brecht loved *The Duchess of Malfi*, but he worked it over so thoroughly that there is hardly a trace of Webster's original left. Basically, only the main lines of the plot have been preserved. A brother is in love with his sister, though she does not realize it. The brother has to go off to war, and he appoints people to watch over her. However, the sister marries her butler and bears him a number of children.

During work a discussion arose that was typical of Brecht. Auden was highly amused by it—as far as I could make out, in that dark and smoky room. The brother wants to make sure that his sister sleeps with no other man while he is away at the war. We asked ourselves: What can a man do to be certain that his wife sleeps with nobody else? Auden thought she should swear on the Bible. Brecht laughed: "Then nobody is safe. An oath has no aftereffects." He suggested putting poison on the Bible, so that she dies: "That's the only way to be completely certain."

Later, when the play was in rehearsal, Elisabeth Bergner could not be persuaded to adopt the epic style. In my opinion she had the ability for it. She succeeded in only one scene, where there was no other way. The duchess is pregnant again (an idea of Brecht's that is not in Webster). Since the clothes women wore at that time prevented her condition being discovered at once, her brother arranges for a large basket of apricots to be brought in. She flings herself on the fruit, thus betraying herself. Elisabeth Bergner was at her best in this scene. There was nothing she could spoil, since she had no words to say.

Elisabeth Bergner took a very active part in the adaptation of the play. It would, of course, have been unthinkable to invite her to Auden's apartment, so we met in her house. Brecht showed her what he had written, and she made suggestions of her own. I will give an example of their method of working together. One scene takes place in a lunatic asylum. In his half-crazy pursuit of his sister, the brother has her locked up. Brecht found the scene unnecessary and wanted to omit it, but it contained one line that Elisabeth Bergner decided she must speak at all costs. Seated on a bench, she asks a fellow inmate, "Art thou mad, too?" Elisabeth found this line so wonderful that we had to retain the whole scene. But how she spoke that line! I can still hear her. Brecht melted whenever he heard her speak. He was crazy about her, like everybody else who ever heard her. She could turn the most innocuous of drawing-room comedies into a work of art. Brecht would very much have liked to have her in his Berliner Ensemble, but she would not come. She could have chosen any role she wanted. Perhaps in the meantime she has regretted her decision.

It was impossible to stage the production immediately, owing to lack of money, so Brecht returned to Santa Monica. I happened by chance to be with him when news came that rehearsals had begun and that, for reasons of economy, decorations from a recent English production of *The Duchess* (in Webster's original version, of course) were to be imported. When these were unpacked, they proved to be old-fashioned junk, quite unsuitable for Broadway. Brecht had in mind decorations of quite another kind; he wanted them to be modern and very bold. He found no difficulty in adapting himself to the Broadway style, for he loved those quick-moving, colorful musicals. *The Duchess*, he felt, must also be presented in splendid, colorful costumes and at a spanking pace if American audiences were to be expected to sit through it. Unfortunately, the settings were wrong and the pace was not maintained.

I have been told that Brecht's name does not appear

in the program, which states merely, "Adapted by W. H. Auden." I did not notice that at the time, or perhaps I have just forgotten it. Certainly it was not due to any attempt on Brecht's part to disassociate himself from the work, but either to modesty or to political considerations—possibly out of concern for Elisabeth Bergner. Nevertheless, she was called before the House Committee on Un-American Activities on account of having worked with Brecht on the play, which shows that some people, at any rate, had registered the fact that Brecht was the author or co-author.

The production was a complete fiasco. It was performed only two or three times. After the premiere I was asked to listen for comments from the audience. All I heard was, over and over again, "Say what you like about Bergner, but a brother has no right to be in love with his sister, not even when she's played by Elisabeth Bergner." The project cost Elisabeth's husband, Paul Czinner, a fortune; he had invested a lot of money in it. Brecht thought he and Elisabeth had only themselves to blame; they should have listened to him. After the premiere there was a tremendous row. Brecht vowed never to see Elisabeth Bergner again, not on any condition, and he declared he would never again do a play with her. However, I continued to stand up for her, despite Brecht's furious outbursts. She and I were close friends then, and we still are. When I fell ill and was put in a mental home, nobody helped me more than she did. She is very devout, but she never parades her religion. She is the kindest, most helpful, most unselfish, and most loving person I have ever met. I have often looked to her to raise me to my feet after a fall, and when, during difficult times in Berlin, she came to visit me, I was in a seventh heaven of delight.

Brecht's condemnation of Elisabeth Bergner did not last forever. Secretly I had some sympathy for him. What had been achieved was not, in his opinion, what might have been achieved. It was not the financial loss that worried him, though money meant a lot to us in those days. What always irritated Brecht most of all was to have invested work and time for no return. This experience caused him much suffering.

One can never know in advance whether expectations will be fulfilled. Brecht's hopes for *The Duchess* were not fulfilled, but with the working out of the American version of *Life of Galileo* the exact opposite was the case. The play had in fact already been completed, but the original version was too long for American tastes. For two years Brecht worked with Charles Laughton on a translation, which in the process grew into an adaptation of the play. They would meet either in Brecht's home or in Charles Laughton's fantastic house. For both it was a period of work as intensive as it was enjoyable. Their way of working together is not easy to describe. Laughton knew no German—literally not a single word!—and Brecht had too little English to be able to express himself with full authority in that language. Speaking half German, half English, Brecht would use gestures to convey what he was after, and Laughton would put into words what he had seen with his eyes. At some point Brecht would then say, "That's it!" and the words would be written down. This led to what in my opinion is the best translation of any of Brecht's plays.

I was invited to join in this work and was able to help with the translation, since my English was quite good—better than Brecht's at any rate. In the Office of War Information I had to translate my Danish scripts into English for the censors, so I had quickly learned to dictate translations straight on to the typewriter.

A lucky accident made it possible for me to be in Santa

Monica at this time. I had made friends with a woman who worked in the Norwegian section of the Office of War Information. She had a very rich father in Oslo, an oil magnate with American dollars. One day, by a round-about route, she received a communication from him telling her to buy herself a house in America, in order that the dollars should not lie idle or lose their value during the war. I advised my friend to buy a house in Santa Monica—to her I naturally said: in Hollywood—and we set off at once to find one. I told her, "If I am to live with you, the house must be as close to Twenty-sixth Street as possible." This was where Brecht was living. She then bought one of the finest houses in Pacific Palisades and gave me the largest room in it.

The house had French windows reaching right down to the floor. Brecht, when he visited me, never entered through the door, but walked round the house to the windows overlooking the lawn. I had a few steps placed there so that he could easily get in through the window. In this way he avoided meeting anybody. He came regularly at two o'clock, by which time I had lunch ready. After the meal he would lie down and rest for a short while—his method of dividing up the day and, as he said, sitting down fresh to work twice daily. When he rose, we would prepare the installment we wanted to work through with Charles Laughton. We would then drive off at four or four-thirty to meet him.

The American version of *Galileo* is very short, just two and a half hours, including one intermission. In Berlin the performance lasted over three hours. This the Americans would never accept—they would simply walk out of the theater. Our greatest difficulties were with Galileo's monologues at the beginning and end of the play. We worked particularly long on the final scene, as one can see from a phonograph record Laughton made after Brecht had already returned to Europe. Laughton put forward several different versions. The necessary cuts often drove Brecht to despair. To make long passages seem less long, we employed all the usual smart American tricks. One of these was to have Galileo perform his morning toilet while speaking to Andrea. Since Laughton appeared stripped to the waist, the audience was willing to swallow it. Like every other woman I was in love with Laughton, but one thing about him disturbed me: he had no hair at all on his body. The make-up artist had to stick it on in the studio before every appearance.

In America we also met the writer Erich Maria Remarque. He was very well off and lived in very exclusive surroundings, though always in the best of taste. Remarque was a real Don Juan, and much less inhibited than Brecht. I remember one evening when we visited Remarque and his current lady friend, who was very beautiful. She was wearing next to nothing. Brecht was greatly amused. It all went well, for she, though a typical American, realized at once what a comical man this was who was flirting with her. Brecht was in very good humor, and for once it was an evening of chat rather than of work. Brecht was scarcely recognizable in the way he adapted himself to the conversational Ping-Pong. Incidentally, quite by accident, I left my gloves—long white ones—in Remarque's house and afterward had great difficulty in recovering them from him.

Another resident in Santa Monica was a world-famous dancer, a highly interesting, very expressive, and remarkably handsome woman. Brecht had known her in Berlin and wanted very much to see her. I had a car at that time, and I drove Brecht to her home. I had arranged to go with Alexander Granach to see a Mexican film that was being shown only on this one evening, so I arranged to pick Brecht up afterward. I could not find the right entrance, I went round the house—nearly all the houses in Hollywood are built in a bungalow style—with the result that I entered through the back door, and came on a sight such as I have seldom seen. Brecht always liked a chair to himself, and I had never seen him share one, but now I surprised him and the dancer together on a chair that was really too narrow for two people. However, they were sitting there quite respectably, each with a glass of whiskey on the table in front of them. I knew then that Brecht had enjoyed a pleasant evening. It was a dignified flirtation, nothing silly or trivial about it, and it looked very nice. He and she were discussing a ballet, probably *The Seven Deadly Sins*, which he wanted to see performed. As always, Brecht's amours were tied up with work. Up till now he had possessed no driving license. By the following morning he had decided to take a driving test, and I had quickly to instruct him in all he needed to know. That evening Brecht drove alone to the dancer's house, and he did not ask to be picked up.

Brecht's closest contact, whenever possible, was with Hanns Eisler. Eisler's house stood on the coast at Malibu, one of the loveliest spots in California. He was professor of music at a university, and he wrote music for films. He earned a lot of money and was doing better than Brecht was.

Brecht and I attended one of Eisler's lectures at the university. On our way home we had great fun recalling Eisler's baffling manner of talking. If he could not immediately find the right English word, he would use the German one, pronouncing it in the American way—"and never a sign of any embarrassment," Brecht observed, much impressed.

I had met Eisler for the first time in Denmark, when

he arrived there with Lou, his future wife. Brecht was always against his friends getting married, for from then on they seemed always to be otherwise occupied. At the very moment Brecht needed them they would have no time, or one thing or another would not be convenient, since it was inconvenient for their wives. In almost all cases Brecht treated the wives of his friends with a certain reserve. In America I did not realize that at once. The various tactical measures he employed were not easy to spot, for they were never talked about. When Brecht was unwilling to talk to Lou, Helli had to take her off to drink coffee. Lou then thought Helli was trying to keep her away from Brecht, but she completely misinterpreted Helli's action—Helli had no other choice. During their exile the deciding factor was simply whom Brecht was willing to admit to his workroom, and whom he was not.

The Eislers were always entertaining large numbers of famous guests. Lou now arranged things so that on the afternoons Charlie Chaplin came, the Brechts were not invited. In retaliation against this curious—and sometimes unfortunate—strategy, Helli excluded the Eislers from her own dinners for famous guests. Each wife held a trump card: Helli had Laughton in tow, but Lou had Chaplin. The Chaplin afternoons were of course Lou's pride and glory. I myself was invited, and I implored her, "For heaven's sake, give Brecht a chance sometimes!" I got on very well with Lou. Later, in Berlin, Brecht also made a friend of her, knowing how nicely she had always behaved toward me in America.

One day it clicked at last, and Brecht met Chaplin at the Eislers' house. Brecht admired Chaplin greatly. He considered him a genius in his own sphere and wanted terribly to work with him. But Chaplin said, "What can I do? I am my own scriptwriter, my own dramaturge, my own director, my own leading man, my own composer"—

141

here he glanced at Eisler—"and my own best audience."
He was right about that. We visited him a few times in
his studio and saw the way he worked. Brecht was also
invited to pre-pre-previews of Chaplin's films. Brecht really
enjoyed laughing, and he laughed a lot, but the one who
laughed most was Chaplin himself. I found that fascinating. Brecht had seen *The Great Dictator*, but only after
he had written his *Arturo Ui. Ui* had come into existence
in Finland, at a time when, with the Nazis sitting everywhere, Chaplin's *Dictator* could not be shown in Europe.

Once, in the period before his emigration, Brecht wrote
a poem about a Chaplin film. This film was *The Face on
the Barroom Floor*, which he had then just seen. In it
Chaplin is sitting on the pavement outside a beer saloon,
trying to draw a picture of his beloved with a piece of
chalk. But he can no longer remember what her face
looks like. At the end he is in despair. Brecht thought a
new, longer film could be made of so fine an idea. Chaplin was interested in the suggestion, but he was in a period
of transition. He no longer wanted to play the old Chaplin
role in which he had become so famous. I once did a
long interview with him for my Danish newspaper. He
said then, "Since Roosevelt's New Deal nobody runs
around any more with holes in his trousers and in boots
like mine." In other words, he felt that Roosevelt had
destroyed his image. (Now he can begin to play it again,
for I hear that since then the unemployment figures in
America have again risen to eleven million.) Brecht was
very interested in Chaplin's attitude and found it exciting
that Chaplin was planning to do something new.

I remember conversations between Brecht and Chaplin
during the McCarthy era, when many people were being
arrested. Despite the fact that the McCarthy hearings
were very dangerous for us, arousing as they did fears of

a Moscow-inspired communist infiltration of America, both Chaplin and Brecht saw the comic side of them. In the course of a conversation they improvised—each reacting to the words of the other—a story about Chaplin leaving America. He is already on the ship when the emigration officials appear. They want to establish whether he is a "security risk" and begin to grill him, but nobody can understand the language in which he replies. They bring in a Chinese interpreter, then a Japanese one, then a Korean, and so on, but all come to grief. No wonder, since Chaplin is speaking a language of his own invention. When he played the scene to us, our jaws ached with laughing. At the end, he showed us the emigration officials giving up the ghost. As the ship is leaving the harbor, Chaplin casts a last look at the Statue of Liberty through a porthole and sees the goddess close one eye in a wink.

Chaplin also demonstrated to us how he planned to conduct himself in Washington when summoned to a hearing. He reckoned with a large audience, and it is certain that the chamber would have been filled to capacity. Chaplin intended, when seated before the senators, to put his thumb to his nose: "Odd, how my nose itches since coming to Washington!" But no doubt something of the kind had been anticipated, and he was not summoned. Rather no hearing at all than to be made fools of by Chaplin!

One was not brought before the committee in Washington in the role of an accused person, but simply summoned to undergo questioning. Accusations, if any, followed the conclusion of the hearing—on grounds, for example, of showing disrespect toward the committee. Brecht was not escorted to Washington from California;

he went there "voluntarily." He was advised to be punctual, otherwise he would indeed have been put under escort.

Brecht was heard along with eighteen other writers, most of them scriptwriters from Hollywood. The "Eighteen," as they were dubbed after the hearing, were wealthy enough to afford expensive lawyers. They took Brecht into their group as number 19, though none of them really knew who he was. They gave him a lawyer whom he would never have been able to pay out of his own pocket. However, when this lawyer heard that he had written poems, he withdrew from the defense. Probably he thought a poet too enigmatic a figure for him. Brecht was given another lawyer.

I later made inquiries about the identity of the films through which these "Eighteen" were alleged to have infected America with communism, thus "threatening the freedom of the state." Nobody could give me an answer, for there had been no such films. Someone told me that from the very start the producers had taken good care to ensure their films were free of political dynamite. If a bank director was fat, disagreeable, and spiteful, then his wife at least must be a nice lady who gave alms to the poor. That would represent social justice, nothing other than which could be shown.

The hearings were set up in order to intimidate the public. The object was to induce a state of psychosis against the Soviet Union. Though it proved impossible to unmask the Eighteen as communists, a way was found to put some of them behind bars. After the hearing they were found guilty of refusing to make statements or—as it was officially called—"contempt of a Committee of Congress."

What they had done was refuse to answer the so-called sixty-sixth question, which was: "Are you a communist?"

Instead, they pleaded the American constitution, which forbids prying into the opinions of individuals. The victims immediately lodged appeals, which delayed the imposition of sentences for a long time, in the hope that the congressional committee would be dissolved before they could be sent to prison. Unfortunately they hoped in vain, for the committee clung obstinately to life. A number of the Eighteen, regrettably, did not manage to hold out, since they faced difficulties at work, being refused writing or directing engagements. They caved in and turned traitor.

At the time, however, it was a splendid fighting force. They defended themselves with great spirit. They came well prepared for the hearing, having decided on their answers in advance. When we first visited the chamber in order to study the nature of the proceedings, we saw a curious sight. The Eighteen were sitting there with their lawyers, in shirt-sleeves and with their feet on the table. As they talked, they kept snapping their fingers. At first we could not understand why, but later we learned that the F.B.I. had installed microphones all over the place. The recordings would be virtually useless if one made a noise with one's fingers while speaking. Some of the writers were in fact members of the communist party or in sympathy with it; others were not. Whichever, they stuck wonderfully together at the hearings.

As an emigrant, Brecht could not plead the American constitution: he had to answer this sixty-sixth question. That too had been prearranged with the party and with the lawyers of the Eighteen. All the same, some German comrades came to me after the hearing and grumbled about Brecht's behavior. They thought it wrong that he should have been the only one to answer the question about party membership—"and then to answer no to it!" The answer was correct, I replied. "Yes," they admitted, "but he also said he had always thought it right to be an independent writer." These comrades had heard extracts from the hearing on the radio, where the reporter had naturally selected only those passages that supported his own point of view.

The broadcast of Brecht's hearing led to what eventually became a national joke in America. Brecht was confronted with evidence as to when and where he had met Gerhart Eisler, and he was asked what they had talked about on these occasions. Brecht replied, "I played chess with him." This answer was quoted in all news reports as a "classical excuse." In American eyes Gerhart Eisler was Moscow's principal agent, working ceaselessly behind the scenes for the communist party, and Brecht's answer became a byword. When a man returned home late and his wife asked, "Where have you been?" he would reply, "I've been playing chess." *Life* magazine published a picture of Brecht at the microphone, surrounded by a cloud of smoke from his own cigar.

Of course there were also many German communists who approved Brecht's behavior, among them Hermann Budzislawski. He had rehearsed the hearing with Brecht beforehand, and he was always relating with great pride that almost all the questions he thought up himself had in fact been put to Brecht.

The day after the hearing Brecht left by air for Europe. Helli and Barbara followed shortly after by sea. I remained alone in America, where I was to await the production of *Galileo* in New York and report on it to Brecht. It was at this time that all the niggling complaints about Brecht's behavior at the hearing were made, and I had the job of defending him.

I thought it might be useful to get hold of the original records of the hearings. There were sound recordings and shorthand notes and, of course, photographs. Those wonderful little shorthand machines, with which one can write much faster than one can speak, I have so far seen only in America. All the transcripts of the hearings were prepared with the help of these, for the benefit of the committee, the lawyers, the police, the press, and heaven knows whom else. In addition, the whole proceedings from beginning to end were preserved on phonograph records.

I went to the police. My passport was still made out in the name of Lund, and nothing had been discovered against me. I said I was thinking of returning to Denmark. "But," I added, "I want to show them there the kind of people who have been trying to smuggle themselves into this wonderful country." On the strength of that I was handed the complete material, for which I paid forty dollars.

We had a very good friend in America. Ella Winter was a member of the party, but she was also a millionairess, and lived in a large house with her husband, the writer Donald Ogden Stewart. Before I left America, Ella and I invited a large number of people, chiefly American and German communists, to her home to listen to the phonograph records of the hearing. There they heard how cleverly Brecht had replied and how well he had conducted himself. The Americans were utterly delighted. "That's the right way to fight!" they said. Our German comrades too were now satisfied.

The record label bore the inscription "Hearing in Washington" and the date of the recording. I stuck another label on top of it, on which I wrote "Hollywood-Dialog." This proved a wise move, for on the ship all my luggage was searched. The records labeled "Hollywood-Dialog" were not played back, whereas sample tests were made on almost all the others in an attempt to discover whether I was taking out anything contraband.

Hanns Eisler had been summoned to Washington somewhat earlier than Brecht. After receiving the summons he was in a great state of nerves. Naturally, he was no keener than Brecht on spending several years in American prisons, now that the Nazis had at last been defeated. As a composer of film music he was in no real danger. But he was in danger for being Gerhart Eisler's brother, as well as for having written the music for Brecht's *The Mother*.

They showed him a photograph, on which he could be seen standing among a crowd of comrades in New York harbor. "What are you doing there with your hand?" they asked him. Eisler, seated before them, looked at the picture and demonstrated what he had been doing with his hand: making the "Red Front" sign, the greeting of all communist workers. He had been caught by the press photographers on the dock in the very act, and we had the dubious pleasure of seeing him next day on the front page of the newspapers making this sign to the members of the Committee on Un-American Activities. He must at the time have been in a bad state, both mentally and physically, otherwise he would never have allowed himself to be trapped into repeating the gesture. If I had been confronted with such a photograph I would have said, "Is that supposed to be me? I don't recognize it. Have you a magnifying glass?" Hanns argued that this was the greeting used by antifascists all over the world. In the course of the hearing he was called "the Karl Marx of music." That was high praise indeed, even in the opinion of his friends. However, for the senators on the congressional committee it was the equivalent of calling him the devil incarnate. To the question whether he had been or still was a communist he replied neither yes nor no. He said he had paid no subscriptions, and a person who paid no subscriptions could not be a member. One had to do a bit of maneuvering in order not to end up in jail. As a comrade Hanns Eisler conducted himself impeccably; my only worry had been the shaky state of his nerves when he went to the hearing.

The authorities blocked the exit visa that was already in his pocket, and in consequence he was obliged to remain in America longer than he had intended. In this tricky situation Chaplin was of great help to him. He— and Thomas Mann—wrote letters to all and sundry and organized a committee "for the release of Hanns Eisler." Chaplin was also repeatedly interviewed on Eisler's account. He knew Hanns was in great danger, and he declared, "He is my best friend and the greatest composer I know." This was printed in all the newspapers.

When, long after the hearings, I visited Chaplin in Switzerland, he did, however, say to me, "Eisler cost me six million dollars." By this he meant that his film *Monsieur Verdoux* had not brought in the six million it had cost him to make. No movie theater dared show it, a fact that Chaplin attributed to his intervention on Eisler's behalf.

But there had also been other reasons for boycotting *Monsieur Verdoux*. I can clearly remember one of those coffee and whiskey afternoons at Eisler's house in Malibu, when Brecht and Eisler succeeded in inserting a few lines into the script of Chaplin's film. For example, it was Eisler who suggested, "What is war but doing business by other means?" This remark was of course too much for the business people. No major theater would show *Monsieur Verdoux*. I once saw people lining up for tickets in front of a very small movie house. Some men from the Ku Klux Klan came up behind them bearing cudgels, and very soon those in line were lying stretched out on the street. Such happenings defy belief, but this I saw with my own eyes. A fascist organization was behind it. It was the last thing I saw in America before my departure.

The irony regarding the Eisler brothers was that, back in Europe, Hanns was always yearning to return to America, which on account of all this turmoil remained permanently closed to him, while Gerhart wanted to leave America for good, and was not allowed to go. The Department of Justice considered him a security risk, and so held on to him.

For me, Gerhart is not only an outstanding politician, but also one of the most wonderful men I know. One evening I had invited him and his wife Hilde to dinner. I was expecting them at seven o'clock. Hilde, herself a cook, always took care to be punctual. When they failed to arrive, I knew something unexpected had happened. At about nine o'clock I went to my newspaper stand, and there I saw on the front page of all the newspapers the headline: "Soviet spy Gerhart Eisler arrested." So Gerhart and Hilde were forgiven.

Gerhart made a real battle of his arrest. His interrogation—everything he said in evidence and his manner of conducting himself—proved a model of what political activity and personal fearlessness should be. After he was sent to jail Hilde traveled all over the country, giving lectures and declaring that her husband had committed no crimes; all he wanted was to return to Germany, from which the fascists had driven him. Hilde was very slim and she looked wonderful. Everything she said went straight to the hearts of the American women.

In America one can be released from prison on bail. To bail out a murderer cost five thousand dollars at that time. For Gerhart Eisler, however, twenty-five thousand dollars had to be found. The sum was raised, but even then Gerhart was not really free. He was constantly "accompanied" by two or three men in trenchcoats. This was very irksome, even though again and again Gerhart succeeded in shaking off his followers. He developed a technique of transferring from streetcar to subway and disappearing into crowds, and in that way kept giving the F.B.I. people the slip. Now and again we would talk together on the telephone, naturally without mentioning our names, since my telephone had long been under surveillance. Occasionally, observing all the rules of conspiratorial conduct, we would meet.

One evening a Polish ship was due to leave New York for England. As usual, there were big farewell scenes on the dock. Gerhart, who had managed to elude his guards, bought some flowers for twenty-five cents, mingled with the people going on board, and did not return to the dock. Once the ship was outside the harbor, he gave himself up to the captain as a stowaway. An American comrade, Georg Alexan, who now lives in Berlin, paid his fare. Someone on board who worked for American radio discovered what had happened. He cabled a personal description of Gerhart Eisler to America, and from then on the F.B.I. did everything they could to get him back.

Policemen were waiting for him when the ship reached England. We saw pictures in the Swiss newspapers of Gerhart being carried off the ship by four people, two holding his arms and two his legs. We thought he had had a nervous breakdown and was being taken to hospital. What had really happened was that Gerhart decided he would not voluntarily put a foot on English soil. He could be removed from Polish territory—which includes a Polish ship—only by force.

Gentlemanly English conservatism sometimes has its

151

advantages. Gerhart was released and brought back to the ship, since under English law he could not be delivered up to the United States. However, he was obliged to spend some time in prison before the case was settled. Hundreds of English comrades gathered outside the prison, shouting, "Freedom for Gerhart Eisler!" They also sang battle hymns written by Gerhart's brother Hanns. It was a political demonstration that attracted attention throughout the world. News broadcasts everywhere carried reports about Gerhart Eisler.

I have already mentioned how much I admire Gerhart, but there was one occasion when he made me cross.

Here in my Berlin apartment, Brecht once mentioned in Gerhart's presence that he intended to continue with the versification of the Communist Manifesto. He had begun this in America, and he said he had now come to a better understanding of hexameters and would try to complete the work. Instead of encouraging him, Gerhart Eisler observed, "It's hard enough already for workers to read and understand the Communist Manifesto in prose." Such remarks simply had the effect of inhibiting Brecht in his work.

Feuchtwanger too had doubts about the versification. "It won't work," he said. "It can't be done. The Communist Manifesto in hexameters would be impossible." But he then made up for it by adding, "All right, we can try," and he sat down at once with Brecht to begin. Brecht needed encouraging criticism, and Feuchtwanger could make him productive. He would never have said what Gerhart Eisler said, even if it was what he really thought. He pointed out lines in which the meter was defective, and Brecht would accept that from him. I used to watch them working together. It was a collaboration characterized by great friendliness and generosity.

They addressed each other with the formal *Sie*, though

they had known each other well for ages. Feuchtwanger would tap out the hexameter rhythm on the bar table, and Brecht would laugh. In this way the verses we now know came into existence.

Once, while visiting me in New York, Brecht read out a version of his Manifesto to some of our friends, among them Jacob Walcher, Hermann Duncker, Albert Schreiner, and a number of Americans. Unfortunately, he read it in such a curiously stiff manner that nobody could follow it. The American comrades were at a complete loss, and our own comrades had no idea either what Brecht was getting at. All of them were bewildered. Afterward, however, they said in tones of great respect that the poem was wonderful. Such praise meant nothing to Brecht. What he wanted to hear was criticism, material objections. He wanted to know where he should make changes. All the same, polite murmurs were better than the way in which Gerhart Eisler reacted. I am not at all sure, either, whether Eisler's judgment was really correct. He never revised it.

The first production of *Galileo* in California was at least two years in the making. The translation from German into English was already in itself a kind of production draft. Brecht and Laughton settled the text together and shaped the plot.

Right at the start Fritz Kortner was keen to take on the role of Galileo, but it was obvious he had no chance as long as Charles Laughton was available: His German accent alone was enough to disqualify him. At that time Brecht was hoping to conquer Broadway with Laughton in *Galileo*. He offered Kortner the role of the Pope, but Kortner turned it down; for him it must be Galileo or nothing.

During the preparations in California Brecht paid attention to every detail, down to the smallest. What I witnessed there was something that was later completely lost. Brecht played and danced everything himself—the movement around the sun, the drumming, the street singer, and so on. I took photographs of all this. We had to rehearse in a bare room, since the stage would not be available until later. For me these rehearsals were truly great theater.

For stage rehearsals we were in a much worse position than the Berliner Ensemble was at a later date. For financial reasons we had to restrict ourselves to only four or five weeks. The director was Joseph Losey, but Brecht worked alongside him from the very beginning. He arranged the group scenes, decided the movements, and explained to the actors the content of each scene. The street scene with the ballad singer was entirely Brecht's work, and in California, as well as later in New York, it was much clearer and more expressive than in Berlin. Here it is hard to understand exactly what it is meant to convey. I did my best, running through the film I had made in America several times for the benefit of both Erich Engel and the choreographer. Unfortunately, they did not catch on.

In California Helene Weigel designed the costumes for *Galileo*. Such thorough groundwork, based on the study of an enormous number of sources, was something completely unknown over there. Helli's starting point was not those commonplace and tasteless concoctions that were in general use in Hollywood; she gathered together historical prototypes as a springboard for her ideas. Brecht himself sought out the stage props or had them made from sketches drawn by a Danish scientist we had come to know.

It was, I believe, fifteen years since Charles Laughton had last acted in a theater, having in the meantime worked only in films. He was very eager to make contact with a live audience again, but at the same time the prospect made him nervous. What particularly eroded his self-confidence was his inability to come to terms with the epic style of acting. At first he would stick to what he had done in rehearsal, but suddenly he would break out in a sweat when the expected reaction failed to materialize. This became even worse in New York than it had been in California. Laughton and Brecht had a very great respect for each other. Laughton acted for Brecht's benefit, but in New York Brecht was no longer there.

Brecht gave me the task of photographing the Californian production. It was a terrible job, for Laughton was in such a state of hysteria that every click of the camera would upset him. More than once he simply abandoned a rehearsal on account of it. I then had a glass partition built into the wall of the lighting director's room, so that Laughton could not hear when I pressed the shutter. Eager as he was to have pictures, Brecht would in the end have given in to Laughton, as he always did with his big stars. He would simply have told me, "Then I'm afraid we can't do it." But I said to myself, "We really need these pictures—if not in any other way, then through a glass partition!"

Many times, dead tired, I drove home from the theater with my cameras and tripods stacked in a tiny Ford car with a reverse gear that no longer worked. I had made myself a darkroom in the cellar, and each night I would develop my films and make enlargements from them. In the morning, before Brecht went off to rehearsals, I would lay out the pictures on the table. We would examine them carefully and discuss what could or must be changed on the stage. Brecht continued to work on his production even after the opening night. In Berlin we took this as a matter of course, but in America it was not customary.

Brecht was very polite and very circumspect in his treatment of Laughton. He would say, "Wouldn't it perhaps be funnier if you did this or that here? What do you think?" For Laughton this manner of working was very upsetting, and I doubt whether he would have accepted it from anyone but Brecht. I still have my "California lap robe." The two of them once threw it into my little car from their larger one, since it was very cold in my laboratory. They themselves went off to enjoy oysters and caviar.

After the premiere I photographed Chaplin with Brecht and Chaplin with Laughton. I had just put my film into the developer when Brecht arrived. He stayed only a short while, but I was so tired that I fell asleep and forgot my film, which remained in the developer for two hours instead of twenty minutes. However, with a bit of ingenuity and patience it is still possible to make prints from them. Mine is the only existing photograph of Brecht and Chaplin together.

The Californian production of *Galileo* opened at the Coronet Theater, Beverly Hills, on July 30, 1947. Three months later—five weeks before the play opened in New York—Brecht left America. I remained at my post in order, at Brecht's request, to keep an eye on the production.

Unfortunately, Brecht had already departed before the preparations for the New York production began. This was a big disadvantage, since there were many casting changes to be made. America possesses no theater with a permanent ensemble, but it has a great many unemployed actors. With luck, good ones can be found. The California production was brilliantly cast, but in New York we ran into great difficulties in this respect. Joseph Losey now carried full responsibility for the direction, but in fact he had to do as Charles Laughton wished. In my opinion, Losey had no good ideas and his taste was bad, so really it was better for him to rely on Laughton. I sat there, trying to keep records of as much of the work as I could, in order to report to Brecht in Switzerland. The many alterations made me uneasy, but all the same there were perhaps things that might be used. Unfortunately, however, most of the changes arose from Laughton once again getting cold feet—not only on account of the epic style of acting but also from the excitement aroused by Brecht's appearance before the Committee on Un-American Activities.

At last I became fed up with the many changes, and I asked Laughton to write to Brecht himself, telling him about them. Laughton refused, on the grounds that Brecht never wrote directly to him. I then suggested that he make some phonograph recordings on which he could explain to Brecht what he was altering and why. I dragged him by the nose into the studio and arranged for the recordings to be made. These discs containing Laughton's explanations are still in existence.

After I had taken three thousand photographs, most of which I sent to Switzerland, Brecht wrote to me: "There are still two pictures missing in the first scene, four in the seventh scene, and three in the eleventh." In despair, I bought an 8-mm movie camera with what was left of my money, and with that I filmed the entire production. Again Laughton intervened, insisting that neither photographs nor films be made. Before it had been the click of the shutter that had put him off; now it was the whirring of the movie camera. Luckily I had already completed my work by then. I was told that Laughton tore his hair when he heard I had filmed all the changes.

Of all the work Brecht and I did together, the most important to me was *The Caucasian Chalk Circle* (*Der kaukasische Kreidekreis*). Brecht came to New York in the middle of November 1943 and stayed for four months. Once again he lived in my apartment. He was working on many other projects at the time, and he also signed a contract for a version of *The Chalk Circle*. This was arranged by the actress Luise Rainer, who was married to the playwright Clifford Odets and had connections with influential Broadway theater producers. It was a great opportunity for Brecht.

He started work on the play while still in New York. I was at that time pregnant with Brecht's child. I was very happy about it, and so was Brecht, though he was extremely anxious to keep my condition a secret. We had also agreed on names: if a girl, it would be Susanne, if a boy, Michel—like the child in *The Chalk Circle*. Shortly after Brecht completed the play, on September 3, 1944, Michel was born. Brecht wrote in his journal that I had had an "operation" in a hospital in Los Angeles.

I was indeed very ill, and my temperature soared. The doctor called for a decision: mother or child. I said, "Save the child." At that moment Bertolt Brecht came rushing in, dressed in white overalls and cap. "Here I am," he cried, "I've come." He came every day, but it meant little to me, since I was on a breathing machine and more dead than alive. Brecht saw his son in the ward for premature births. He told me later that I had never spoken except to ask after Michel; nothing had mattered to me but my desire to save the child.

One day the doctor came to me. (Peter Lorre was paying for him; we ourselves could not have afforded the hospital charges.) The doctor sat down on my bed. All I could see of him was his tie as he very gently began to say there was something he must tell me. "I know already," I replied, "Michel has died." He lived only a few days.

What follows was told me later by Hanns Eisler. He

said he had no longer found it possible to speak to Brecht. "He was distraught in a way I have never seen him before." Eisler asked him, "What is the matter? Have I offended you in some way? Have I done something wrong politically?" Brecht's only reply was, "No, it's a private matter." Sadly Eisler went off home, knowing that Brecht would never speak of private things. He learned from the women what had happened: "Ruth Berlau has had Brecht's baby. She is very ill. The baby is dead, and we don't know whether Ruth is still alive."

Brecht fetched me from the hospital before I was fully recovered. We were too poor to afford a longer stay. He took me to Berthold Viertel's house, where his wife Salka had prepared a little room for me. Here I gradually regained my strength.

For me, all this is closely tied up with my work on *The Caucasian Chalk Circle*. Brecht said to me, "Don't grieve any more about Michel's death. When we get to Berlin, we'll adopt a child at once. There are a lot of children now with neither father nor mother." We did not adopt a child, but there are always a lot of children in my home. Brecht was right about that: I love them just as much as I loved his and my own child.

Brecht had told me the basic elements of the Azdak story while we were still in Denmark. He had always been interested in the function of a judge during periods of lawless change. The main work in America was the invention of the Grusha plot: how she steals the child, how she comes to love it, and how in the end she cannot bear to be parted from it. Brecht continued the work that he had begun in New York. He sent me each new scene the moment the pages left the typewriter. I too would reply without delay, giving him my opinion. It was as if we were still continuing to work side by side, though Brecht was now living on the West Coast and I on the

East. He opened a file in which he stuck the manuscripts of *The Chalk Circle*, pictures he had collected as models for costumes and stage props, as well as my notes and comments. He adopted many of my suggestions. At that time Grusha and Simon bore the names Katja and Wolodja.

What gave Brecht most trouble was the prologue, "The Struggle for the Valley." He was eager to find something that would connect the "chalk circle" legend with our own times. In my opinion this connection is very effective, but after the premiere in Berlin in 1954 the prologue was attacked on all sides, in East as well as in West Germany. Here in the East the main critics were Fritz Erpenbeck and Alfred Kurella. Kurella even wanted the word "Caucasian" erased from the title, declaring that the conditions in that part of the world were quite different from the way Brecht described them. Erpenbeck objected mainly to the use of masks, insinuating that Brecht was adopting Chinese traditions instead of concentrating his attention on the development of a German national theater. Criticisms of this kind could not be lightly dismissed. Brecht conserved his energies and remained silent. I thoroughly approved of that, but was then astonished when the first performance in West Germany was given in the spring of 1955—with Harry Buckwitz directing and Käthe Reichel playing Grusha—to find Brecht openly assenting to the omission of the prologue. He simply said, "Otherwise the play could not have been done in Frankfurt am Main, or the premiere would have meant the end of Harry Buckwitz as intendant." On the other hand, he insisted that the prologue be printed in the Suhrkamp *Versuche* edition, though Peter Suhrkamp was not at all happy about it.

* * *

In the summer of 1944 I was suddenly summoned to the office of the director of the Office of War Information. Seated behind his large desk, he told me he had discovered that I fought on the wrong side in Spain. The information came from a Danish social democrat who owed his job in the Office of War Information to none other than myself. His name was Hans Bendix.

Over a period of time I had introduced several Danes into the Office, to give them the chance of earning a few dollars. Bendix had two children in need of shoes. Unfortunately he had a falsetto voice, and they were reluctant to engage him. I went to the director and said that since he was so good at training voices—which was by no means true, but he was always proud when one asserted it—maybe he could also succeed with Hans Bendix. Not only did Hans Bendix get his voice put in order, but later he himself became director of the Office.

Bendix managed to denounce Ida Bachmann as well as myself, so that we both found ourselves out of work. I had to leave at once, with two men at my side to ensure I took nothing with me: I was almost begrudged my own hat. To console me, my Norwegian friend took me to an elegant restaurant. When we entered, we saw Peter Lorre sitting there with his wife. I told him I was now out of work. He drew a key from his pocket and gave it to me. "Go to Santa Monica," he said. "You can stay with us." He had a lovely villa there.

I arrived by train in Santa Monica very early in the morning. Knowing that Brecht rose early, I called him at seven o'clock. By ten past seven he was there.

Brecht too was very grateful for Peter Lorre's help. Peter Lorre supported us on many occasions, but Brecht never obtained from him what he really wanted. They often talked about a production of *Schweyk* in America, but Lorre never played Schweyk. I have letters from Brecht in which he declares that his only reason for writing his *Schweyk in the Second World War* was because in America he had Peter Lorre for the main part. But Lorre let him down, as did Kurt Weill, who was to have written the music.

Brecht would have preferred Hanns Eisler for the music, but Eisler told me one day in America, "I am tired of writing music for my bottom drawer." Well, as far as his music for Brecht's plays is concerned, Eisler did not have to leave it in his bottom drawer for long. In the end, shortly before Brecht's death, he did write music for *Schweyk* after all and was able to play his songs to Brecht. In my opinion, however, he should have done more for Brecht than he did.

In contrast to Hanns Eisler, Paul Dessau worked for his bottom drawer without grumbling. While in Hollywood he made a start on the music for *The Chalk Circle*, and a number of the "War Verses" ("*Kriegsfibel*") were also composed in exile. But of course Dessau was not as well known in America as Eisler. He was not working in the film studios, and so he had time to spare. Brecht had a very high regard for Dessau, and their work sessions were also full of fun. Dessau is crazy in a very delightful way. He had a complex about making something of Brecht's his own. He offered to marry me at least ten times. In the end he got Elisabeth Hauptmann—also something of Brecht's!

Elisabeth Hauptmann participated in Brecht's development more fully and more closely than any of us, beginning with *In the Jungle of Cities* (*Im Dickicht der Städte*). She was a comrade, and during Brecht's early years in Berlin she collaborated in all his works and knew everybody—Eisler and Dudow, Weisenborn and Suhrkamp,

162

Emil Hesse-Burri, the boxer Samson Körner, Caspar Neher, and the other childhood friends from Augsburg— it is impossible to name them all. It is vitally important that Elisabeth should write about her experiences, otherwise much will be lost.

She could, for example, tell us about work on *The Step* (*Die Massnahme*), in which she was involved. I think of that because it proved a particularly tricky subject during Brecht's hearing in Washington. Brecht was accused of glorifying murder in it, but he got the committee into a tangle by claiming it was based on a Japanese play. In fact, the Japanese play was the basis not of *The Step* but of *He Who Said Yes* (*Der Jasager*). *The Step* was concerned with adherence to party discipline, indispensable in times of political struggle outside the law.

The break between Brecht and Elisabeth Hauptmann came even before he went into exile. The reason was almost certainly Brecht's act of bringing Margarete Steffin in as a collaborator. This was too much for Elisabeth Hauptmann, who temporarily suspended their relationship.

When she arrived in Denmark, where he had then been living for some time, Brecht wanted her to stay on. However, she went to America, where she became a teacher. She told me later why she had felt unable to comply with Brecht's wish. Helene Weigel was there with the children, then she saw Grete Steffin working together with Brecht, and finally she met me.

In 1935 she gave up her teaching work to assist Brecht with the production of *The Mother* in New York. Brecht wanted her, since Grete Steffin had not accompanied him to New York. She took a small apartment in which she furnished one room for Brecht and another for herself. She knew the play well, had an excellent command of English, and could be of great help in many ways. But the old relationship had gone forever, and life in the little apartment was no longer very pleasant. According to what Elisabeth told me, he immediately started an affair with the translator: "She weighed a couple of hundredweight." Elisabeth took a dim view of that. After the production she returned to her teaching.

When we came to America in 1941 and Brecht then visited me in New York, I asked Elisabeth to work something like two hours each week for Brecht, writing letters and interpreting for business discussions. I have already mentioned that she was not prepared to do it, and so it fell to me, with my bad English and bad German, to type his letters. Today I know that Elisabeth was right. She wanted to live her own life at last. She became friendly with Horst Bärensprung, an emigrant social democrat who had been a police chief in the Weimar Republic, and eventually she married him. She kept on marrying— I believe four times in all: Hauptmann, the reciter Ludwig Hardt, Bärensprung, and Dessau. She had more sense than many others, even during the nine years preceding Brecht's emigration, when he and she were living in adjacent apartments.

After the emigration period Elisabeth was relatively late in coming to Berlin. Brecht much looked forward to her arrival, for he needed her urgently for his work. Though she had decided to work with him again, Elisabeth had probably kept him waiting too long. Regrettably, when she at last arrived Brecht treated her badly. At that time we still had no theater of our own, and our only permanent place of work was an office in the back premises of the artists' club Die Möwe. There—apart, naturally, from Helene Weigel's director's office—I had the best room, since Brecht and Neher used to meet in my room for their daily discussions. Brecht went to no trouble on Elisabeth's behalf. She had to find a room for herself.

There was only a very tiny one available, smaller even than my lavatory. Elisabeth took it over without any sign of resentment. Before long everybody in the company discovered what a great personality she was. Brecht's assistants, his "young people," took to visiting her regularly. They would sit with her in her little room, picking her brain. She helped many of them with her advice. What came out then about Brecht's early life was thanks entirely to her. But for a long time life was none too pleasant for her; she had little money, and on top of that she was ill. But despite this she worked for Brecht with great modesty and admirable persistence. Now everybody knows how important she was—and still is—to Brecht.

7 ❧

Once *Galileo* had opened in New York I could
fold my tents, and I headed for Switzerland with
a case of cigars for Brecht in my luggage. In the meantime
Brecht had given up the studio in which I had hoped to
find him. He was now living in Feldmeilen. Helene Weigel had set up a home for them to share, so Brecht was
once more enjoying warmth, good food, and the little
comforts of life.

I arrived in Zurich on January 22, 1948. In the evening
he came by train to welcome me back to Europe. We got
down at once to work. This is literally what happened;
there was no time for settling in, for Brecht and Caspar
Neher were deep in their production of *Antigone*. They
were working together as they had always done, Neher
sitting with a drawing block, not very large, making
sketches, while Brecht held forth and worked out ideas
for the staging. At the finish, Neher would hand over a
bundle of sketches showing groupings, postures, gestures, scenic designs, and so on. While planning a production, Brecht made swifter progress when he had Neher's "protocols" in front of him as reminders. (I put

California, 1942.

omen From Nazi-Occupied Nations

ch actress, formerly of the Royal Theatre in Copenhagen, broadcasting from the O.
...ions Branch studios in New York

...ect and Broadcast Facts for O. W. I.

Ruth Berlau
broadcasting to
Denmark from
New York, 1942.

California, 1942.

W. H. Auden
with Brecht in
New York, 1944.
RUTH BERLAU

Charles Laughton
with Ruth Berlau,
1945. ARCHIV BUNGE

Brecht and
Charles Laughton,
1944. RUTH BERLAU

Ruth Berlau in 1945.
ARCHIV BUNGE

Charles Chaplin in 1946.
RUTH BERLAU

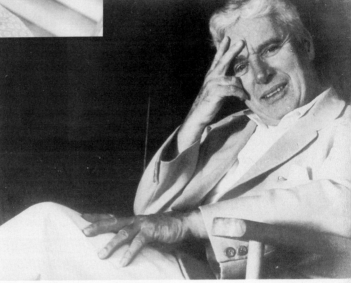

Charles Chaplin
and Brecht, 1947.
RUTH BERLAU

Brecht rehearsing *Antigone* in Chur
with Hans Gaugler and Helene Weigel,
1948. RUTH BERLAU

Helene Weigel as Mother Courage,
Berlin, 1949. RUTH BERLAU

Brecht (center) and Ruth Berlau, the director (right), rehearsing
The Mother in Leipzig, 1950. ARCHIV JOHANNES HOFFMANN

Ruth Berlau, Berlin, 1950.
ARCHIV BUNGE

Brecht and Helene Weigel
in 1953. HERBERT HENSKY

Brecht and Helene Weigel on the stage of
the Berliner Ensemble, 1954. PERCY PAUKSCHTA

Ruth Berlau (Brecht's iron ring on her finger) with her Leica camera, 1954. ARCHIV BUNGE

Caspar Neher in Switzerland, 1948. RUTH BERLAU

Brecht at a rehearsal of *The Caucasian Chalk Circle* in 1954, with Hans Bunge (foreground), Manfred Wekwerth (at back), Ernst Busch (right). ARCHIV BUNGE

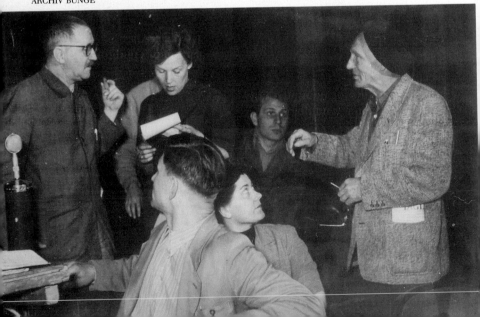

Brecht and Hella Wuolijoki
at a performance of *Puntila*, 1949.
ARCHIV BUNGE

Elisabeth Hauptmann in
1970. RENÉ HILL

Ruth Berlau (second row at left) talking with Swedish student actors,
Berlin, 1971. ARCHIV BUNGE

Ruth Berlau in her
Berlin apartment, 1973.
ROGER MELIS

"protocols" in quotes because in fact they included many of Neher's own ideas.)

The text of the play was already written down, but as always with Brecht, it was not yet finalized. He had gone through various translations of Sophocles, and there was even a Greek text on hand, Brecht having found someone with a slight knowledge of Greek. In the end he decided on the Hölderlin version, which he considered to be more than a straight translation. If only for its folklorish Swabian idiom, which he was constantly pointing out as he read it to me, Brecht found Hölderlin's text "the strongest and the most amusing."

We were very happy. The war was over, the Washington hearings had passed without any dire consequences for Brecht, he had Caspar Neher back at his side and many other friends within reach, and he had a number of plays ready for staging. All was in order except for one thing: Brecht wanted Helene Weigel to resume her acting career at last, but the theater in Zurich, the Schauspielhaus, turned a deaf ear. Kurt Hirschfeld had begun rehearsals on *Puntila*, and Brecht wished Helene to take on the role of Bootleg Emma. Hirschfeld, however, was against it. I do not know why; perhaps he lacked confidence in her after so long an absence from the stage. Anyway, he gave the role to Therese Giehse.

I was full of admiration for the way in which Helene overcame this disappointment. It cannot have been easy for her, having to content herself merely with the role of housewife that had been forced on her by emigration. But she remained cheerful and patient, receiving guests and playing hostess with all her usual charm. In the narrow space she had furnished as a dining room she served up meals for at least ten people. The progressively minded Swiss citizens who visited Brecht were for the most part penniless, and Helene was concerned to ensure that in her house they should at least have something to eat.

If Helene had been allowed to play in *Puntila*, Brecht would possibly never have written *Antigone*. Because of that refusal, he had to find something else for her to do. He was determined to stage *Mother Courage and Her Children* with her, and felt that she must first be given a chance, after the long break in her acting career, to stretch her wings on the stage. He himself was in no doubt about her talent, but he felt she would be helped by the reassurance. The character of Antigone was one she might have been born for. Maybe Brecht remembered her performance as the maid in *Oedipus*, which had made such a huge impression on him in 1929.

I arrived in Switzerland at exactly the right time to take photographs of the *Antigone* production. We had of course worked with photographic models before, in my productions of *The Mother* and *Señora Carrar's Rifles* in Denmark, but now we were thinking in terms of a real, printed model book with text, photographs, and annotations.

The production labored under many difficulties. The Schauspielhaus in Zurich was not available to us. Hans Curjel, who had been dramaturge at the Kroll Opera House in Berlin before being forced to emigrate, was now in charge of the little theater in Chur. He offered Brecht his stage for the experiment, but we did not get the use of it until shortly before the premiere, and had in the meantime to make do with various rehearsal rooms. Another snag was that neither Brecht nor Neher could rehearse continuously, since many of the players had touring engagements.

For the first time I saw what directing a play meant to Brecht. In America he had always worked under handicaps. I was fascinated by the amount of enjoyment he brought to the rehearsals of *Antigone*. There was no feeling of haste, though time was short; it was all amusing, courteous, and enlivened by a willing and precise attention to detail. Helene Weigel was good-humored and very gracious; quite forgotten was the fact that she had not stood on a stage for more than fifteen years. Brecht was expecting a big star actor for the role of Kreon—first it was to be Gustav Knuth, I believe, then Walter Richter. But the stars did not appear, and Brecht entrusted the role to a young actor who had stood in for Kreon at rehearsals. His name was Hans Gaugler, and better casting for the role cannot be imagined. Brecht considered his performance in the scene with the dance around the seer Tiresias as exemplary in every way. Gaugler, who had been a substitute for a star, became a star himself. Later on Brecht brought him to Berlin to play the title role in his adaptation of Lenz's play *The Tutor* (*Der Hofmeister*).

Owing to other engagements, Caspar Neher was not in Chur for the final rehearsals. However, he had done an immense amount of preliminary work and had personally helped prepare the decorations. I can still see him painting the hessian backcloths blood red with the help of a scrubbing brush. Around the acting area were wooden columns, on which skeletons of horses' heads were impaled. I remember with horror the arrival of those fresh horses' heads, which were then put into a laundry tub to boil. Brecht and Neher were anxious to put Curjel's theater to as little expense as possible.

Unfortunately, the audience was not on its toes. The opening night was passable, since people had come in from Zurich and Basel, but the usual Chur audience found the performance odd, and I believe no one understood it at all. In consequence, it was done only five times, to which can be added a single matinee in Zurich. Hans Curjel could not afford to keep the production going, and he invited two financiers to come and see it, in the hope of persuading them to support us. However, the financiers did not take to the idea.

Immediately after the *Antigone* premiere Brecht and I set about preparing a model book of the production under the title *Antigonemodell 1948*. Brecht sold it to the publishing firm Gebrüder-Weiss-Verlag. Weiss, who dearly wished to publish something by Brecht, departed happily. Maybe he was less happy later, for the book had no success at all. I was still working on the last photographs in the night preceding his departure. On top of that, in 1948 there was no paper suitable for reproductions to be found. So Weiss cannot be blamed.

The *Antigonemodell* was the only manuscript Brecht succeeded in selling in Switzerland. He had dealings with many publishers there, but they dragged on and in the end dried up. Our financial situation in Switzerland was anything but good. Since money was short, I was obliged to continue writing for reactionary newspapers.

Brecht would have liked to visit Augsburg or Munich. He wanted to see his native city and meet the friends of his youth; he wanted to discuss joint projects with Erich Engel and his friend, the theater director Jakob Geis; and he wanted to become involved in productions already in preparation: *Mr. Puntila and His Man Matti* in Munich and a touring production of *The Threepenny Opera* with Hans Albers. However, the Americans would not allow him inside their occupation zone. So Brecht sent me to West Germany to report on the productions and to negotiate with publishers. Since I still possessed an American press pass, I could not only travel around freely but could also live at the Munich press center. Thus I had the advantage of a swift, uncensored postal service and could make telephone calls to Zurich, something Germans were not allowed to do. I also had no difficulties about food, which for the native population was strictly rationed by the occupying power.

I still have a suspicion that Brecht's main purpose in sending me to Germany was to obtain a car for him. The Nazis had confiscated his car in 1933, and he was determined to get his hands on another. We talked frequently on the phone and exchanged many letters, and on each occasion the car was his main concern. He did not have enough money to buy a car in Switzerland, so I was instructed to contact the publisher Desch in Munich and offer him the rights to *The Threepenny Opera* novel and to the *Puntila* play, and then with the advance to buy a car for him. It should be a cabriolet, and if possible a Steyr of the kind he had previously owned. Desch took the novel and the play, but in spite of his good connections nothing could be done about the car. Gradually I realized why Brecht was still holding off the Swiss publishers. He wanted to be sure of his car before closing with them.

I spent about three months in the American occupation zone, where I took a good look round. I also attended the Nuremberg trials and reported on them for Danish newspapers. My impressions of the Germans were conflicting. I met old comrades and incorrigible Nazis. The towns were mostly in ruins. Life immediately after the war was very complicated. I wrote Brecht detailed letters that were probably frequently too long, and he failed to read them to the end. By the time I returned to Switzerland he had written his *Little Organon for the Theater* (*Kleines Organon für das Theater*). We did not foresee then how hysterically some theater people would react to it. They feared—rightly—that Brecht was out to destroy the old red plush theater with all its emotionalism.

As time went by, Brecht's longing to return to Berlin

grew. Eventually he found friends who could help him to get there: Gottfried von Einem in Austria, Egon Erwin Kisch in Czechoslovakia, and Günther Weisenborn, who had good contacts with the Soviet headquarters in Berlin. In the middle of October 1948 Brecht and Helene Weigel set off on their journey, traveling via Salzburg, Prague, and Dresden. It proved arduous, with many stops along the way. Brecht was oppressed by the terrible scenes of destruction he saw everywhere. But he was returning to Germany. He was excited by the prospect of again seeing Berlin, from which he had been forced to flee so abruptly fifteen years ago. He had decided on an attitude of reserve; above all, he was unwilling to say anything in public until he had cast an eye over conditions as they were in the Soviet-occupied part of Germany. However, he consented to take part in a reception that had been arranged for him in the Haus der Kulturbund. There is a story about that, which I cannot confirm, since I was still in Switzerland at the time, but I have no reason to doubt its authenticity. Awaiting his arrival in the Kulturbund were Johannes R. Becher, Ludwig Renn, Alexander Abusch, Slatan Dudow, Herbert Ihering, Arnold Zweig, Jacob Walcher, his school friend Otto Müllereisert, the intendant of the Deutsches Theater Wolfgang Langhoff, the cultural officer of the Soviet military administration Alexander Dymschitz, and other prominent guests. Now only Brecht was missing. The company became restless. Eventually Becher went to the hall porter to inquire. "Yes," the porter said, "a man was here, but he looked like a *Heimkehrer*, not suitable for present company. I wouldn't let him in, and he went off without a word." The porter had probably been upset by Brecht's sloppy clothing and his haircut, suspecting him of being another type of returnee, an ex-prisoner of war. Becher then arranged for Brecht to be fetched from his hotel.

172

Brecht and Helene spent their first days in the famous Hotel Adlon—or what was left of it after the bombing. Wolfgang Langhoff at once accepted Brecht's proposal to stage *Mother Courage and Her Children* in the Deutsches Theater, with Brecht himself as director. He had not been more than two weeks in Berlin, I believe, when he began rehearsals. He got Erich Engel to co-direct. The atmosphere at rehearsals was fantastic. Brecht had found players with whom he could work splendidly: Paul Bildt, for instance, Werner Hinz, Paul Esser, Gerda Müller, Gerhard Bienert, and Friedrich Gnass. He also had new young players such as Ernst Kahler, Joachim Teege, and Angelika Hurwicz. The opening night was a triumph for Brecht's work in the theater. After the performance Brecht wrote to Helene Weigel: "When Mother Courage's covered wagon trundled across the stage of the Deutsches Theater, a new theatrical era began."

I saw Brecht at rehearsal and knew at once that he would remain in Berlin. With Wolfgang Langhoff he discussed the setting up of a studio theater to be attached to the Deutsches Theater. Brecht's main desire at the beginning was to bring back the great actors who had gone into exile, inviting them to give guest performances in Berlin. At the same time he wanted to establish a permanent company of his own. The discussions were held for the most part in the Hotel Adlon. Helene Weigel was earmarked as head of the company. Others who took part in the discussions were the stage director Erich Engel, the scenic designer Caspar Neher, and occasionally Slatan Dudow. Later on, Hanns Eisler and Paul Dessau arrived in Berlin. Brecht saw them too as future members of the ensemble.

The idea of naming our company the Berliner Ensemble came from me. It arose quite simply. Since it was always being said that what we needed above all, if we were to produce good theater, was an ensemble, the name more or less suggested itself. It was just that I was the first to say, "Then let's call ourselves the Berliner Ensemble." It became evident later on that the idea was not such a good one after all, since there is no one in Germany who can pronounce the word "ensemble" properly.

Shortly before the *Mother Courage* premiere Brecht was summoned to the office of the mayor, Oberbürgermeister Ebert. There he found Wolfgang Langhoff and Fritz Wisten, who was at that time intendant of the Theater am Schiffbauerdamm, as well as representatives of the Central Committee and the head of the cultural office, Kurt Bock. Brecht returned from this meeting disappointed. The response to his theater project had not been as enthusiastic as he had thought it would be. All the same, a green light had been given for the establishment of the Berliner Ensemble. Helene Weigel took over an office in the artists' club Die Möwe and began work on its organization. We were to be given the right to appear as guests in the Deutsches Theater until Brecht was provided with a theater of his own. The plan was to give him the Theater am Schiffbauerdamm, but first the Volksbühne am Luxemburgplatz must be rebuilt for Wisten to take over.

Unfortunately, difficulties soon arose with Langhoff. Every trivial detail led to a quarrel. Brecht was very sensitive; if a request of his was not granted, he imagined he was being boycotted and made a fuss. In turn, Langhoff regarded this as outrageous. In the end the two men took to avoiding each other. Since work on the rebuilding of the Volksbühne took so long, this uncomfortable relationship persisted for five years. At one time Wisten had already moved into the new theater, but it had to be rebuilt yet again, the acoustics were so atrocious. (In my opinion the theater was not much better even then. On that stage an actor cannot speak; he has to shout.) It was not until 1954 that Brecht took over his "Schiff." Surprisingly, he did not open it with a play of his own but with Molière's *Don Juan*, directed by Benno Besson.

Fortunately we were given, shortly after the founding of the Ensemble, a rehearsal building in which Brecht could be his own master. This was the former gymnasium of a demolished barracks in the Reinhardtstrasse, opposite the Deutsches Theater. Now, where fascist soldiers had once drilled, antiwar plays like *Mother Courage* were being rehearsed. The rehearsal stage was the same size as the stage of the Deutsches Theater, so we did not need to bother Langhoff until the time came for technical rehearsals. Beneath the roof of the rehearsal building we also had our own workshops, two of which in time became famous: those of the scenic artist Eduard Fischer and the carpenter Toni Schubert.

While Helene was arranging her office in the Möwe and their house in Berlin Weissensee, Brecht and I went back to Switzerland to prepare the model book for *Life of Galileo*. In addition, Brecht was planning a play about the Paris Commune, with which he originally intended to launch the Berliner Ensemble. In fact, it was not performed until after his death.

The idea for *The Days of the Commune (Die Tage der Commune)* had already come to Brecht in Scandinavia, and it was suggested by Margarete Steffin's translation of Nordahl Grieg's play *The Defeat*. Brecht never read it, but Grete had discussed it with him, and I also talked to him about it, for we had staged it in the Royal Theater. I introduced Grieg and Brecht to each other in Denmark. Brecht on that occasion criticized Grieg's work. He pointed to a page in Marx about "the civil war in France" and said, "There is more about the communards on this one page than in the whole of your play." He looked at Grieg: "*Your* play is called *The Defeat*. What *I* want to know is: What have we *learned* from the defeat?" He had posed the same question at the end of the Spanish Civil War. Nordahl Grieg said to me, "Brecht is right, but once I start arguing with him, I can't write a single sentence more."

On the plane to Zurich Brecht at last read Grieg's play, if only perfunctorily. Afterward he said, "It's quite impossible. Now I understand why the King of Denmark and the gentlemen in tails clapped when the communards died." It was clear to me that Brecht would never present the play unedited—I remembered his reservations about Nordahl Grieg too well for that. He thought the rats at the beginning of the play were good, and that was the very part I wanted him to cut, out of consideration for Grieg's copyright holders. Brecht thrust my objections aside. "That's rubbish," he said. "There actually were rats in Paris, and during the siege rats were eaten. There's nothing copyright in that." I replied, "Then at least don't insist on keeping the schoolmistress. Make her a librarian." "No, I need the schoolmistress. The rats stay in, and the schoolmistress too."

Brecht had decided to write a counterargument to Grieg's *The Defeat*. My collaboration had less to do with studying historical accounts of the communards (Brecht of course already knew all those) than with finding out, in conjunction with him, what consequences could be drawn from their defeat. Our original title was *The Seventy-two Days (Die zweiundsiebzig Tage)*. I thought (and still think) this better than *The Days of the Commune*, since, as we worked on it, Brecht several times said, "We won't have very many more days either, unless . . ." He thought it would be impossible for us to survive without the use of force. It is not the communards' historical achievements, such as higher wages and better working hours for bakers' apprentices, that matter; it is, above all, the necessity of hanging on to power once gained, and defending it by all possible means. That, I think, is the message of *The Days of the Commune*.

When Brecht had spent as long thinking about his material as he had with the story of the communards, he could, circumstances permitting, write a play within three weeks. This was the case with *The Days of the Commune*. All he needed was someone to produce the right material at the right time, and that was my task. I rode my borrowed bicycle to the library and fetched him book after book. This, incidentally, was his reason for writing the play in Switzerland, since the most important libraries in Berlin had either been destroyed or their books were still stored away. Zurich was the easiest place to find what we wanted. It was my job to go through the books and mark the relevant passages, for Brecht did not enjoy reading thick books. In addition, he expected suggestions from me for the next scene. That was my night work, for Brecht retired early to bed. Next morning he would find the marked books outside his door, together with my suggestions. I felt proud if among them Brecht found two sentences he could use. He had to have something to get him started, even if it was only two sentences. The balloon scene was drafted by me.

Brecht stuck to his usual working rhythm. He rose at seven, made his own breakfast, and worked until about ten o'clock. Then he would come to my room—I was living in the same boardinghouse—and we would discuss his work. He enjoyed showing me what he had produced between the hours of seven and ten. Somewhat later Caspar Neher would arrive and the scenes would be gone through with him, Neher as usual making sketches throughout. His sketches could persuade Brecht to change his text. If Neher had not understood what Brecht was aiming at, either something was wrong or it was unclearly phrased. At noon Benno Besson came along to join in the discussions. Brecht wanted to form an impression of him, for he was thinking of engaging him and his wife Eva for the Berliner Ensemble. In the same way, during his first stay in Zurich, he "hooked" Therese Giehse, Leonard Steckel, Hans Gaugler, and Regine Lutz for his theater.

Originally Brecht intended to publish the play under a pseudonym. On one occasion he wrote beneath the title: "from the French of Jacques Duchesne," on another he named the author as Jacques Malorne. Unlike me, he was suffering no qualms of conscience on Nordahl Grieg's account. His reason for choosing anonymity was a quite different one. As I have already related, Brecht always had in mind what people would be saying about him fifty years later. He might be writing for his own time, but his plays were designed for lasting effect. With *The Days of the Commune*, however, his aim was to engage directly in current political events and to provoke discussion. How can we manage to hold out longer than seventy-two days? How much force will be necessary? What can we learn from the communards' mistakes? Brecht used the story of the Paris Commune as a vehicle for drawing conclusions on current affairs. *The Days of the Commune*, like *Señora Carrar's Rifles* during the Spanish Civil War, was written for the present, and Brecht was at first uncertain whether the play was strong enough, or whether it would remain valid. As it neared completion, he abandoned the idea of a pseudonym.

Back in Berlin, the *Commune* was severely criticized. The plot was held to be obscure and incomprehensible. Even Herbert Ihering came out against a production. All of them saw the text as a first draft, in need of revision before a production could be contemplated. I, on the other hand, was certain that, at the moment Brecht decided to put his own name to the play, he acknowledged the present version as the final one. However, having no wish for major arguments at that time, he decided to launch the newly founded Berlin Ensemble with a production of the comedy *Mr. Puntila and His Man Matti*. The first night was a great success, and that was probably of more importance to the start of the Ensemble than any demonstration of principles would have been. Even at that time Brecht had the idea at the back of his mind of staging *The Days of the Commune* in another theater before producing it in Berlin. Shortly before his death he commissioned Peter Palitzsch and Manfred Wekwerth to produce the play in Karl-Marx-Stadt, and together with them, he evolved the manner in which it should be done.

I believe Brecht would have liked to try out all his plays elsewhere before bringing them to Berlin. He never attached any importance to reserving first performances for his own theater. He preferred to gather experiences outside beforehand, producing a model that could then be adapted. This was the reason why I directed *The Mother* in Leipzig long before it was done in Berlin. Brecht had *Señora Carrar's Rifles* tried out on amateur stages, and *The Good Person of Szechwan* was first produced by Benno Besson at the Volkstheater in Rostock. In this case Brecht attended a few rehearsals shortly before the premiere at the beginning of January 1956. The play came out in Berlin in October 1957, again with Benno Besson as director and Käthe Reichel in the main role. After Brecht's death Helene Weigel kept to this procedure. Benno Besson also produced *Man Equals Man* (*Mann ist Mann*) and *The Threepenny Opera* in Rostock, and *Turandot* in

Zurich, before they had their Ensemble premieres in Berlin.

There was yet another reason, besides those I have already mentioned, why Brecht did not insist on an immediate production of *The Days of the Commune*. In Switzerland he had made an agreement with Leonard Steckel to produce *Puntila* in Berlin, with Steckel in the main role. In those days Brecht still honored such agreements, so he found no difficulty in giving preference to *Puntila*. The rehearsals led to a fiasco for which I must take part of the blame. In Hamburg I had seen Willy A. Kleinau, whom many people at that time regarded as Germany's greatest actor, play Puntila. His wife Ursula Burg was Eva. Both of them were terrible, but they had an enormous success with the audience. I thought Kleinau, under good direction, could still be good. When I arrived in Berlin, I suggested that both he and his wife be engaged, knowing Kleinau to be unwilling to come without her. And that is what happened. Since Steckel was not immediately available, Brecht started rehearsals with Kleinau. It was decided that after the premiere he and Steckel should alternate in the role. Kleinau agreed.

During the first rehearsals Brecht, Engel, and I sat on chairs on the stage, close to the footlights. This was odd, for I never again saw Brecht rehearsing with an actor at such close range. Usually he sat in the tenth row of the auditorium, so as to have a general view of the stage. At these rehearsals Kleinau behaved as abominably as it is possible to imagine. Time and again he broke in with remarks such as, "In Hamburg I did it like this," or, "In Hamburg the audience laughed here," or, "In Hamburg I got applause on stage there." This was the very worst way to handle Brecht. He forced himself to be polite, but he was becoming increasingly desperate. I had brought along cigars for Kleinau in the hope that they would at least help to keep his mouth shut, but it was no use. One day Kleinau declared, "There's no question about it: I shall do the premiere. Steckel is the alternative casting." With that, Brecht threw him out. Kleinau went to the Deutsches Theater, where he became a great star and where he probably fitted in much better.

Our rehearsals were so far advanced that when Steckel arrived he had not much more work to do. He had already learned his lines during the *Puntila* rehearsals in Switzerland. Brecht had changed quite a lot and made some additions for the Berlin performance, but Steckel accepted it all without complaint, recognizing them as improvements. He quickly adapted himself to the new scene settings. I find this worth mentioning, for it is not easy for an actor, having once played a role, to be obliged shortly afterward to do it differently. Kleinau did not succeed. Steckel was superb.

My main task, once the Berliner Ensemble was established, was to build up an archive. Brecht wanted everything connected with his work to be preserved. Unfortunately, I believed him when he told me I was the right person to take charge of the archive. It is true I was interested in all that Brecht thought and wrote, and I collected everything that came into my hands, but I have never learned how to arrange this material for general use. The significance of my work was neither recognized nor appreciated by the members of the Ensemble. It was a true labor of Hercules.

The archive had already been begun in America. Brecht was looking for a way of transporting his papers in a light and compact form. We decided to establish a photographic archive and started work on it at the beginning of 1945. Brecht took a very active part, carefully noting down every exposure time, focal length, and shutter setting in a truly scientific manner. I had to learn it all from the beginning, for I was no photographer—I just took snapshots like any other amateur.

At this time Brecht happened to be working on the theme of "the god of fortune," which was not yet envisaged as the subject of an opera. He returned one day from the Chinese district of Los Angeles bearing a small figure. The photograph of this god of fortune was my first exposure on my very first roll of film. The second exposure, taken by Brecht, shows me, looking horribly emaciated. After Michel's death my weight was down to under one hundred pounds. The third exposure is of Carola Neher, drawn by Caspar Neher. Brecht bought a little cabinet with twenty-five compartments, in each of which a roll of film was kept. He wrote the inscriptions himself.

At the same time Brecht was working on his versification of the Communist Manifesto. I photographed the manuscript each time after Brecht had made corrections on it. Thus one can follow accurately, step by step, the work's progress. Prints of the exposures were sent off at once to Karl Korsch and to Stefan, with both of whom Brecht was in correspondence regarding his work.

We gave the films I made in America to a library for safekeeping. They contain pictures of almost all Brecht's works up to that time, both in print and in manuscript.

In Berlin the archive grew rapidly. I photographed every stage production, at rehearsals and also at many performances following the premiere. I have never counted the rolls, but there must be several thousand exposures. With the help of these photographs Brecht and I reconstructed the precise sequence of a performance. The photographs were then pasted carefully into albums with inscriptions of the matching text. We lent these illustrated model books to theaters wishing, subsequent to our own production, to perform the play. They thus have a double significance: they document the work of the Berliner Ensemble and at the same time act as a support and inspiration to directors working on the same material. Regrettably, these model books have often been misconstrued as Brecht's desire to have his work slavishly copied. He himself regarded them as an invitation to build on what he had already done.

Brecht had a weakness for clean, uncorrected manuscripts. In order to avoid the task of recopying corrected pages in full, he would write the new text on a fresh page, cut it out neatly, and stick it to the old manuscript. In his view that was not pedantic frivolity but a rational working method. He called it *Klebologie* (after the German word *kleben*, meaning "to stick"), and it was a word he liked to use, since it so exactly described what was an important part of his working technique, peculiar to himself. I do not know whether this method saved him time, for it involved much laborious handiwork, but Brecht enjoyed that; it gave him a good opportunity for thought and reflection. There are pages in his manuscripts consisting of five or six cuttings stuck together, yet the page as a whole is of normal size. In this respect he was fussy in the extreme. If a page had a line too many, he would cut it off and stick a blank piece of paper in its place. But he would not then just copy out the displaced line at the top of the following page. He took another strip of blank paper as top margin, stuck the single line to it, and then another sheet of blank paper. He then shortened this at the bottom to make a page of normal size. The process is difficult to describe; one must see the manuscripts for oneself.

As meticulously as Brecht looked after his manuscripts after losing Grete Steffin, it could happen now and again that a manuscript or a particular verse would go astray. This text he then regarded as gone forever; he did not attempt to reconstruct it. Since I myself have again begun to write, I can understand his attitude. Brecht never cared to do anything a second time. There is only one exception I know of. All of a sudden his marked copy of Becher's *Winterschlacht* vanished without trace from the Berliner Ensemble office. This time Brecht had to reconstruct his adaptation, for he had committed himself to a production. Maybe he had even better ideas than the first time, but he felt unsure of himself. He was always afraid that something would be lost. In my opinion this was just bluff, for Brecht was never at a loss for new ideas. He could write in any style, and maintained that he could copy any writer you cared to name. That was his reason for writing *Edward the Second* (*Leben Eduards des Zweiten von England*, loosely based on Marlowe's play). Together with Caspar Neher and some other friends he saw a Shakespeare production in the Deutsches Theater, and said after the performance, "I can do that too."

The working relationship between Brecht and myself was a peculiar one. I was a one-hundred-and-twenty-percent party communist, and I was always asking him to write something for us. I believe I can pride myself that it was at my bidding he began work on the Communist Manifesto. I have already spoken of the other works I demanded of him. Once the spark had struck, Brecht would work on the project as if it had been his own idea. It is wrong to think that Brecht worked in a cool and detached manner. Once he had begun something new, he worked feverishly on it. He would tear the pages from the typewriter and show them to me or to whomever else happened to be there: "I've done it!" he would cry. When I once asked him how his poems originated, he replied, "By short-circuit!"

I was not the only one to set him going. I know that he wrote *Señora Carrar's Rifles* in response to a request by Slatan Dudow for a play on that theme. And the poem *"Die Erziehung der Hirse"* ("The Cultivation of the Millet") came into existence after Hermann Duncker had sent him a copy of Gennadi Fisch's book *Die Volksakademie*.

Hanns and Gerhart Eisler—particularly Gerhart—were always demanding plays on topical themes from him. It is our great loss that he did not do more in this line. There is only one topical play: *Report from Herrnburg (Herrnburger Bericht)*. In 1950 thousands of young people from West Germany took part in the Whitsun meeting of the Freie Deutsche Jugend (Free German Youth) in the G.D.R. On their return to West Germany they were arrested, and the police spent two days questioning them. The headline in our newspaper read, "Germans Held by Germans for Crossing the Border from Germany into Germany." Dessau called Brecht on the phone: "We must do something on this at once." Brecht sat down and wrote, while Dessau composed the music. But *Report from Herrnburg* was not performed at the World Festival of Youth, to which it was dedicated. Brecht was asked to make some changes that he considered unnecessary. He said to me at the time, "That's what happens when I make shoes to measure." He wrote *Report from Herrnburg* as a line of argument for comrades. But the comrades were used to a different kind of struggle with their opponents. It was not until a disappointed Brecht had gone off to Ahrenshoop on holiday that work began on a staging in Berlin. President Wilhelm Pieck had come out in support of it. When Brecht returned to Berlin for the performance, he found the president sitting in the front row. In my opinion *Report from Herrnburg* is one of the finest things Brecht ever wrote. But it was the last work he ever wrote to order.

Of the young co-workers Brecht took on over the years I best remember Peter Palitzsch. We had returned from Switzerland, and Brecht had moved into the large house with fourteen rooms in Weissensee that he never liked, while I stayed on at the Hotel Adlon. One day a tall, thin youngster came to see me—he had been sent by Brecht to look at photographs. I was up to my ears in pictures destined for the first *Mother Courage* model book, and I allowed Palitzsch to look through them. He showed outstanding skill in assessing pictures. He sat poring for hours over three of them, expressing his opinion of this and that. I told Brecht about it, and he engaged Palitzsch as a dramaturge for program design, printed papers, placards, coloring, etc. Palitzsch came from Dresden. I can still remember my first conversations with him: horribly bourgeois, typical Dresden provinciality, although he occupied quite an important post in the theater there.

Palitzsch had many disputes with Brecht. He was never one to sit still with open mouth, drinking everything in— a type that, to my regret, Brecht in his later years had come to favor. Palitzsch always had objections to make and questions to ask. "Why that exactly?" In such cases Brecht would very soon adopt a dictatorial tone toward his pupils. He would accuse them of not being communists. And in many cases he turned out to be right.

He brought Benno Besson along with him from Switzerland. Besson was soon given directing tasks; he staged, for instance, the skating scene in *The Tutor*. Brecht and Besson got on very well together, except on one occasion, when Besson lost a folder containing manuscripts and notes. Brecht was very angry and would not speak to him for weeks. However, that passed over, for Besson did not play the injured martyr—something Brecht could not stand at any price—but continued to attend all the rehearsals. Brecht regarded Besson as a stage director, a qualification he refused to recognize in Palitzsch. Later on he divided the work up, allowing one person to try out a certain scene on the rehearsal stage, another to do a different scene, and he would then look at the results.

Egon Monk, a typical Berliner with an entrancingly Berlinish sense of humor, had the easiest path. He was the first to be given a directing job all to himself: a production of Goethe's *Urfaust*. Unfortunately, the project went completely wrong, though not through any fault of Monk's. Brecht wanted to try something out, and it was a failure. Neither the critics nor the public could make anything of it, and Brecht himself was far from satisfied. I believe the trouble was that Brecht concentrated too much on the character of Gretchen.

Gert Schäfer was required to present a modern Mephisto. He brought many ideas to the rehearsals, but was given little help. He is an excellent actor, and he had thoughts about how a young Faust should be played. As a general rule an actor is not given this role until he is at least seventy. Unfortunately, no one would listen to Schäfer, and Brecht suddenly decided he could no longer do anything with him. Johannes Schmidt was playing Faust, and now it was Monk who could not get along with him. Brecht concerned himself only with certain specific players: Heinz Schubert, who played the student; Carola Braunbock, who was cast as Martha; and most of all, Käthe Reichel, who was Gretchen. Käthe Reichel was discovered and made famous by Brecht, and he had perhaps chosen the *Urfaust* because of the Gretchen story.

The first discussions regarding the *Urfaust* were held in my apartment. It was New Year's Day, and Brecht was in a good humor. Hans Tombrock, who was there too, fetched some wine. Brecht felt the urge to explain to everyone once and for all what the play is about. I still remember almost word for word his account of the plot: "Here is a man who is feeling old and wants to be young again. He summons the devil and is made young. Then he goes out into the street, falls in love with a girl, and makes her pregnant. She kills her baby and is sent to prison. He tries to rescue her, but she refuses, oh heavens!" It made the young people's hair stand on end, but that is the way Monk produced it. The premiere was in 1952 at the Landestheater in Potsdam. The play was not done in Berlin.

That same year Egon Monk directed *Señora Carrar's Rifles*. This was not really successful either, otherwise it would have remained longer in the repertory. The reason probably was that Helene Weigel was in a bad humor during rehearsals. It must be admitted that Brecht had been much nicer to her during the *Carrar* rehearsals in Copenhagen than he was in Berlin. There were a lot of disputes. However, despite this, Monk had no reason to complain, for he was given the job of directing the television film of *Carrar*, and that, with Brecht lending his help, turned out well. Brecht liked Monk, simply on account of his humor. There was never anything tragic or complicated about their relationship, as there was with Palitzsch.

One day Monk told me he was being given a chance to do a production of Shakespeare in Stuttgart. We thought it fantastic news. For quite a while afterward I heard nothing from him. I did not find that odd, for he had an apartment in the palace at Potsdam that he was keen to keep, in spite of its being so far away. After all, he did not have to be in Berlin every day. But then we heard that the apartment was locked up, and a delivery of firewood had not been taken in. Monk had simply left without telling any of us—not even Brecht. It was not a nice thing to do, simply to disappear like that. But Brecht did not take his breach of trust too seriously. He just asked which of us would be willing to cross the border to speak to him and ask him to come back. At that time anyone returning from abroad was sent to a transit camp for three weeks. Brecht intended to take steps to ensure that Monk would have to spend only a few days there. As far as Brecht was concerned, his departure was nothing more than a foolish escapade. He made another attempt later to get Monk back.

In 1950 I managed to acquire Wolfgang E. Struck for the Berliner Ensemble. He was the intendant of the Maxim Gorki Theater in Schwerin. Brecht had sent me there to attend rehearsals of *The Mother*, for in Berlin the rumor had gone around that a formalistic production was being prepared. This was indeed the case. Everybody was wearing a black suit and playing behind bars. We changed all that, and in the process Struck gave me every support. He also had the brilliant idea of giving the official in the copper collection center a limp, to explain why the man is not serving as a soldier. Brecht loved ideas like this. Struck was engaged as a dramaturge, but he was used mainly as an actor. To amuse me, he came to each rehearsal wearing a different costume and a different beard. It did amuse me too, very much. Brecht liked him a great deal. In *The Caucasian Chalk Circle* he gave him the small child to carry in the church procession, and in Azdak's scene with the farmers and the old peasant woman he was given the role of the bandit Irakli. Struck later went on to the Metropoltheater and subsequently took over the Friedrichstadtpalast.

At the end of 1951 I went to Greiz, where *Antigone* was being staged along the lines of our model. It was the first opportunity of testing the value of a model book.

The play was directed by Ernst Otto Tickhardt, who was the theater's intendant. Brecht did not know him personally, only through letters and my reports on the work in Greiz. He would have liked to have Tickhardt in the Deutsches Theater, but his efforts to get him proved unsuccessful.

In Greiz I met Hans Bunge, a student from Greifswald who, having made a study of Brecht's adaptation of *Antigone*, wanted to see the play on the stage. Following the first performance I took him back to Berlin with me and introduced him to Brecht. Brecht found it interesting that a man who had served as an officer in the fascist Wehrmacht and then spent more than six years as a prisoner of war in Soviet hands should now be studying in the G.D.R. and have done some work on *Antigone*. Bunge invited me to Greifswald, where he ran a students' theater that wanted to do *Señora Carrar's Rifles*. Many students were objecting to military training and service in the armed forces. The *Carrar* production was designed to show them why a resort to arms was necessary.

We rehearsed in accordance with the model I had made in Copenhagen. I believe I stayed only three or four days in Greifswald, in order to lay the foundations of the production. They were strenuous days for the students, for we had to work in a very concentrated fashion. Brecht had told me to come back as soon as possible. In those days he still wanted me in Berlin.

By the last day of my stay in Greifswald we had assembled all the stage properties we needed. It had been a very difficult task, for the group had no money and everything had to be made or borrowed, from the stage settings and costumes down to the props. Bunge, whom I always called Blitz, managed to prize various objects out of the municipal theater—above all, the three rifles we needed at all costs. After our last rehearsal, we all went out to celebrate. It must have been after midnight when, the celebrations over, we emerged onto the street. There I saw a sight I shall never forget. The moon was shining, and in its clear light I distinctly saw a figure come striding down the road, loaded with a rucksack and three rifles. It was Bunge with all the stage props, and for this play we needed a lot: rifles, a fishing net, jug, beakers, and so on. When I returned to Berlin, I told Brecht what I had seen and said, "We need that man." Brecht replied at once, "Good, let's have him." After Brecht's death Bunge built up the Bertolt Brecht archives.

A *Carrar* production was also responsible for bringing Manfred Wekwerth to the Berliner Ensemble. He had staged the play in Köthen, with Erich Franz in the role of the worker Pedro. On Helene Weigel's invitation the company gave a performance on our rehearsal stage, and as a result Brecht engaged both Wekwerth and Franz. As far as I am concerned, Wekwerth has been the real head of the Ensemble since Brecht's death—in conjunction, of course, with Helene Weigel.

I have always wanted to write a handbook for apprentice theater directors and actors, basing it on Brecht's work in the theater. The book has not yet been written, but I should like to give an outline of the opening chapter as I see it:

Brecht comes fresh to rehearsals—and usually ahead of his fellow workers. From the very moment he enters the theater he is in his element, a fish in water. He starts with a reading rehearsal, asking the actors to read out their roles, with neither expression nor accentuation but concentrating instead on the implications of the words. After that comes the positioning. Brecht sits there with a cap on his head and a cigar in his mouth, knowing nothing. For me this is the fundamental difference between him and those many other theater directors who know everything—and always better than anyone else. This makes the actors lazy. They either wait to be positioned somewhere, or they are too nervous to display ideas of their own. Brecht is wiser. With his method he gets more out of his actors as well as out of himself. When an actor asks, "Should I stand up here?" everybody is always astounded by Brecht's typical response: "I don't know." He does not make up his mind in advance but tries out several possible solutions. The actor can make suggestions of his own. What Brecht likes most of all is to have suggestions demonstrated, not discussed. As soon as someone starts explaining his intentions at great length, Brecht breaks in and says, "Show us." For Brecht an actor's technique is not a matter for discussion.

In his theoretical works Brecht has written about alienation (*Verfremdung*) and alienation effects. Many believe this to be a very complicated affair, but in fact it is very simple. A statement is "alienated" by being made to appear strange, and therefore striking. Things that are so general, so everyday, so usual that they are no longer noticed—since one knows them too well—are presented as remarkable and worthy of attention. In this way facts, procedures, and conventional forms of behavior are made more transparent. Curiosity is aroused about what lies behind them: What is it exactly, and why is it so? Brecht induces the attitude of an explorer who has come on something remarkable.

I could say that in rehearsal Brecht begins by "alienating" his own play. He appears to be familiar with not a single word of his text, and with each rereading he discovers it anew. I am convinced that he really does possess the ability to see his plays as if they had been written by someone else, thus allowing him to listen to them with critical curiosity. Certainly he has no wish to stick obstinately to what is written on the page; what he wants is to see and hear what actors using the text can show him. When a sentence or even a whole scene has been thoroughly examined in this way, it can come as no surprise to learn that up to the very last rehearsal Brecht is always making changes in his plays. He conducts rehearsals in sections, initially treating each matter entirely for its own sake. Someone knowing the play as a whole might then say to him, "The third scene explains what has already been indicated in the first scene. So how can the actor throw away his line in the first scene so lightly?" Brecht will listen, then laugh and reply, "Is that so? That's good. Well, we shall see." It might really become necessary to make changes in the first scene while we are already working on the third, but now we know why. In this way, rehearsals remain constantly productive. Nothing is ever glossed over; everything is checked and rechecked again and again.

I will give an example, taken from Brecht's play *Mother Courage and Her Children*, which deals with the seventeenth-century Thirty Years' War. In one scene a young man and his mother decide to sell their bedding in order to get money to live on. How does the young man remove the sack containing the precious blankets from his shoulder? And what is the expression on the mother's face as he does so? Now, in summertime, they can, if they must, do without blankets. But will she not also be wondering how, when winter comes, they will manage to find blankets again? It is a very tiny scene in a long play, but it has much to say.

The young actor and the older actress have only a few words to speak. When they were given their roles, they were very disappointed. But during rehearsals both players, as well as we in the auditorium, gained the impression that the roles are important ones. There are no small roles when Brecht is rehearsing. The scene could be played on its own, to show that in wartime people are driven to the point of having to sell even their bedclothes. Just as mother and son have decided to do this, the bells ring out, proclaiming peace, and they are able to return home with their blankets. The episode could bear the inscription: In peacetime the humble family's sleep is assured.

When the bells ring out, the young man has only a single word to say: "*Frieden*..." ("Peace...") The actor dragged the word out, saying very expressively: "*Früü-deen!*" Brecht suggested, "Listen when you hear the bells start to ring. After you have made sure they really are peace bells, you tell yourself, 'Now it's peace.' What you really want to say to your mother is, 'Did you hear? It's peace.' But of the whole sentence you bring out only the last word, and only the first syllable of that is clearly heard. Surprise makes the second syllable stick in your throat, so to speak. When the excitement makes your mother ill, you oughtn't to act pity for her, but just ask her, in a kind but factual way, 'Can you walk?' The line must be spoken quickly, for now there is a lot to be done. Yet all the time something of the glory of the news of peace can be expressed in your tone."

Several times during rehearsals Brecht asked the player not to act a man older than himself. This seems to me an important point. Young actors tend to speak their lines slowly and weightily. The object is to stress their significance, but all it achieves is to make the actor seem old. Of course, all this is connected with the actor himself having at last reached the stage and wanting to make the most of the few minutes he has been given. Brecht is adamant in combating this wish. He gives his actors their chance in a different way, presenting them with one of his famous pauses. These pauses are not there to express feeling but to allow something to be shown while silence reigns, thus giving the audience a chance to reflect and to understand.

How does it come about that young players working with Brecht achieve fame overnight? Why are actors who have never enjoyed a reputation and have scarcely ever stood on a stage suddenly "discovered"? It is because Brecht never ceases to make demands on them and to help them. For example, he demonstrates to them ways of walking on stage—the walk of weariness, of sensuality, of vanity, of injured pride. In that way he gives the actor a basis to work on, for the manner of walking reveals the attitude. How does an overworked woman hold her shoulders, when life has already given her too much to bear? Brecht makes the poor woman's arms hang lower through too much carrying, her shoulders droop, her stomach protrude. Or he sends for cheap steel-rimmed spectacles to make the eyes look tired. The mouth may also be held a little open, to indicate difficulty in breathing.

If the actor has talent, he will not just imitate Brecht but make use of the suggestions in his own way. Sometimes one can hear Brecht give a sudden laugh—even when a scene is being rehearsed for the first time—for he has observed that the actor is offering something new and interesting, even if nothing more than a silent walk across the stage. This laugh means much to the actor. From then on his colleagues will say: Now for the walk, or the gesture, or the look.

In such an event the principal actor may become uneasy. What is happening behind his back? There is only one thing he can do: take this walk into account in his own performance. He is forced to take the subsidiary roles seriously. His fellow players are not there just to build bridges for the principal actor or to feed him his cues. Each has his own thing to do. Thus the quality of the performance is raised, to the advantage of all.

Should one young actor or another still consider his role too small for his talents, Brecht is quick to prove to him that his talents are not even up to the small role he has. Brecht is merciless and harsh toward young people who have no talent for the stage. He considers it antisocial not to advise them immediately to take up some other occupation.

Talent is essential for the actor's art, but most important of all is hard work. One must learn how to observe; one must learn how to read and how to prepare oneself; one must learn how to learn; one must learn how to involve oneself in everything. Brecht has no time at all for nonpolitical actors.

Brecht once sent some young people who wished to take up acting to the theater to see a performance of *Mother Courage and Her Children*. Afterward he sat down with them to discuss both play and production. These young people then behaved like senile professors, who always know best and are opposed to everything but the cut of their own beards. Their opinions were fixed, and they just sat there, looking bored. They had not studied the play, had observed nothing, understood nothing, learned nothing, and possessed not an ounce of modesty—and they were quite unaware even of that. These young people had no desire to know anything; they just gabbled out opinions they had heard or read somewhere before.

An actor must know why he wants to be an actor. Brecht put this question to the young people. I should say in advance that when talking to young people, Brecht was always especially courteous, indeed, respectful. I have seldom seen him—as he did during this discussion—lose all his patience and with it his politeness. He received no immediate answer to his question. At last a few managed to stammer out that they wanted to show what they themselves felt. They wanted to act themselves. Thereupon Brecht seized his cap and, as he left the room, said, "Then think again!"

Afterward I asked Brecht what answer young people like that could be expected to give. "At least that they want to demonstrate what is right and what is wrong in people's attitudes. The purpose of our theater is to effect change." If one has not grasped that, there is nothing to be gained from learning roles by heart or seeking interviews.

As far as I am concerned, the greatest living actress is Helene Weigel—at any rate the greatest I have ever seen on stage. She is also the hardest worker of anyone I know. And she has strong feelings. But she does not merely yield herself up to them; she conveys them, purified, fresh and clean, straight across the footlights into our hearts and heads, making us laugh or making us cry. For fifteen years this great actress was condemned to complete silence. But what was inside her she preserved, and when—as Antigone in Switzerland—she appeared for the first time on the stage again, it was evident that her art had become still richer and more mature. From the very beginning I modeled myself on her, and not only in relation to my work as an actress at the Danish Royal Theater, where she helped me with my costumes and makeup and taught me how to build up my role. Regrettably, she is unable to accept pupils, her work as intendant and actress, as member of the Academy and mother of the Ensemble leaving her no time for that. All one can do is go to her performances.

My own greatest success was not on stage, but in a circus ring. It happened quite a while ago, when I met a clown and rode with him on a streetcar. We were standing on the rear platform. In order to pass the time, but also to see what effect Danish humor would have on Germans, I told him a few Danish jokes. The effect was tremendous! The whole streetcar was soon laughing with us, so infectious was the laughter of this great clown, for it was the only thing the people at the far end of the streetcar could hear. That made me envious.

Unfortunately, this clown then substituted my jokes, taken straight from life, for all his ancient and traditional circus routines. In the process he got it all mixed up and did not get the kind of reception he was used to. He came to tell me of his misfortune. He then of course returned to his old character and enjoyed all his old success. We remained in touch.

One day I found him in a state of great distress. Weeping, he showed me his clown's costumes locked away in a cupboard. He was weeping because the traditional clown had been condemned as "undesirable," on the grounds that the public could no longer be regarded as stupid. We went along to the circus ring, a few people joined us, and we began to argue, while behind us a bear tamer was rehearsing a new act with his animals. I defended the traditional clown figure, maintaining that he was wiser than all the rest of us and in addition was part of our nation's cultural heritage. I probably became rather overheated and fierce, for suddenly there came a shout from the tamer: "Quiet, please, or the bears will start listening over there"—and he pointed his whip straight in my direction—"and not to me!"

Maybe young actors can learn something from this story. You must be able to speak loud enough to make even bears listen. But you must also be able to speak so softly that (as the Germans say) fleas can be heard coughing in the wings. It is in this sense that you must com-

mand the entire range of human emotions, be able to adapt to the whole spectrum of human temperaments, and understand all human characteristics without surrendering your own personality. And then, of course, you must practice, practice, practice! Brecht has taught me this: the important thing is for each of us to pass on his knowledge, like an athlete passing on the baton in a relay race.

Whenever I went to see Hanns Eisler, he would always jump up to greet me with his own peculiar brand of expansive friendliness. His voice was fresh, sparkling like champagne, and it had the same enlivening effect. At a stroke I would be transported to another world. All cares, great and small, were forgotten. I always had something to ask him. Eisler took laymen's questions seriously, and there was no need to feel ashamed if the question was naive. "Why is a certain kind of American jazz harmful?" Eisler showed me by simply dancing to it. Unforgettable. When I return to Denmark, my native land, and see the jazz dives, I always think of Hanns Eisler's little dance— how his face altered to assume an expression of imbecility, as if his brain had suddenly lost all its blood. Afterward he said, "I've nothing against sensuality, as I hope you can see from my music. But mindless sensuality has no point."

It was astounding how quickly Eisler could adapt to the conversational level of his interlocutor. With his Viennese courtesy he would stay with a theme, clarifying it through examples and explanations, until he saw that the other person understood. I noticed how keenly he would observe his partner. Although he was usually pacing up and down with short, rapid steps, he would keep a sharp eye on the reactions of the person he was addressing. Listening to Eisler was like being at a lecture.

199

He could describe fourteen different kinds of rain—and point out the nastinesses of the petty bourgeois in at least as many ways.

I once watched him composing. He was sitting at his desk, an ordinary pencil in his hand. The paper in front of him was not even musical notation paper. Eisler drew the staffs himself. Writing fairly fast, he filled up two or three pages. Then he put the pencil down, pressed the knob of a stopwatch, and read the notes he had written, listening to the music nobody else could hear. Then he stopped the watch and compared the time with some scribbles on a piece of paper—no, not even that: on the back of an old envelope. Apparently all was in order. He rose, fresh and lively as ever. We went out onto the terrace, where he liked to sit, and began our conversation.

At our first meeting following Brecht's death Hanns Eisler told me, "It was a Sunday. He got out of bed when I arrived. I could see he found talking an effort, yet the afternoon passed cheerfully enough. But the thought kept going through my head: It was a great mistake on my part not to have responded to his repeated invitations to move closer to him. I did not pay sufficient attention to the state of his health. When he found the energy to visit me, and I played to him a piece of music I had written, I let myself be taken in by his pleasure and his gaiety. It was only when I met him for the last time that I realized how even that fifteen minutes' drive to my house in Niederschönhausen appeared to him like a mountain he was scarcely in a condition to climb. Who seriously thought that Brecht might ever die? He was tired, yes, but—to die!" We were both silent for a long while. Then Hanns Eisler continued, "Brecht went with me to the door and, as we said goodbye, he remarked, 'Forgive me, I have not done enough for your great music.' Those were his last words to me. I never saw my friend again. Could he

200

have known on that Sunday how ill he already was? Why, otherwise, did he say that to me?"

I was very close to Hanns Eisler, as also to others of Brecht's friends—Walter Benjamin, Karl Korsch, Caspar Neher, Gerhart Eisler, Jacob Walcher, Hans Tombrock. They all knew that my decision to follow Brecht into exile had not been taken frivolously. At that time I was very good-looking, but that was of no advantage to me. There were people who accused me of having used my beauty to make an impression on Brecht. But his old friends knew that this had not been Brecht's reason for wanting me close to him.

8

O nce, in Denmark, Brecht and I stood looking up at the night sky. Brecht pointed above his head and asked me, "Do you see that *W* there? Cassiopeia is made up of five stars. From now on that is our celestial sign, Lai-tu. Wherever we are, our eyes will meet up there."

Thus he brought heaven down to our earth. Under Cassiopeia we kissed, a cautious kiss, heavenly in its lightness, a starborn, an eternal kiss. Oh, I know what love is! Brecht wrote to me once, "Your love could bring happiness to five continents."

What I have told is a love story, and love is a rare thing in these days since the Second World War. Today is October 12, 1959. I have said that love is a rare thing. By that I mean an old-fashioned, passionate, powerful, and tender love such as ours was. Perhaps I should say: Thank God it is rare.

I see Brecht sitting in front of me. His feet, strikingly small and narrow for a man, nestle in shoes of soft leather. One leg is crossed over the other, exposing his slim ankles. Two—at least two—parts of his body are my favorites: his shoulders, which fit exactly within my hands, and these ankles with their prominent ankle bones. Since he hates elastic, he wears gray woollen socks. They are never pulled up, but slide down to form little bunches. His trousers have bulging knees. They are a shade darker than his socks, but of course gray as well. They are made of a good and expensive woollen material. Even when they have just been ironed, they lose their form within a day and hang on him. But that suits him to perfection; he never looks shabby.

I see a dark blue poplin jacket, tailored to his own specifications, with buttons up to the collar and many pockets. The jacket looks comfortable, for it too is shapeless. Brecht has grown stouter around the hips and has developed a paunch from so much sitting and so little exercise. Not even love can conceal that he is no longer the slim figure I met for the first time in Denmark. Only his eyes are the same, though not always. Sometimes there is a veil over them that frightens me.

The blue jacket is open, revealing a shirt of a yet darker blue. It is made not of silk, as in Denmark, but of coarse linen. His spectacles have brown rims.

His hands are very white, but they too are fleshier than they used to be. They are no longer the slim hands that at seven in the morning would be busy writing against the oppressors. Yet in conversation they have lost none of their expressiveness. His right hand holds his cigar carefully, to prevent the ash from falling. His left hand, when he is arguing, is in constant motion. When Brecht speaks, the hand speaks too. But even when he is not speaking, the little finger of his left hand continues to move unceasingly. Then the costly cigar is transferred to his left hand, and the right hand starts to argue. Brecht clutches his forehead, strokes his black, closely cut hair, which in winter is slightly longer than in summer. At the back of his neck it bursts out in tight little curls, now white, and it was always my task to trim these off.

Sharpest in my memory are his gesticulating hands and his eyes.

I see Brecht surrounded by thirteen people, his entire staff of production assistants and dramaturges. But closest to him is Rolf, a German shepherd dog that years ago attached himself to him. Rolf wedges his beautiful head with its glittering, intelligent eyes between Brecht's knees. The understanding between them resembles that of two friends. If some other person strokes Rolf and Rolf looks up at him, Brecht raises his shoulders, betraying a touch of jealousy. I truly believe there is no other living creature he loves as much as he loves Rolf, who is always in a good mood and who never reproaches him.

PART II

Occasional
Writings

In my passport I am described as *Schriftstellerin* (writer). I should have liked to change this to *Aufschreiberin* (chronicler), but everyone told me the word does not exist in German as a description of an occupation. Brecht was the only one who liked it. "It's true there is no such word," he said, "but it should be taken into the language."

A GIFT

He had found a particularly beautiful pebble beside the Svendborg Sound. With a knife he engraved on it the letters *e.p.e.p.* He told me they stood for *"et prope et procul"* and meant "near and far."

The largest diamond, all the glistening rubies in the world, are nothing to me compared with this gift. The small, cool stone helped me through the times I was separated from him. This wonderful gift soothed the yearning in my burning womb.

And the manner in which it was given to me! With

great kindness, so infectious that I could have jumped over the moon.

(Undated)

Notes on *The Chalk Circle*

The Judge. Speech on chaos.
I (The noble child)

Hard times are coming. Only those who go about in rags will be safe. The poor child must fear hunger—the rich child the hungry.
Constant change among the governors breeds fear.

II, 2 (In the caravansary)

The first conversation, where the innkeeper emerges, is fine. But I would cut the reference to the ground being stony there and the farmers using it to graze their sheep. It is unsettling, since involuntarily one thinks of the prologue and wonders whether there is a connection. And that is a pity, for the old man describes things so well.

I also think it a pity that the elder lady pursues the conversation so politely. She should interrupt the innkeeper and carry on with her speech.

Then I think Katja should give herself away by dragging something. Couldn't there be a haysack in the corner, which she carries to the center of the room, then spreads the blankets over it? It might not be enough that she is shown up just by spreading the blankets. On the other hand, it would be fine if she threw the sack lightly over her shoulder and carried it from the corner.

I am convinced it is wrong for her to continue playing the grand lady there. It makes us laugh, and that destroys the effect of Katja betraying herself by working. I think one feels the fine ladies are also wondering why Katja is playing at being a lady. Of course it is a wonderful scene, with her playing the grand lady and complaining of migraine. But can that not be at the beginning? Then suddenly she starts working, and perhaps even sings as she works, since that is something she is used to. Then it will certainly be easier, Bertolt, to understand why the ladies are surprised. However, if you want to keep it as it is, couldn't you make Katja work harder? She could, for instance, go down on her knees to wipe the floor before dragging in the sacks.

On the chalk circle act:

Since once before Katja was prepared to give the child away, I think it must be very clearly shown that her attitude toward the child has changed. It is in the song, but that is not enough. It is essential we are told exactly why she is no longer prepared to give the child up at any price.

III, 2 (In the scullery)

I find the scene in the brother's room a bit long-winded. Of course there are wonderful things in it—for example, the song about her soldier—and it is also funny when the brother keeps saying his wife is "very sensitive." But could it not be shown in this scene that Katja in the meantime has become completely attached to the child? Could her brother, when he hears that the child has nothing to do with her soldier, not suggest that she should hand it over to the nuns in the convent? Or when Katja refuses to marry the dying peasant, couldn't her brother tell her she must leave with the child and seek a job in the city? When she then replies that with the child she wouldn't find work, the brother could then urge her to find a home for the child until she has found a job and is able to pay a little something for the child's upkeep. It must be something that makes it clear she is determined to keep the child with her. When she later agrees to the marriage, will she then be able to keep the child, or even to take it with her when they go to the wedding? She cannot bring herself to leave the child with strangers. It is now a poor woman's child.

III, 5 (In the bedroom)

I find the scene in which the peasant complains of Katja's unwillingness to sleep with him very fine and very strong. I realize how difficult it must have been to write, but you have succeeded. It is also good that the peasant is so human, since we then understand him as well as Katja. The line "It was not conceived in joy" is very good.

I just feel that the horrible mother-in-law should not be allowed to have the child with her during the night. That's not right. Katja would not wish it, and we don't wish it either. What I really mean is: I don't wish it! I realize that the child would have a mat in the mother-in-law's room. But could not Katja too have patched something together for the child?

The change in tone I find very good. It is all nice and light.

There is something else I venture to suggest. I feel it is not good for Katja to be there when the peasant rises from his deathbed. I know we have already discussed this, and that you didn't want her to return to her brother's house. But why shouldn't she after all go with her brother, the mother-in-law promising to let her know as soon as the peasant is dead? After the splendid scene with the mourning guests, in which Katja is completely out of place, the peasant sets out to fetch his wife. Instead of a message, he arrives in person. If you don't want her to return to her brother's house, you could just make the singer tell it in song. As it now stands, I miss the feeling of Katja's love for the child. You'll find you will need this later.

On the other hand, I find the conversation between the two people during the night very fine. I have not yet received the end of the scene, and naturally am wishing for Katja to be filled with joy when it becomes light. She takes up the child, and standing in the doorway, shows him the new day.

II (Flight into the northern mountains)

Bertolt, I find all this absolutely splendid and lovely. I haven't a single criticism to make. It is now complete in every sense, and all so light. You have really brought it off.

It is good that we already know the two ironshirts before they meet up with Katja. And it is very important for us to have heard the corporal's theory when Katja later says, "But those men are worse." And I always find your similes so amusing, as for example when the corporal calls the other soldier a "hollow reed."

And I love the poem after Katja lays the child on the doorstep and the peasant woman takes it in. Also the singer's song beforehand is very, very beautiful: "The little burden in whom a heart was beating."

And the fact that she now hits the corporal over the head is tremendously good. The more risks she takes, the better. Then one also sees the crossing of the glacier bridge in the proper light. Bertolt, the poem she sings beforehand is so full of kindness! I mean the one as she is wrapping the child in rags.

II, 8 (Glacier bridge)

But I do, after all, have one small though very definite criticism to make. When Grusha [Katja] has crossed the bridge and from the other bank sees the ironshirts arrive, she cannot laugh, and on no account thumb her nose. I, anyway, believe she was afraid of crossing the bridge, and now, with it all behind her, she is angry with the ironshirts. I could well believe she would reply with a few words on the corporal's monologue. Of course, I realize she could not have heard him speak it, but all the same. In any case, she should be serious and angry, and after her comment go on her way relieved and singing. Don't you feel?

III, 6 (By a little stream)

The scene by the stream is splendid.

I hardly dare make a suggestion. But how would this be: Wolodja goes off and Katja calls after him, "It's not mine." Then the ironshirts arrive. While she is speaking to the ironshirts, Wolodja returns to ask for the cross he gave her earlier. He sees the ironshirts going off with the child. In Wolodja's presence Katja calls out to the ironshirts, "Leave it here, please! It's mine!" And she knows that Wolodja has heard her. Then Wolodja says, "Throw the cross in the stream!"

Do you believe, incidentally, that Katja would say "it," when the child is so big? "It's mine. Leave it here"? Forgive me, I suppose that's the way it has to be in German?

I think "Chalk Circle" wonderful. It really is a very good story. Send more soon. I'm now looking forward to the judge.

III, 5 (Bathtub)

I do think the scene with the peasant in the bathtub better than the earlier version. Of course that was a good scene, I just felt it might be better—even perhaps for Katja—if the peasant is a sympathetic character. It's good too when we hear he has beaten Katja, for we then know what she has had to go through. But in my opinion it would be better still if you were to restore the friendliness.

II (Flight into the northern mountains)

I find the flight very successful now, the sequence of each successive stage and the rising tension up to the glacier bridge.

Katja is a very lovely person.

But would it perhaps be worth considering whether it should not be the peasant who betrays the child—and not his wife? Or, if it remains the peasant woman who betrays the child, would it not be possible to make her say, in her conversation with Katja, that she would be willing to protect the child, if only the soldiers would not take away her home and her silver? Then it becomes the fear of losing her property that causes her to break down. Forgive me.

IV (Azdak act)

I don't know whether Azdak's disappointment at the failure of the new era to arrive is made clear enough, and it is an important point.

I fear a bit too much happens in the scene with the ironshirts, and it is not clear what is really going on. But I shall study the scene more closely once more, and then write to you about it.

Azdak is so comical, and his messy way of doing the right thing is very amusing.

The tour of inspection is splendid. What I particularly like is his meeting with the Grand Duke.

(1944)

GOING IN CIRCLES

Through all the years
there is much I have learned
from you
and much I have unlearned.

I love you
I love you
I love you.

You have written
that you need me.
Then you were a stranger
in strange lands.
Now you are here
in your own Berlin.
What I photographed
has appeared in print.
My work is
ended.

I thank you.
I love you.
Jeg elsker dig.

(February 1950)

A class-war courtesan gets into difficulties, since she
cannot decide who best serves the third cause.

Is it then the standard bearer
or he who wove the standard?

Is it he who bore the flag
outside Madrid and for that is still
being persecuted?

Or should it be he who
far from the battlefield
beneath a thatched roof
wove the flag?

WAITING

The copper kettle may hang there yet
and the small iron bond
stay on my hand.

The leather-bound notebook
lies open to your will.
In my black widow's weeds
I'll sit beside it still.

The pipe and the chessmen
and I, need I say,
will wait as, for the cause
that is mine and yours,
you leave the house and go away.

MY BACKSIDE IS TOO GOOD

Someone sat in my best chair.
He spoke:
I am great and mighty,
I am a master.

I sit now on my footstool,
my backside is too good for that chair!
(February 1950)

From a Letter to Professor Th.

Charité, Berlin,
Sunday evening, March 5, 1950

[. . .] Today only your assistants were with me. They are of course nice, good people, but we both know that young doctors cannot have the same scientific knowledge and great experience that you have. Now I am writing you this, since I do not know whether you will find time for me tomorrow.

I thank you for having done all that is humanly possible for me here. I hope that both you and Brecht will speak to me tomorrow, but I want to send you this in advance, not because I have "an uncontrollable urge to write letters," but because it will be difficult for me, since:

If I weep for joy at seeing B., you will say I am depressive—if I am gay, you will say I am manic. If I am quiet, you will say: She is content, so she can stay here. So I am completely helpless. You would have more pity for a bird that has flown into your room and is trying to get out.

And I cannot even compare myself to a bird, because I am myself to blame, and I am so ashamed. But I did not mean to take my own life, and it is something I shall never do. I had been drinking a terribly strong, 45 percent vodka, and I put on an Ophelia act with the object of getting B. at last to spend a night with me, which he had so long been promising to do. B. and Dr. M. knew I had some sleeping pills, which I had had for a long time—I had not got hold of them in secret. The one bottle I had from Dr. M. six months ago, and the other Brecht mislaid in my bed. I told them both about it, in a joking way— that was at least ten or twelve days ago. All they needed to do would have been to take them away from me. After all, there were three men there that evening. It was easy enough to take the pills away. There is surely a big difference between a suicide who has once taken pills and a person who just says she will (while drunk, too). I shouldn't have said it if I had really meant to take them. I would have known in that case they would find me and pump me out. I would just have taken the pills without saying a word to anybody—what else? I DID NOT WANT TO DIE, and I do not want to die. I beg you, Professor Th., to make a distinction between a suicide and someone who just says he means to take some pills. I know I have deserved it all, that it is all my fault, that it was despicable, and that Ophelia should be played on a stage and not on a terrace. But now I have been punished enough and have learned my lesson enough. Now I want to leave this place. I realize exactly how unpleasant it will be for me, but I would rather bring the Danish consulate into the matter than remain here with this uncertainty hanging over me. Brecht knows the whole story of my sister, after all, and I hope he has told you, Professor Th., why I don't wish to stay here. That is not meant as a reflection on the hospital or the nurses. On the contrary, I know you are the best German doctor in the field of nervous disorders. I know it and I recognize your responsibility, but

217

you can help get me transferred to a clinic in which I can talk everything over with my own Danish countrymen. I cannot even telephone Professor Robert Lund from here. Now I am begging you, Professor Th. and Brecht, to talk this over. And please help me. Thank you.

R. B.

THE SNOB

> He has a horrible voice—
> the voice of a superman—
> who knows it all.
> One hour he spoke.
> Beneath the sky we sat.
> He spoke.
> We drove.
> He spoke and spoke.
> And I did so want to ask something.

From a Letter to the Publisher Peter Suhrkamp

Tuesday, January 16, 1951

[. . .] I took a copy of Maria Sten's *Jedes Tier kann es* home with me. I turned over a few pages, read a bit here and there. Let me tell you: it is a good book! Really. After all, I wrote it with Brecht [. . .]

If you give it to a translator or a reader—or whatever the people are called who recommend or reject books in foreign language for a publisher—you must give it to a sensible man; the book is modern and new and Brechtian. It is also a fact that men do not enjoy reading it, since it is a critique of men. But above all I should tell you that an important chapter is missing, a final chapter that I have already written together with Brecht (not quite complete). That is a critique of women. And believe me, in it Brecht is really great. Actually, he deeply despises us women: nothing in favor can be squeezed out of him except about Rosa Luxemburg and Krupskaya, Lenin's wife. Oh, and Helene Weigel, of course!!! He has always treated me like dirt—but unfortunately I love him [. . .]

It was only after working with him for two years that I discovered it was not just our poet Brecht I loved, but Bertolt too. I separated from Robert Lund, though he said and believed it would only be for six months or so. He did not want a divorce. He told me, "You can't play second fiddle." Alas, Peter Suhrkamp, with Brecht I have learned to play fifth fiddle. I love him.

Well, what I really meant to talk about was Maria Sten's book, but it's just that I have no friends here— they are all in Denmark, good, great, splendid people like yourself. And I would so much like to have one person who knows who I am and what I am capable of. To the people here I am just Brecht's lady friend, who was once very beautiful, but now Brecht is out after younger blood. That's how people talk. And—now I am forty-four years old—what is most important to me in the final analysis is my work. But I no longer wish to be a photographer. I did it only because I wanted to help Brecht make a record of his plays. There are surely enough good photographers in Berlin, and now he is in a position to pay them. In America I was cheap labor, and I worked my fingers to the bone.

I want to write, and also to direct plays. That is my field of activity, my profession. It is what I can do!

But the final chapter of my book *Jedes Tier kann es* is important, otherwise it will be thought the book is written by a homosexual woman, and in that case it is worthless. I love men. But for fifteen years Brecht forbade me to smile. "Your whore's smile," he called it. My hair turned gray.

In fact I did leave him once. I held out for a year in Hollywood, from 1941 to 1942. I had no friends and lived in a small rented room. One day Helene Weigel said to me, "Why don't you go to your Danish friends?" There was a Danish consulate in California. The consul was always sending me invitations, but he was a Nazi! There were also two Danish nurses living there. I should go to them, Helene Weigel suggested, and not be around when Charles Laughton or Feuchtwanger or Brecht's friends came to visit him. Brecht told me, "Better not come: it upsets Helli." One day I left for New York [. . .] The rest of the story you shall have another time—or never. For you have not the time to read such long letters.

But the final chapter of my book is important. It is a powerful chapter, for of course women carry as much of the "blame" (if one can talk of blame in this connection) as the dear men.

I had forgotten the book because the world situation became so to speak stronger and graver, and sexuality or personal happiness retreated to the background. But it would be a pity if the book were to be available only in Danish. Perhaps there might just be time to publish it before the atom bomb.

It has done me good to talk you. Thanks.

Ever your R. B.

THE BLOOD-RED CLOTH

Then she knelt down
and wiped up
the red drops:
she had struck him.

ONE HALF FOR ME

In the night she took the scissors
and cut the cloth
in two:
But the shame
was hers alone.

FAILINGS

You had none.
I had one:
I loved.

                    (January 28, 1951)

MY BOILERMAN

Seventy years old is my boilerman.
Yet he must be a wonderman, for
he has a son of seven.
"He has no pants," he tells me,
my boilerman of seventy.

Tomorrow the great German poet
will be fifty-three—I

shall not see him. But pants
I give my boilerman's son
in the name of Bertolt Brecht.
Thus do I celebrate
the great German poet's
birthday.

So many people will he have around him,
yet none like my boilerman.
His people all have pants.

I went with him because he wrote:
"Should we meet again,
I am ready to be taught."
He has need of it.

(February 9, 1951)

From the Diaries

February 1951

Whether I shall now be declared sick or fit, the fact
remains that since I left Denmark I have usually been by
myself, through long evenings and Sundays, at Christmas, on New Year's Day, on my birthdays and on his.
During the three years in Berlin I have not been invited
out once. Just now and again I have been allowed to go
along too, if it happened to be convenient, and if it could
be assumed I would not be in the way, and if there maybe
happened to be a seat vacant in the car. Should a guest
be treated like dirt?

This is a ruined country inhabited by ruined people. I
hear that Jürgen Fehling, the theater director, simply sat
down and crapped wherever he pleased. A talented fellow, but crushed, like the city of Berlin itself.

And yet I love Berlin. Nowhere else in the whole world would you find such class-conscious workers. I really love them all. Yesterday one of them said to me, "We shall soon have to mount the barricades again." Then we sang the "United Front Song." They tell me about their families, and we laugh a lot. Yet really they have nothing to laugh about. They earn one mark and fifty-nine pfennigs an hour—trained workers. I might also add: They have little to eat.

My door is always open. Everybody knows it, but not once has anything been stolen, not even a hairpin. And not one of these workers has ever laid hands on me. I say that as a woman who lives alone. We talk together as friends. They tell me their troubles. I often think to myself: If only Brecht were here! If only, at least once, he would take a look at these workers' hands as they talked! I think I must take photographs for Brecht of these hands and these eyes.

I see old men in the street dragging handcarts. I revere old people, and it makes me ill to see such things. I help pull their handcarts. I am an idiot.

All you who were once persecuted and are now great and powerful, do you feel comfortable as you drive along in your cars, able to sound your horns when you see an old man blocking the way with his few potatoes and lumps of coal? All he wants is to warm his old bones. Get out of your cars for once and ask the old man where he wants to go and whether you can help him. Then you will learn something about his misery. He lives in some cellar or other, his children were killed in the war, his wife has died, his sister is ill . . .

However, it is possible that he will have no wish at all to talk to great people like yourselves. Berlin working men have said to me, "We are still the feeding troughs from which they grow rich and fat, they get their cars from us." I have worked out my own version of that saying: The feeding troughs are the same, only the oxen have changed.

There is no reason why our comrades shouldn't drive around in cars. They have much to do, and they are doing a good job. But they shouldn't sound their horns so much. All these people on foot, or on bicycles, or dragging something behind them, are they not the ones who build our houses, cook our food, repair our cars, and dig our coal? Without them, everybody would live as wretchedly as they do.

In Denmark I once allowed myself to be stopped from giving a lift in my car to a man standing out in the rain. Bertolt Brecht said, "No, we can't give anyone a lift." But he sent me the following poem:

> Traveling in a comfortable car
> Down a rainy road in the country
> We saw a ragged fellow at nightfall
> Signal to us for a ride, with a low bow.
> We had a roof and we had room and we drove on
> And we heard me say, in a grumpy voice: no
> We can't take anyone with us.
> We had gone on a long way, perhaps a day's march
> When suddenly I was shocked by this voice of mine
> This behavior of mine and this
> Whole world.

Brecht forgot to mention that, after obeying my important guest and for the first time in my life leaving a fellow being stranded on a country road, I said, sharply and distinctly, "Despicable!" It was after that that Brecht sent me his poem. My reason for putting it in my diary at this time is because he now sounds his horn too much for me to bear. He no longer sees nor helps anybody. However,

I no longer let him forbid me anything. I help where I can.

"Charity?" the great ones ask. "No, we won't go along with that." Lenin asked everyone, "Have you any tea? Shouldn't your brother go into hospital?"

January 17, 1952

Yesterday, calmly and with much earnestness, Brecht said to me, "I must now tell you something very bad, Ruth, but it is something you must know: If tomorrow I fall dead in the street, the fault will be yours. You have cost me five years of my life. I am now fifty-three, and I look five years older."

Brecht is convinced of the truth of what he said, and it was very kind of him to tell me what he thinks. I am not referring to the fact that, in making this statement, he showed me I am not a matter of indifference to him. What I am saying is that his reasoning is wrong. Those five years were stolen from him by his work and by his struggles. I believe that if he had allowed me to share in his work and struggles, I might even have been able to help him.

March 26, 1952

Bertolt Brecht informed me today that I am unable to provide him with the inner peace he needs.

It is new for me to hear Brecht talking about inner things. "Peace is something you get in the grave," my teacher once told me.

Three Telephone Conversations

1.

I am in the tower in Buckow that Brecht has put at my disposal. He himself lives in his garden house. We are not connected by telephone, but my neighbor has a telephone on which I can reach Brecht.

I have been waiting for him all day, keeping of course his habits in mind. He could have come at nine in the morning, if he felt bored—he did not come. Then, if he had done some work, he could have come at eleven—he did not come. Then he could have been here at four in the afternoon, after his siesta—he did not come. Perhaps he will look in quickly just before supper? No. So I call him.

HE: Are you here? I didn't know whether you'd come . . .

I: Yes . . . What are you doing?

HE: Sorting through old manuscripts . . . Got to be done sometime . . .

I: Yes . . . When are you going to Berlin?

HE: Tomorrow . . . Tomorrow morning . . . How's the stove doing?

I: Wonderfully. A splendid stove. Starts at once and keeps on burning . . .

HE: Is the bath working?

I: Yes. Everything's fine.

HE: I tried to call you, but no one answered.

I: My neighbors were away on Saturday and Sunday, they've just returned.

HE: I thought you'd gone out for a walk, but . . . I could get you a lift to Strausberg tomorrow. Would that be a help?

I: Very much so. The journey here was horrible.

HE: Yes, I know . . . I know . . .

I: I suppose there's no room in your car?

HE: I? Ha! Mine's not here, and the other is full.

I: Right, then. When can the chauffeur pick me up?

HE: At eight o'clock.

I: That's a great relief. Then I'll see you tomorrow in the office.

HE: Yes, I shall go straight to the office and be there all morning.

I: There's something I'd like to show you. Good night . . .

HE: Good night, Ruth.

Ten minutes on foot, two by car—that is the distance between our houses. As I walked back to my tower following this conversation, the moon was lighting up two slender poplars, and the verse came into my mind: "Our ceaseless discourse, like two poplars communing, our discourse over many years has fallen silent . . ."

"You should be glad to see me enjoying myself," he told me. Am I frigid? Only a frigid woman can meet this demand: to look on cheerfully as he kisses other women. He has also said in a letter, "Loving people are great people . . ." So why does he trample on something great for the sake of three or four silly bitches?

(October 29, 1954)

2.

My telephone rings. A glance at the clock. Right: seven P.M., call time.

HE: I've got the contract for the *Antigone* model book. What's the name of the people?

227

I: The Henschelverlag.

HE: This is how I've done it: I take five percent, since it includes the play, you get five, and that leaves five to cover the photographic work and the fees.

I: I think that's wrong. The publishers should pay the photo costs. You always take too little for yourself.

HE: I'm paid for the plays anyway by the Aufbau-Verlag.

I: Where have you been all day? What are you doing?

HE: Oh, general things for the theater. Rehearsals . . .

I: You haven't been to the *Winterschlacht* rehearsals at all, have you?

HE: No. *Don Juan* and *Carrar*: there's so much to do. I'm tired. I'll call you later.

I: Thanks. I sleep so much better when you say good night, Bertolt.

By "call time" I mean the time he rings everybody up, one after the other. That is seven P.M. And then a short "Good night" at eleven. If you have forgotten to say something and try to ring back, the line is already engaged.

(November 3, 1954)

3.

I had given him the first thirty pages of my record of our time together to read. I did not want to go on writing behind his back. I wanted to know what he thought of it and whether it was worth continuing. Above all, however, I had gradually realized that I cannot delude myself; what I write, I write for him, about him, to him. My telephone woke me up. I took up the receiver with no hope that it might be he, for it was outside any call time.

HE: I've read it . . . the thirty pages.

I: Well, is it worth continuing?

HE: Definitely . . . Only I'd like to keep off the tragedy.

I: I can always cut it out.

HE: So long as you're describing, it's all very good. But the tragic bits then become like a conventional novel.

I: Consider them cut.

HE: Then that bit about the silk shirt in Denmark that you nearly stole . . . There you should describe how else I was dressed. Otherwise it sounds so elegant . . . with a silk shirt . . .

I: Yes, but after all I'm only stealing it. That's not tragic—I meant it to be funny.

HE: Yes, but why is it a silk shirt lying there . . .

I: Tell me, then, why do you wear silk shirts? Do they feel good on your skin?

HE: (murmurs something).

I: You've just had some new silk shirts made, haven't you?

HE: I don't know, it just seems to me too elegant. Write another page, telling how I'm dressed. It's a pity too that you don't describe my workroom in Skovsbostrand.

I: At the point I've reached in my manuscript I've not even been in your workroom.

HE: The point where Helli takes the architect along . . .

I: But I wasn't in the room with them. Why can't you write me half a page, describing your workroom?

HE: All right, I'll try . . . You must also write why I'm important . . .

I: Why you're important? I could write why you were important to me . . . how you became important to me during my work on *The Mother* and *Carrar* and *Fear and Misery*, and with the translations.

HE: Oh yes, you must do that, otherwise one can't really follow.

I: I'll do it.

HE: And the tragedy isn't good. Immediately you start describing events, it gets interesting . . .

I: Then I'll concentrate on describing things. But of course I'm not as merry and cheerful as I was then. You've now begun a new life. Just as you helped me move out when I left Robert Lund, now you're helping her move out on her husband. All according to pattern . . .

HE: I help many people, all the time. It means nothing.

I: No?

HE: Nothing at all.

I: All right, then let me join in your work. There's a lot to be done. I'm looking forward to the model books.

HE: Why don't you go and photograph the perfor-mance this evening, even if it's only for half an hour?

I: I'm frightened of taking photographs. I can't do it any more. I'm afraid you might be disappointed with what I've got out of *The Mother*.

The conversation ended as usual: "I'll ring later . . . ," "Many thanks . . . ," and so on.

I sat back. What went through my poor head did not go along the telephone line. I should describe why he is important, but by the time this is read, people will surely know already why Bertolt Brecht was important. My God, is he still frightened he might be forgotten, in the way he described it in his poem "Visit to the Exiled Poets"? In Denmark he once asked me to learn his poems by heart. Was he thinking even then of the atom bomb? Was I to wander around, a piece of human wreckage, murmuring his poems to the survivors?

(November 7, 1954)

TRUTH IS CONCRETE

Looking through my old script about the possibilities of making a photographic record of stage performances, I see in my mind's eye the smiles of my fellow photographers. Well, regrettably I never became a photographer—a professional photographer, I mean. And I say "regrettably" because, having taken to heart the maxim TRUTH IS CONCRETE on the beam in Bertolt Brecht's Danish workroom, I regard photography as an important and tremendously serious profession. It is also useful for my professions as author and theater director, and can indeed be essential, for I have now become a "chronicler" rather than an author. What I write down is what I have seen and heard, but often enough it is believed only when I can produce concrete proof of what I have written—in the shape of pictures.

I resorted to a Leica and even to a movie camera in the USA, since in countries where art is controlled by soap, cheese, or toothpaste manufacturers—that is to say, in capitalist countries—no professional photographer, however great the art, would make around five thousand exposures, when at most only five of them are saleable.

It was a matter at that time of Brecht's production of

his play *Life of Galileo* with Charles Laughton, providing a unique opportunity to make a photographic record of three branches of art at one go: stage direction, drama, and acting. Is it in fact possible to recapture a drama, a play, in photographs? Direction, acting, decorations, costumes—certainly. But a drama? Yes, it can be done. It is possible, I maintain, if one photographs the action directly, particularly when one is dealing with epic plays, epic stage direction, and epic acting. If the takes are posed, the pictures that emerge may be very sharply focused, but they are unrealistic, counterfeit.

Dear colleagues and readers, do not judge my pictures too severely. I did what I could in the conditions available to me in capitalist countries, working behind glass, in a small projection room in California or, as in the Zurich Schauspielhaus, during the single matinee performance of Brecht's *Antigone*, where the taking of photographs was forbidden. I photographed from the prompter's box, and the outcome was one of my most successful pictures: Helene Weigel as a Berlin woman.

The intendant in Greiz, Ernst Otto Tickhardt, was the first man to make use of our *Antigonemodell 1948*. The whole company willingly adopted everything that seemed worthy of imitation. There I saw the first fruits of my shabby and inadequate photographic activities, and I added to my collection—at present confined to the archives—a thousand exposures from this first so-called "model" production.

The pictures of a collaboration between Brecht, Neher, and Weigel that I am presenting here comprise only a small selection from a total of two thousand photographs. In the archives we have successful color exposures that reveal the beauty of the decorations and the costumes. We also have short film clips of Helene Weigel's ways of walking. But the little I have learned as a photographer was spoiled, not only by lack of money, but by the fact that, regrettably, I am no cold-blooded professional photographer. While focusing my lens on Weigel as Antigone, I had only too often to wipe the little glass viewfinder of my Leica dry. I was seeing for the first time, as if through a veil, the burning torch of the actor's art in the small, eloquent, and now so famous hands of Helene Weigel. Up till then I had known this artist only as a communist, mother, cook, and bookbinder. Now for the first time I saw her holding high the torch of her great profession. She had never let the flame go out, but in the many lands in which she was forced to seek refuge, the interest in and need for her art was minimal. Here is a remark I once overheard in a Hollywood studio: "No, no, and no again, not Weigel. With dialogue or without, I can't cast her. That woman"—the producer was going through Helene's screen tests at the time—"colors everything red, even with her eyes. She's a communist!"

I was of course familiar with Helene's voice, but not from a stage, at a distance. Consequently two performances went by before I grew accustomed to that warning voice, at least to the extent that my hands stopped shaking as I fed film into our shabby old Leica, the only camera we then had. I vividly remember—and shall always remember—how an important roll of film broke on the line "Whoever seeks power drinks salt water which he cannot hold . . ." At that point, dear colleagues, the film stuck, and on "Woe is me!" it snapped. In the darkness I could feel the damage. Later on I made many exposures with cotton wool stuffed in my ears, but it was too late, my auditory nerves were already affected by this unprofessional photographic activity. That is why I admire those calm and cold-blooded professional photographers. Now— I set it down as a warning—I photograph with a listening aid that I can turn off when *logos* (the word, the teaching) assails *psyche* (the soul). But a switch to turn off our tears has not yet been invented.

Should Helene Weigel play Antigone again—and I hear there is a prospect of that in the Academy of Arts—then I beg you, try to photograph her so as to show her complete command of mime, for in my pictures little of her face can be seen.

Do it better! We have better facilities in the G.D.R. For example, Max Reinhardt's Deutsches Theater has a new lighting apparatus. Maybe a brightly lit performance could be put on there, especially for photographers. Here we are not forced to watch every penny we spend, as I was in Switzerland.

But above all: Do it! Place your photos in front of the greatest of playwrights and coax from him verses of the kind he gave us in his *Kriegsfibel* (*War Verses*)—or demand them from him. Surely that is a photographer's greatest triumph, when his productions stir our poets into celebrating his concrete snapshots in verses, songs, and ballads!

What really happens on stage can be checked only with the help of photographs. A picture can be examined at length in quiet morning hours far from the director's desk. Once the curtain goes up, it is already too late. And it is not without good reason that the Berliner Ensemble possesses a larger photographic laboratory and archive than any other theater in the world. In none of the countries in which we have worked has there been a photo lab devoted to the needs of stage direction and dramaturgy. None of this—to avoid any further misunderstanding—has anything to do with naturalism or formalism. From photographs of postures, gestures, walks, and groupings we take what we need to achieve truth on the stage, bad postures as well as good postures: the bad ones in order to change them, the good to make them worth copying. We must show our new, critical, knowledgeable audiences, entering the theater straight from the fields and the people's factories, that we are at least making efforts to present the truth. The photographer's profession is an important one in 1955, the year in which I am writing. All that is needed is for it to be properly appreciated, understood, respected, and above all, supported.

For me this work has proved more than rewarding, and perhaps one day people will be grateful to me for it. The poet himself wrote the "bridging verses" to my wretched photographs in the *Antigonemodell 1948*. I demanded them from him.

(Draft of an unpublished article for the *Antigonemodell 1948* by Bertolt Brecht and Caspar Neher, 1955)

YOU

You mean so much to me.
To have such a friend in times like these.
What I gaze on with ever new surprise:
The stars, the sea, and your face.
Your face, your eyes—stronger than sea and stars.
You know my misery, this deadly longing.
I have held your shoulders in my hands.
Ute weeps, too terrified to understand that you were here,
You, Bertolt.

(End of July 1957)

WHAT WAS BERTOLT BRECHT LIKE?

What was he like as a person?
Ask me rather how he worked.
Did he not write in cold blood, utterly without
feeling?
No.
What did he feel when he was writing?
He said: I feel only when I have a headache, not
when I am writing. Then I am thinking.
Was he a genius?
Yes, a hard-working, Marxist, normal genius.
What was his motivating force?
To put it briefly: class warfare.
What was he working for?
For the oppressed, against the exploiters.
And how did he write?
Sympathetically and humorously for the former,
openly and harshly and intolerantly against the
latter.
Did he have private problems?
He said he had none, and that anyway it was
nobody else's business.
Was he not strange?
All that struck me was that, even in
the depth of a hard
Finnish winter, he never wore gloves.
His hands were
always warm, and he loved fresh
air on his hands and
forehead. Then, of course, that he worked
like no other person I have ever known.
He knew no Sundays, no
vacations, no public holidays. But he did
want to have a Christmas tree.

BRECHT AND COURTESY

One morning, as Brecht arrived at the theater in his car, our house manager leaped forward to open the car door. Brecht gave him a friendly nod and a "Good morning"—and got out through the other door.

WHAT HE HATED

Somebody holding his coat for him. Somebody offering him a light for his cigar. Disputes about who should go first through a door.

ARGUMENTS

Brecht was hurrying from one rehearsal to another:

B.: Why isn't the scene I ordered being rehearsed?
R.: We've already rehearsed it.
B.: I gave clear instructions that the new scene should not be rehearsed before I was there.
R.: Yes, but—
B.: I forbade the scene to be rehearsed without me.
R.: The actress wanted to go home, and—
B.: There are no prima donnas here—except for me!

HIS OWN SON

When Brecht returned to Germany from his long exile, the younger generation often did not even know his name. His books had been burned, and he himself deprived of his nationality by Hitler.

One day we had to fetch some papers from some authority or other, and—as usual—we had to apply to the doorkeeper for a pass. The doorkeeper was thoroughly enjoying his position of power. He made his way slowly, letter by letter, through the name B-e-r-t-o-l-t B-r-e-c-h-t, fixed Brecht with a sharp eye and asked, "Are you any relation to Bert Brecht?" "Yes, I am my own son," Brecht replied, seized his pass and murmured as we went in, "There's a Kaiser Wilhelm still sitting in every corner."

ON LAUGHTER

There was always much laughter during rehearsals and script conferences. Once a pupil had to describe the difficulties we were having with the stage settings for our production of *The Mother*. It was his first job with our company, and his colleagues, already hardened by Brechtian schooling, almost died laughing at the poor wretch's helpless manner of expressing himself. One sentence was seized on, and it made even Brecht laugh until he cried: "The stove in the mother's small room expanded into a problem."

The clumsy pupil attempted to join in the laughter, but he was actually nearer to tears. Then Brecht, with his proverbial kindness, came to his rescue. He pointed to him, tears of laughter still in his eyes, and called out, "A man who can laugh at himself is halfway to being a god. God spends all day laughing at himself."

BRECHT'S EVERYDAY VOCABULARY

A Small Dictionary

Words of Praise
normal
kind
useful
helpful
gifted
amusing
genuine

Words of Condemnation
corrupt
sold
exploiter
non-dialectical
non-Marxist

In the Theater
show
try out
contradiction
to speak drily
plot
why?
why?
and again and again: why?

FAVORITE ANIMAL

His dog Rolf

FAVORITE COLOR

Gray

FAVORITE MATERIALS

Leather
Wood

WHAT HE ENJOYED

a) eating:
new potatoes in spring
asparagus with vinegar and oil
carp
beef broth
dumplings of all kinds
horseradish
cheese, as much and as many sorts as possible
raspberries, raspberries, ah, raspberries!
b) drinking:
lemon juice, morning, afternoon, and evening
beer in the quiet of evening, at the end alone
whiskey, but only in London fogs
tea for his guests
never, on any account, water
schnapps, if necessary, with screwed-up face, to ward
off colds
Over champagne the great man fell asleep

WHAT HE LIKED

old copper things
old clocks
fine pipes
farmhouse cutlery
old knives
old Chinese rugs

WHAT HE NEEDED

many tables
typewriter
reading lamp
light
good typing paper
scissors for cutting out pictures
adhesives for mounting

WHAT HE NEEDED IN ADDITION

pupils
gifted actors
composers
discussions
scientists
detective stories
to be left in peace

WHAT WAS NEVER TO BE FORGOTTEN

that a young tree must be given water
that in winter birds have a hard time finding food
that a sick person needs help

a starving person food
a freezing person warmth

(1958)

An Unaddressed Letter

Copenhagen, August 6, 1962

Today I received a letter from the secretary's office of the Suhrkamp Verlag (Dr. Unseld). It will be printed in my chapter about Brecht and Peter Suhrkamp. And it will be printed with or without permission. I have now had enough of "permissions."

So it was an "oversight," was it? It was not known that I have no exchange facilities? When my feet touch Danish soil, I get no Öre. So my "participation in the *Simone* royalties is not recognized by Brecht's heirs," is it? "The royalties will be divided only between Feuchtwanger and Brecht's heirs," will they? "The contract was drawn up in the USA simply in order to save tax." Is that so? Dr. Unseld has got his people to write me: "There is nothing I can do to change that." But could he not at least read the contract, a copy of which Marta Feuchtwanger has sent me?

For the stage production in Frankfurt am Main I sought and found a Simone, since Brecht had always wanted a child for this role. I worked with this Simone and recorded our work on tape, so that no one could deny it. Nothing of this has appeared in the press, curiously enough. On the contrary, it was reported that the intendant Harry Buckwitz made this truly great discovery himself. Buckwitz has written to me, saying this is not correct, but he is not to blame for the mistake. That's funny. Brecht was always praising my Danish sense of humor, but now it has vanished. I have to remain in Denmark, because my eighty-year-old mother is ill. But I have no idea where the money is supposed to come from to support her and cover my own living costs. Brecht was fond of my mother, and I am now selling some handwritten letters and a manuscript of his. The great man would approve, since he was always glad to be of use. Now I am using him on my mother's behalf.

And at the same time I am looking forward to being back in Berlin soon, in Charitéstrasse, among Brecht's things. There I wish to die in peace and, what is more, in his own bed.

BERTOLT BRECHT AND THE VIRTUES

He was always cheerful and gay. For him cheerfulness was a virtue that helps one through the hardest of tasks. "A cheerful person always finds a way out." When I said not everyone possessed this gift, he replied, "Cheerfulness must be worked on."

He despised people who crept miserably out of bed in the morning. "One must prepare next day's enjoyment the evening before, even if it only means watering green plants or feeding the birds in the window."

Most important of all to Brecht was regular application. He spoke crossly of people who labored spontaneously and then let it all lie for days on end, simply because they had not been praised or criticized. It meant that for a few days they were completely out of the reckoning. To apply oneself without enjoyment was something Brecht found unbearable, though of course he too had tasks to perform which he called with a sigh "duties."

Brecht also possessed the virtue of punctuality. If someone arrived late, Brecht would say, "It is disgraceful to waste other people's time by making them wait."

Modesty, for Brecht, was a double-edged virtue. He said, "It is false modesty to underrate one's own abilities. A woodworker loves his wood and must take pride in being able to shape it so well. A mechanic must be conscious of his manual dexterity. In such matters one should not be modest. But an actor, however great he is, should, for my taste, keep at least a pinch of modesty in his pocket." I have been asked whether Brecht himself was modest. He enjoyed being used—and not only on stage, after the curtain is up, but in real life as well. Tell me, is that not a part of modesty—the urge to make oneself useful?

Once we were sitting talking to some building workers. Next to Brecht sat an old, gray-haired working man. Brecht asked him, "What work do you do on the building?" "I carry up the mortar and the stones." "Isn't that too heavy work for you?" Laughing, the old man replied, "I could carry you up there ten times, and back again." There was a short pause. Brecht, bashful and ashamed, looked away. Then the man said, "But not your mind." Brecht gave a pleased laugh.

Helpfulness. Brecht said, "A readiness to help is bound up with imagination and, above all, with kindness." He did not like it when a task was carried out as if it were slave labor. "It makes me feel like an exploiter." He made no demands, was always ready to give advice, but never more than once, even to his closest collaborators. If his advice was not followed, he would not repeat it.

Maybe someone would like to know what Brecht's attitude was toward love. Among my notes I have found the following sentence: "Loving people are great people." If anyone can make anything of that, Brecht would have been pleased.

(1966)

A DREAM

The roof falls in, and I feel myself on fire. Strange that my pubic hairs are the first to catch alight. This I can extinguish. I seize them in both hands and attempt to douse the flames with the waters of my womb. I raise my right hand, which is burning like a torch. I point to him, for he is now there too. He is standing a few yards away and is talking to many people. He glances obliquely across at me. I take in sentences. What is worrying him is the life and death of his works. Once again I raise the torch, my burning right hand, on high, and call softly through the night, "Bertolt." He looks round once more, then speaks some lines from his poem "Ardens sed virens": "Splendid, what the lovely fire cannot turn to chilly ash! Sister, you're my heart's desire, burning, and yet still intact." Then he says threateningly to me, "Chilly ash is no use to me!" I attempt to give him a sign: in Cassiopeia a star is missing. It is this missing star that has struck me and sparked off the fire. He shakes his head and does not even look up to the sky. He thinks I have once again gone out of my mind. Then W. grabs him by the arm and says, "Send for the fire brigade! Only the fire brigade can deal with this. When fire breaks out, one must send for the fire brigade: You cannot help!"

I see him giving instructions to telephone for the fire brigade. Then from Cassiopeia a second star falls. But the firemen are already there. They carry me out and cover me up.

(Undated)

245

PART III

Afterword

R uth Berlau was an unusual woman. There were times when I admired her, others when I hated her. For she lived only in extremes. Her demands on the people around her were as hazardous to them as to herself. Her relations with her friends were always poised on a razor's edge. She played for high stakes, but she was no gambler; she fought for what she considered reasonable. Even when she lost, she emerged the stronger, for she had fought without reserve. Her persistence was astonishing. After whole nights of exhausting argument she would find herself in the morning in sole possession of the field. In her best days she could drink the toughest of men under the table. Doctors, whom she had to deal with quite often, were themselves ripe for hospital treatment after treating her. Ruth Berlau personally helped to get them back on their feet. She harassed bureaucrats, shirkers, offhand shopkeepers, and rude waiters. Nobody possessed the courage to stand up to her because her reproaches were both definite and to the point. Say what one will against her, she sticks in the memory as a great personality, along with all her contradictions, strengths, and weaknesses.

Ruth Berlau's behavior was difficult to predict. The switch from one attitude to its opposite always took one by surprise. And it was all unconditional: love and devotion, contempt and tyranny, tact and discretion on the one hand, angry abuse and condemnation on the other. One had to spend years living and working with her before one could hope to understand her. In Brecht's case this turbulent relationship lasted for twenty-two years.

Those who experienced Ruth Berlau only in a giving mood, and not when—in the same uncompromising way— she was demanding something, did not know her at all. Looked at from the other side, those who turned tail and fled when she was angry and unjust toward them had no idea how self-sacrificingly helpful and tender she could be.

If it suited her purpose, Ruth Berlau could put a dispute right out of her mind and carry on as if nothing had happened, relying on an unspoken reconciliation. Only understanding and good-natured friends found this easy to accept. The uninitiated could seldom hide their confusion, and in consequence reaped mockery and scorn for their obstinacy and pigheadedness. They could even find themselves thrown out of her apartment. Because of her unpredictability, many people, including some important contemporaries, preferred to make a wide detour rather than risk the danger of a meeting with this human volcano. A famous Danish lawyer once spent hours hiding in the toilet when he set eyes on her in the foyer of his hotel. She wrecked a birthday party by engaging in a heated argument with other guests, to whom Brecht meant less than he did to her. In reply to her host's protests, she insisted on her right to defend Brecht to the death and demanded approval of her wild behavior. But on another occasion, when she felt that Brecht had wounded a colleague by failing to appreciate something she had done, she went, dressed just as she was, to the afflicted woman to hand over flowers Brecht had shortly before presented to her. Clad only in a nightdress, she hurried through the crowded streets like an avenging goddess.

Ruth Berlau had many squabbles with Helene Weigel, especially in Berlin, and always stoutly maintained that she was in the right. But when a cabaret singer once sang a satiric song against Helene Weigel to her in the expectation of earning her applause for this proof of solidarity, she kicked him on the shin and broke off all further contact with him. She saw his act as an attempt to curry favor, for which she had no time at all. Whom or what she herself chose to criticize was not to be regarded as fair game for every Tom, Dick, and Harry. That right depended on a lifetime of experience, which she measured in terms of her own.

The whole house shivered when Ruth Berlau slammed the door behind a visitor with whom she had just quarreled. I myself can tell a tale about that. Five times she appointed me her heir, and five times she just as impulsively disinherited me. She wrote down touching stories about my solicitude toward her and sent me many letters expressing her gratitude, but she also abused me as an incorrigible Nazi. Yet despite this, we remained close friends for more than twenty years. I was often her only confidant, and not infrequently I found myself alone when it came to the point of standing up for her. There is only one thing that for a long time I found it difficult to forgive. Wrongly imagining that I too might be deserting her, she once denounced me to the authorities. I had gone to a theater conference in Yugoslavia, and she declared that I had no intention of returning. This was a dangerous charge, and Ruth Berlau was not the only person against whose suspicions I was obliged to clear myself. Today I find it touching to recall to what lengths she would go just to ensure that she did not lose me.

In the fifties many people formed a negative impression of Ruth Berlau. All they saw was her bitterness, her self-righteousness, her quarrelsomeness, and her desperate destructiveness. They failed to see that all this was a form of self-defense, arising from the fact that Brecht had ceased to involve her in his work. Nothing worse could have happened to her. She had long since bound her life to Brecht's, and she had no desire to lose her identity. To wage a campaign of malice was exhausting work, but Ruth Berlau held this mask before her true face from the moment she began to suspect the tragic turn her relationship with her idol Brecht was taking. She felt her behavior justified, if causing scandals was the only way of drawing attention to herself. And for a time the method even worked: Brecht began again to take more trouble with her. Gradually, however, he came to feel she was blackmailing him and that his work was suffering in consequence. He grew weary and was no longer ready to seek her support. He did not understand that it was an attempt to preserve the meaning of her life that made her clutch at every straw. And Ruth Berlau herself did not understand that her hopes of influencing Brecht's feelings for her by applying maximum pressure were self-deluding.

Throughout her life Ruth Berlau relied on her phenomenal instinct—in her political convictions, in her acknowledgment of friendships, in her working ambitions, in warding off dangers—and she never reckoned in advance how to set about achieving success. She could be infinitely happy and infinitely sad, infinitely proud, and infinitely depressed. But she never gave up. In high spirits or in low, she retained an untamable will to survive, and, even when lying flat on the ground, never forgot her sense of humor. When she pointed to the hook in the crossbeam above her door and the rope in a drawer of her commode, she did so amid laughter. None of us interpreted this macabre demonstration as a threat, for suicide was the last thing one could associate with Ruth Berlau.

It is possible now to form a clearer view of Ruth Berlau's life. In writing about her one need omit nothing, nor is there anything one should gloss over. Gossip about her will continue to circulate for a while, for there is material enough at hand. But it will do her little harm, and she will continue, despite it, to live on in literary and theatrical annals. So long as Brecht is talked about, the name of Ruth Berlau will continue to be mentioned. Her place is with the great inspirers, whose contribution lies in the realms of empathy, understanding, and loyalty. Next to Helene Weigel, she, of all the women associated with Brecht, spent the longest time with him, and she must be named as one of his most important collaborators, along with Elisabeth Hauptmann and Margarete Steffin. Ruth Berlau never overestimated her allotted function, but such as it was, she performed it with all the powers at her command, and thus had a definite share in Brecht's work. This Brecht himself always recognized, even after he abandoned her.

Ruth Berlau has described how important discussion partners and collaborators were for Brecht. While working, he needed an audience to act as a sounding board. What collaboration actually meant to him is difficult to define. The word can be understood simply in its normal sense, but it is also collaboration when a writer's work is helped by the presence of some other person who independently assumes all the attendant organizational duties. Brecht was a manuscript fetishist. He set to work more willingly and wrote with more enjoyment when the pages he had amended the previous day lay in a clean copy on his desk the following morning. An ordinary typist would not have been up to the task; it needed the critical attitude of a Margarete Steffin, who herself put forward suggestions for amendments. When each evening Ruth Berlau photographed anew the heavily corrected and pasted-over manuscript of the versified Communist Manifesto and spent the night making prints of it, Brecht considered this to be more than mere manual assistance. He could now send the work off to his discussion partners Karl Korsch and Stefan Brecht. It was collaboration, too, when someone went off unbidden to seek out relevant books, documents, pictures, and photographs, or contacted scientists, writers, and artists for discussions.

A collaboration has many intangible aspects. Whose idea was it? Was it accepted? Was it used? And in what way was it used? Maybe it was just a passing remark that proved important, and possibly only long afterward, by which time the speaker might already have forgotten it. Cause and effect are almost never distinguishable from one another. Inspirational ideas, some quite definite, others perhaps only vague, were accepted or rejected by Brecht, usually with no reasons given, and some might also have subconsciously taken root. Nobody could judge in advance whether the time was favorable for suggestions or unfavorable. What could prove decisive was from whom they came, and to whose advice Brecht was at that particular moment vulnerable. But the overall conception was always safe in his own keeping.

The play *Mr. Puntila and His Man Matti* was written in exile in Finland. It was completed in September 1940. During this period Ruth Berlau was in daily contact with Brecht, but she took no significant part in his work on the play. She herself always acknowledged Hella Wuolijoki as the inspiration and Margarete Steffin as the collaborator. Yet in 1943 Brecht wrote to Ruth Berlau, "Without our walks in the woods [at Marlebäck] I should never have been able to write the play." One may wonder what his reasons may have been for making this assertion, but one must assume that, when he wrote these words, he meant them seriously.

An explanation can be found in Brecht's story "A Production of Lai-tu's": "The poet Kin-jeh said: It is hard to say what Lai-tu produced. Perhaps it was the twenty-two lines about the countryside that I added to my play. Without her they would not have been written. Naturally, we never spoke about the countryside. I was also influenced by what she called funny. It was not what other people call funny [. . .] If she did no more than produce what caused and allowed me to produce, she would still have demonstrated her worth. (Kin-jeh did not suffer from modesty.)"

It is unlikely that Brecht intended in this story to reveal his vanity. He himself was unaware of it, otherwise he would surely have deleted the final sentence at least. His aim was rather to help Ruth Berlau overcome her existential doubts. And this is the meaning she herself found in the story, for she had learned from Brecht that love is a production, and that a production demands love. She firmly believed that Brecht did everything for love, and that is why she did all she could to protect this love.

Later on she tended rather to feel that Brecht, when he ascribed to her a productivity that inspired and furthered his own production, was interested above all in helping himself. She interpreted Brecht's disguise as Kin-jeh thus: His love was first of all for himself. Brecht's aim was always to establish a certain point and then to prove its validity. In this way his truth would remain the whole truth. Even when he was making excuses for himself (something that rarely happened) he would in the end still be in the right.

When he went into exile Brecht was forced to abandon his favorite method of working—collective writing—and adapt himself to new ways. Collaborators, their numbers hitherto all but limitless, were no longer on hand. Even Elisabeth Hauptmann, the only woman among his various working groups, had dropped out, having chosen a route into exile other than Brecht's own. He must have found this loss particularly painful, for no other person had worked with Brecht as uninterruptedly as Elisabeth Hauptmann. She was involved in practically all his productions between 1923 and 1933. Brecht named her as collaborator in nine of his eleven plays. Clearly she succeeded best of all in adapting herself to Brecht's methods of working—or encountered the least difficulties. The problems besetting his male collaborators—how best to get on with a man who always assumed the dominating role—did not exist for her. Neither Caspar Neher nor Kurt Weill, not even Hanns Eisler, held firm throughout, and there were other reasons for this beside the simple fact that each of them had other work of his own to do or had meanwhile moved to another country. The relationship with his female collaborators was basically different for as long as Brecht remained loyal to them. They invariably formed a symbiosis with him. That was what Brecht needed, and since the women did it of their own free will, they may have felt at times overstretched, but never overexploited.

It is remarkable (if from this point of view not really strange) that throughout the whole period of exile Brecht's permanent collaborators were women who were at the same time in love with him: first Margarete Steffin, then Ruth Berlau.

Margarete Steffin took over seamlessly from Elisabeth Hauptmann in the middle of work on *Round Heads and Pointed Heads*. During the following eight years—up to her death in 1941 in Moscow—she was involved in almost all the plays Brecht wrote. He names her seven times as collaborator. To these works may be added several fragments, her work in connection with the publication of *Lieder Gedichte Chöre* (*Songs Poems Choruses*) and her help with the *Dreigroschenroman*, much of which Brecht dictated to her from his hospital bed.

As a collaborator Ruth Berlau's name appears for the first time, beside that of Margarete Steffin, on the play *The Good Person of Szechwan*. After that come *The Caucasian Chalk Circle*, *The Days of the Commune*, and finally the adaptation of Lenz's *The Tutor*. But it should not be forgotten that she also took charge of the publication of the Berliner Ensemble's four model books, the *Svendborg Poems*, and the *Kriegsfibel*. Even if one adds to these her collaboration on *Theaterarbeit* (an anthology dealing with the work of the Berliner Ensemble) and the countless photographs of Brecht's productions that she made, the record of her participation in Brecht's work is still not complete. Brecht named his collaborators only in respect of his plays, and then only when the texts appeared in print. Consequently one will not find her name attached to *Flüchtlingsgespräche*, and it is also missing from the one-acters *Dansen* and *What's the Price of Iron?*, as well as the full-length plays *The Visions of Simone Machard*, *Schweyk in the Second World War*, and *The Duchess of Malfi*. Her significant contributions to fragments and film scenarios can be seen in the manuscripts in the archives. If one counts everything that has been staged and has since also appeared in print, the total number of plays in which she collaborated amounts to nine. As editor she stands second only to Elisabeth

Hauptmann, who was responsible for the collected edition of Brecht's works. As founder of the Brecht archives and as chronicler of his work in the theater she occupies a unique position among Brecht's female collaborators. None of all this is intended as a value judgment, for many of the opportunities for collaboration were the result of circumstances. Consequently, in regard to what they did for Brecht, none of these three women should be given preference over the others; each was in her time of equal significance. But each made her own distinctive contribution.

To give an impression of Ruth Berlau's collaboration, it might be useful to describe in detail the part she played in the evolution of the play *Schweyk in the Second World War*. She does not speak of it in her memoirs, and Brecht does not mention her name in his working journal, which in any case has little to say about the play. But how close the collaboration was can be discerned from letters he wrote to Ruth Berlau. There are about forty of them, all written between mid-June and mid-November 1943. Only about half of these have yet been published. (A similar proportion, incidentally, applies to the correspondence between the two in the published edition of Brecht's letters.)

Brecht was in New York from March to May 1943. Ruth Berlau had already been living there for a year, and Brecht stayed in her apartment. He met Kurt Weill, and among other things, planned with the composer—by now a producer as well—a version of *Schweyk*. Immediately after returning to Santa Monica, Brecht wrote to Ruth Berlau, telling her that he had begun work on *Schweyk*. "As soon as the first bits are ready, you shall have them." He also gave her notice of his intention to entrust all contractual matters to her. Though he made good progress with his work (by the middle of June he had already completed "almost two of the three acts"), he was unable for lack of writing paper to make more than one carbon copy, which he needed to keep for corrections. Ruth Berlau immediately sent him some typing paper, and soon afterward she had the rough draft in her hands. With it Brecht wrote, "I'm looking forward to hearing whether the play makes you laugh, and whether I've succeeded in keeping the background sufficiently serious." He asked her to negotiate with Kurt Weill, whose draft contract restricted Brecht's rights too severely. "I have no intention of interfering too much in Weill's business arrangements, but I must retain at least some 'influence,' not be there just to fetch the beer." The letter ended with the words, "I need you as much as you need me." When no reasonable compromise could be found—"I am not just a librettist," Brecht wrote—Ruth Berlau was instructed to make tactful and cautious inquiries whether Josef Aufricht might be interested in a production. She should also talk to Erwin Piscator with a view to his directing it, and try to get Alfred Kreymborg as translator. But Brecht wanted "to keep the last word" in regard to the direction on stage, and the translation would need to be ready in six or at the most eight weeks. "If not Kreymborg, then Reyher, but no waiting around for a year." It was already the middle of July, but Brecht was still reckoning on a production in autumn. If Peter Lorre should not be available for the main role, Ruth Berlau should find out whether the comedian Zero Mostel could take over, "since I am always against wasting time." Then Ruth Berlau was told to apply to the Czech Mission—Brecht did not know in which city it was situated, but "it is urgent"—for permission to dramatize Jaroslav Hašek's novel, and at the same time inquire whether there were any English translations of Czech folksongs available, since he wanted to include some in his play. In the meantime she continued to receive further installments of the manuscript. Brecht told her, "Write whatever you think (without reservation, circumspection, etc.), it's all helpful. Small details as well, Ruth. I can still make use of everything." At the same time he told her he was very happy with the way she was handling the *Schweyk* affair. Without her help, he wrote, the whole project would already have foundered. A few days later he was even writing, "It is true that you are so clever with my affairs. It would be best if you were simply to take over the management of all my affairs. When you write as you do about *Schweyk*, you are so friendly and wise and so close to me, as if you were wearing that long white thing." (Brecht meant by this the long white nightgown that Ruth Berlau wore during his visit to New York.)

Kreymborg's translation arrived in the middle of September—later than Brecht had hoped. Ruth Berlau was dissatisfied with the result, but Brecht consoled her: "Of course there are as many mistakes in it as fleas on a dog, but that's quite natural, it's dialect, not simple German." Despite this, "Kreymborg has found the right tone and shown that it's possible. The mistakes are simple to put right, the tone would not be so easy to correct. Thank you for once again getting things done." But his optimism did not last. After subjecting the text to a serious examination, he was "in despair over the translation," which he described as "colossally irresponsible." He did not blame Ruth Berlau for the fiasco but set her a new task: "I know you did everything you could possibly do, Ruth, and I am extremely grateful. But now you must at all costs help me to achieve a presentable version." Brecht's only worry was that his expenses were mounting at a time when no royalties from a production were coming in to cover them. He racked his brains over ways of keeping her "in freedom," so that she would no longer have to earn her living but could devote herself exclusively to managing his affairs. He expressed admiration for her "gigantic achievements" in such difficult circumstances. Others, he told her, would have capitulated long ago and found themselves a profitable job. With her at his side, he believed, he would still be able to win through.

Hopes of making some quick earnings with a *Schweyk* production proved illusory. Hanns Eisler's promise to his friend to take over from Kurt Weill and to write some music for the play was no more than a crumb of comfort. In the meantime the people who would have been in a position to stage a production, either through influence or with their own money, had withdrawn. Brecht would have been ready to abandon the whole project if Ruth Berlau had not so obstinately persisted with it. She forced Alfred Kreymborg to make a thorough revision of his translation and herself joined in the laborious work. But for Brecht himself it was no longer the matter of urgency it had formerly been. While again living with Ruth Berlau in New York, from the middle of November 1943 to the middle of March 1944, he occupied himself with all manner of things rather than with *Schweyk*.

Suddenly, however, his hopes rose again. In the spring of 1944 he made the acquaintance of Charles Laughton and gave him the play to read. At the beginning of April he wrote to Ruth Berlau, "Just to show you what a good thing it was that you had *Schweyk* retranslated: I gave it to Laughton yesterday, he read it straight away during the night and, at first reading at any rate, seems to be truly enthusiastic. Perhaps something may come of it." Two weeks later he reported that on the previous day Laughton "read out two acts of your translation to Eisler, me and Winge, and said that 98 percent of the play came through, the translation was much better than we thought. In fact, we laughed ourselves silly, he understood literally *all* the jokes! So you see!" Brecht thought so highly of Ruth Berlau's contribution that he ceased to mention Kreymborg's name and gave her the entire credit for the new translation. "*Your* translation," he wrote.

But once more their efforts came to nothing. In July 1943 Brecht listed in his working journal the ten plays he had written during his ten years of exile, the last being *Schweyk*, and he added, "Not a bad repertoire for an utterly defeated class." Ten months later he drew up a "procession of figures" in the same place, naming a total of thirty main characters in his plays, from Baal to Azdak. Schweyk is not among them; evidently Brecht had given up. However, he wished at least to protect his rights in his dramatization, and for that he once more made use of Ruth Berlau. He asked her to procure an extension of the *Schweyk* agreement, making it valid indefinitely in Europe, and for at least two further years in America. She should take particular care to ensure that he would not have to share the rights with anyone else. Besides that, he mentioned other possible tasks for the future. He wished Ruth Berlau to be his "liaison officer" with Elisabeth Bergner in connection with a production of *The Duchess of Malfi*, also with a publisher who was planning a complete edition of his works in English. Looking far ahead, he even gave her the responsibility for his works and contacts in Germany. For all this and much more besides he had nobody but her, he said. "So you must be fresh, friendly, cheerful, and loving."

Ruth Berlau enjoyed working for Brecht and was happy when she could help him by making useful suggestions. Nevertheless, she suffered at times from her dependence on him and was always fearful of becoming more and more dependent. She made no secret of this to Brecht. But they were complexes with which Brecht was unwilling to concern himself. As so often before, he tried to dispose of them by literary means. In the story *"Lai-tu's Wert"* ("Lai-tu's Value") he wrote: "Lai-tu thought little of herself, since she had not written any great work . . . That works of literature had been written with her in mind, and that good people behaved better than they would otherwise have done, she considered of no importance. Me-ti said to her: It is correct that you have not yet delivered any wares. But that does not mean you have made no contribution. Your goodness is established and valued by reason of being called upon. Thus, by being eaten, does an apple achieve its fame."

This was the alpha and omega of her life with Brecht: to be used, worn out, and consumed. She had no time to reflect on it. She never counted the cost to herself.

In the spring of 1950, a time of conflict between the two of them, Brecht attempted to objectivize their relationship. The "third cause," socialism, should be put at the forefront, rather than personal and private matters. In a letter without greeting or signature Brecht set down under four headings his thoughts about "what we can do for socialism on this basis and during these years." He summed it up at the end: "Neither owes the other anything, each owes all to *the third cause*. Thus, as if we were meeting for the first time, should we try to make ourselves pleasant to one another." But only four days later Brecht had evidently forgotten the principles he had— not without bitterness—set down. In one of his most personal letters he acknowledged the following qualities in his irreplaceable collaborator and friend: generosity such as he had never before encountered; tremendous modesty, which invariably worked to his advantage; Chinese industry in all work done for him; fearlessness in her unwavering support for him, regardless of intrigues against herself; "independence of spirit, such as one rarely finds elsewhere"; and "an instinct for what is important, which is equally rare."

The published edition of Brecht's poems contains a quatrain that runs: "Failings / You had none / I had one: / I loved." This poem was discovered in two places: in a letter to Brecht from Ruth Berlau and among her manuscripts on a page containing others of her poems. Ruth Berlau might even have been the author of these lines. What they express applies to them both.

Ruth Berlau signed many of her letters to Brecht "your creature." She regarded Brecht as her teacher and accepted her role as pupil. She was willing to be his creation. The process that led to her becoming dependent on him was not foreseen, and for a long time she fought against it.

When Brecht met her in 1933 she was an actress at the Royal Theater in Copenhagen, an accredited journalist, and she occupied a respected position in bourgeois society as the wife of a skillful and prosperous physician, Dr. Robert Lund. At the same time she was regarded affectionately by members of the progressive workers' movement, as much on account of her disregard for privilege as for her initiative in founding and running a workers' theater. Her beauty attracted attention wherever she went, and her willingness to help ensured that she was much sought after. Under the sobriquet of "Red Ruth" she even achieved a certain amount of fame throughout the country.

Brecht found himself at that time in a completely different situation. His fame lay behind him, he was just an unknown emigrant. He was living outside the language area in which he could articulate his ideas, he had no theater in which to try out his plays in his own way,

and there was no publisher greedily awaiting his manuscripts. The friends he wished to consult were scattered
all over the world, either entirely out of reach or available
only for short periods when he could persuade them to
visit him in Denmark. Keeping in touch through letters
was never anything but a poor substitute. He wrote at
that time: "Teaching without pupils / Writing without
fame / Are difficult," and "There speaks the man to whom
no one is listening: / He speaks too loud / He repeats
himself / He says things that are wrong: / He goes uncorrected."

When Brecht met Ruth Berlau, he must have looked
on her as a gift from heaven. He lost no time in making
use of her as an interpreter and assistant in a foreign
land. Ruth Berlau arranged and ordered and mediated
whenever she was asked or herself saw the need. She put
up Brecht's guests and looked after them, supplied him
with an old Ford car, organized journeys, introduced him
to various people, helped to obtain visas. All of this had
to be learned, for she was not by nature practical, and
up till then she herself had always been looked after by
others. But she concealed her lack of experience so as
not to discourage Brecht from making his requests. She
quickly grasped what was needed.

There was yet another aspect of Ruth Berlau that Brecht
found fascinating. He enjoyed the uninhibited glee with
which she flung herself on his manuscripts and kept on
demanding more. She could also listen to him for hours
on end. Participation in and approval of his work always
acted on Brecht like an elixir, in the same way that the
absence of an echo could produce boredom and atrophy.
The significance to Brecht of Ruth Berlau's activities in
translating and producing his plays can scarcely be overestimated. There were few opportunities in exile for put-

ting his work to the test. He saw that he was needed, and that he was in a position to help. Each production provided the impulse for further work together.

In 1939, no longer feeling secure in Denmark, Brecht moved to Sweden. When he decided to leave that country as well and flee farther into Finland (where he also did not intend to stay), he feared that his ties with Ruth Berlau could be broken, and he asked her to follow him into exile. In her memoirs Ruth Berlau quotes from a letter Brecht sent her at that time: "It is not for your sake, Ruth, that I am reckoning on your coming, but for my own." That left her no other choice. She abandoned husband and family, put country and native language behind her, gave up her financial independence, and from then on was bound to Brecht entirely, for better or for worse. From that time on, she wore an iron ring on her finger. The compact it symbolized she honored her whole life long, *et prope et procul*, near and far.

Ruth Berlau had to accept the immeasurable consequences of her decision. In later years she often asked whether what she did had been right, and she wondered what her life would have been if she had rejected Brecht's plea. There was of course no possible answer to that. She even put the question to Brecht himself. He was not embarrassed, and he had no scruples. In his opinion Ruth Berlau had already made up her mind to follow him when she turned away from Robert Lund and transferred her love to him. The fact that he had forced her into this "act of liberation" was forgotten. But in 1938 he himself described the process in a poem which he dedicated to Ruth Berlau:

THE CRUTCHES

Seven years I could not walk a step.
When I to the great physician came
He demanded: Why the crutches?
And I told him: I am lame.

He replied: That's not surprising.
Be so good and try once more.
If you're lame, it's these contraptions.
Fall then! Crawl across the floor!

And he took my lovely crutches
Laughing with a fiend's grimace
Broke them both across my back and
Threw them in the fireplace.

Well, I'm cured now: I can walk.
Cured by nothing more than laughter.
Sometimes, though, when I see sticks
I walk worse for some hours after.

Before, Ruth Berlau had always returned to Copenhagen after a meeting with Brecht. Now there was nowhere to return to. The consequences affected not only her and Brecht; Helene Weigel found her generosity and patience put to a new and severe test. She had already been obliged to accede to Margarete Steffin's accompanying the family wherever they went. Now she tried at least to keep Ruth Berlau at arm's length. She relied on her knowledge that Brecht shied away from radical decisions. And she had the sympathetic understanding of Hella Wuolijoki, on whose summer estate in Marlebäck Brecht and Margarete Steffin were living. When a third woman arrived, Brecht felt the need of an explanation.

He wrote to Hella Wuolijoki, "Just to help you understand why I feel to some extent responsible for Ruth: When the Nazi machine starts to function properly in Copenhagen, it will be quite impossible to conceal all the things she did in cooperation with me. Not just that Helli and I stayed with her in Copenhagen and she with us in Svendborg—she also staged *Señora Carrar*, got two plays put on in the Royal Theater (*St. Joan of the Stockyards* and a ballet), and above all published the *Svendborg Poems* as a private subscription. And there are evil things in those about the Nazis. And on top of that she appeared in many anti-Nazi shows, reciting poems by me! In my opinion she cannot go back until the war is over."

Brecht failed to mention their intimate personal relationship. Curiously enough, he was always convinced that he had camouflaged all his love affairs so effectively that no one around him had the least idea. In fact, they were as clear as daylight. The women themselves took care of that. Ruth Berlau, too, saw no reason to conceal herself and play the game according to Brecht's rules. Thus she was obliged to suffer hurts she had done nothing to deserve. When in America life among the emigrants started to return to normal, she was no longer prepared to put up with Brecht's uncertainty with regard to their relationship. After spending a year in Santa Monica, sometimes needed, sometimes merely tolerated, but at all times dependent on Brecht's decisions, she went off to a women's congress in Washington. It was an excuse for putting a distance between Brecht and herself without causing an argument. She had no intention of returning to California, but she kept silent about that. A position in the Office of War Information in New York gave her the chance of earning her own living. She went to Santa Monica only on visits of limited duration. But she was successful in persuading Brecht to come to her in New

York, usually twice a year for several months. She then had him entirely to herself.

In his letters Brecht showed a liking for coded formulations. A reference to the constellation of Cassiopeia was among them: where their eyes would meet while they were living far apart; also the initials *e.p.e.p.* (near and far) and *j.e.d.* (I love you), when Brecht would underline the *d* up to seven times according to the current state of his affections; the demand that "the brow must be smooth," his image of a tranquil love for him; and finally the constantly recurring question, "Is everything all right?" the answer to which he expected to be an avowal of sexual fidelity. To this Ruth Berlau always replied frankly and with a clear conscience. She could not bring herself to gloss over the single "slip" of which she had been guilty. Brecht did not praise her for her honesty but reprimanded her for having been unfaithful. All the time she was well aware that if he had anything to admit, he would lie shamelessly. Usually he evaded the question, leaving her to read between the lines. On both sides jealousy reared its head. At times the correspondence petered out in mutual reproaches based on mere suspicions, and at times, for the same reason, it was broken off entirely. Tension and even serious differences developed over "the eternal petty bourgeois problem," which Brecht attempted to brush aside but that nevertheless continued so obstinately to occupy his mind.

His constant efforts to cover his tracks and take the wind out of the sails of the gossips could assume grotesque proportions. Ruth Berlau was sharing an apartment with her friend Ida Bachmann. When Brecht came on a visit, Ida Bachmann moved somewhere else temporarily. The day after his departure Brecht sent an express letter to Ruth Berlau: "On Sunday, in the train, it suddenly occurred to me that I had forgotten to remind you to put the nightgowns out of sight—those white, grandmotherly ones—on account of the Bachmann woman. I hope you did so. But it was nice of you to wear them all the time. I can still see you in them. There is something of the old times in them, yet also something of the new. J.e.d." Such apprehension Ruth Berlau could dismiss as a comic idiosyncrasy. On the other hand, she did not find it comic when, in the summer of 1944, Brecht advised her to leave New York temporarily because two women they both knew in California had given notice of paying her a visit. Brecht did not want her pregnancy known, "since all my acquaintances here are only waiting for a chance to denounce me as a Don Juan." And she never forgave Brecht for the way in which he recorded the birth of their child in his diary: "Ruth had an operation." That he also entered down the price he had paid for Michel's cremation and for the urn—forty dollars—was something she likewise never forgave.

Yet even then Ruth Berlau did not give up. She stayed on in New York when, after the hearing in Washington, Brecht boarded a plane for Europe, in order to document for him the second production of *Galileo*. Her hopes had been set on sharing a home with him in Switzerland. But by the time she arrived there the studio he had told her about had been given up and he had gone to live with Helene Weigel. Ruth Berlau went to Germany, to the American zone of occupation, which Brecht was forbidden to enter, and busied herself on his behalf with publishing contracts and stage productions. She fell down, however, on Brecht's instruction to get hold of a car for him—a truly absurd commission at that particular time. She then pinned her hopes on Berlin, and for a time seemed to be within reach of her goal. After rehearsals Brecht came regularly to her apartment in Charitéstrasse, where he had his lunch and rested and also often received friends and colleagues. In 1953 Helene Weigel decided on a divorce. She was now standing firmly on her own two feet, the children had long left home, and she had had enough of turning a blind eye on Brecht's amorous relationships. The house in Weissensee was given up, and Helene Weigel and Brecht moved to separate apartments close to the theater. However, this arrangement lasted only a short while. Brecht needed Helene Weigel. And he needed her for his work in the theater, not for any vague idea of keeping up the pretense of an idyllic family life. The fact that he had once promised Ruth Berlau, "when the time is ripe," to share his life with her, "even if only in an attic to start with"—all this, even if it had ever been meant seriously, was long forgotten. How often had he assured women that the other "stories" were totally meaningless! In the final run the assurance was valid only for Helene Weigel. Painful as it must often have been, she had exercised remarkable patience in the way she always awaited his return. She was also shrewd. She furnished the house at the rear of Chausseestrasse 125 as a joint home. She herself lived on the second floor, Brecht had his quarters on the first, and the ground floor was designed as a common dining room. This arrangement meant that Brecht was no longer obliged to eat his lunch in Charitéstrasse 3 with Ruth Berlau.

For Ruth Berlau this was a great blow. In her desperation she chose the wrong methods of achieving the aim on which her eyes were so firmly fixed. She tortured Brecht with her boundless jealousy. She hindered him in his work—at home by constantly besieging him with telephone calls, in which she alternately swore her love for him and covered him with abuse; and at conferences in the theater, where she allowed herself to be swept into acts of the maddest sort. She was capable of disrupting a rehearsal to such an extent that Brecht would lose his nerve and break it off. She even struck him. In the hopelessness of her situation she took more and more to drink, and then she would blame Brecht for making her drunk. Several times she had to undergo psychiatric treatment, which served only to exacerbate her nervous excitement. She felt betrayed.

But Brecht too was helpless. His efforts to transform the love relationship into a working relationship proved of no avail. Once, long ago, Ruth Berlau had learned from Brecht that love and collaboration went hand in hand, that one could not be isolated from the other. At this stage it was only on the surface that she appeared, when Brecht gave her a specific task to do, to recover her former confidence. He appointed her to direct *Mother Courage and Her Children* in Holland, and sent her to the Scandinavian countries to seek productions of his plays or to arrange tours for the Berliner Ensemble. She was grateful for this sign of confidence and spent much time and energy preparing for her task. But hardly had she left Berlin when the suspicion would enter her mind that Brecht's only aim was to get rid of her, and that was why he was sending her away. Her suspicions were not without foundation, and she clung tenaciously to her imaginings, with the result that actors and theater managers found themselves faced with a colleague with whom there was no getting on.

For as long as Brecht was alive she remained under his protection. Whenever it was possible, he went to her defense, even against his better judgment. Whoever clashed swords with Ruth Berlau had to keep a careful eye on Brecht. But with his death she lost her whole support. The management of the Berliner Ensemble gave her notice to quit; they did not have to look far for reasons. She was forbidden to enter the theater; for that too there were reasons. The question of moral obligation was conveniently ignored. But what was she now to live on? Hanns Eisler lent his aid, the Writers' Association (*Schriftstellerverband*) provided her with some support, and the Academy of Arts (*Akademie der Künste*) bought Brecht manuscripts from her. It was some time before she received the pension due to her as a victim of Nazi aggression. That at least paid for her keep.

Worst of all, her younger friends turned away from her, the writers and theater people to whom she had been a marvelous counselor, a confidante in regard to their private interests, and a helper always willing to be imposed upon. Ruth Berlau spent the last years of her life in loneliness, deserted, indeed actively avoided, by the very people who had most reason to be grateful to her. I myself was among them at the end. She had given her help to everybody, yet during a long and difficult period when she herself urgently needed affection, there was no one to help her. Certainly her impulsiveness was not easy to bear. But however much patience might be required, it was nothing in comparison with the patience Ruth Berlau herself had shown in helping Brecht's pupils to find their way out of the catastrophe of fascist Germany and to grasp the significance of Brecht, his political outlook, his working methods, and his theater. All that his pupils knew about Brecht's life in exile was learned not from him but from Ruth Berlau.

She had no intention of simply sinking out of sight and leaving the world without a trace. She rose up and spread the fictional news that she was still playing an immensely useful, indeed indispensable, part in the story of Brechtian theater. This chapter in her life, the penultimate one, is perhaps the saddest of all. She told everyone, whether willing to listen or not, what articles and what books about Brecht she was in the process of writing or was planning to write. In fact, she was no longer capable of undertaking any such work. She gave accounts of lectures she had given or intended to give, though nobody had invited her to do so. She reported on her contribution to conferences that had never taken place. She canceled meetings because she had foreign guests to look after, but none of them ever arrived. She answered the telephone in a disguised voice, saying, "Ruth Berlau's office," in order to give an impression of her importance, but the disguised voice was unmistakably her own. Her situation was pitiable.

While Ruth Berlau was thus struggling for survival, she looked in vain for friends to sympathize with her and give her the courage to continue. There were only two exceptions, neither of them belonging to the circle from which morally such help should have come. They came on the scene on their own initiative. One was the great actress Elisabeth Bergner, who had become a close friend in the years of American exile, and who kept up the tie, even though their meetings over twenty-five years were only occasional and of short duration. The other consisted of Johannes Hoffmann and his family, who looked after Ruth Berlau during the final six years of her life. This entitles them to admiration and respect, for it demanded patience and unselfishness, often indeed self-denial. Johannes Hoffmann and his Bulgarian wife were able to give her the help she needed. In their company she recovered her tranquility and her mental balance. She became wise in her old age.

At the beginning of the seventies Ruth Berlau's health declined. A hip complaint that was diagnosed much too late and that obliged her, following an operation, to wear orthopedic shoes and walk with a stick, flared up again. Her body was also weakened in other respects by a way of life that was unsparing toward herself. She suffered from sleeplessness. The doctors decided to send her to the hospital. Ruth Berlau bore the medical examinations and treatments with equanimity, speaking sarcastically of the need for a "general overhaul" and her chances following an "all-round renovation." On January 15, 1974, she learned that a room had been reserved for her in an old people's home for victims of Nazi aggression. The decision to give up forever her apartment in Charité-strasse appeared to cause her no pangs. She needed constant nursing.

On her final evening in the hospital, after the night nurse had made her rounds, she drank one or two glasses of wine and smoked a cigarette. Nobody knows exactly what happened then. She must have fallen asleep while still smoking. The subsequent smoldering fire went unnoticed. She was suffocated before the flames broke through, shattering the window panes. When it was at last possible to enter the room, she was found lying in her bed as on the previous evening. The day of her death was recorded as January 15, 1974.

In my memory she is still living in the apartment in which she so often sat with Brecht, in the room containing the standing desk at which many a work of his was written, the stool that he carried around with him through all the years of exile, the copper and pewter vessels they gave each other as presents, the bureau in which his books and letters were kept, and the tattered red flag that was borne on the stage in her production of *The Mother* in Copenhagen forty years previously, at the time she first met Brecht.

Her wish to have her ashes strewn in the sea at a place from which they would be carried by the waves to Denmark could not be fulfilled. The urn was laid to rest in Berlin, in the Dorotheenstadt cemetery where Bertolt Brecht also lies. She was not in Berlin at the time of his funeral. But over a period of close to eighteen years she paid regular visits to his grave. She still loved him, and she remained full of gratitude toward him, for her life was Brecht's life, her work was Brecht's work, her worries were Brecht's worries, both after his death and up to her own.

In 1939 Brecht wrote a poem for Ruth Berlau that he dedicated to her. Hanns Eisler set it to music, and Ernst Busch sang it to her. For Ruth Berlau herself it was a sacred possession.

ARDENS SED VIRENS

Splendid, what the lovely fire
Cannot turn to chilly ash!
Sister, you're my heart's desire
Burning, and yet still intact.

Many I saw slyly cooling
Hotheads stunned by ignoring fact.
Sister, you repay my schooling
Burning, and yet still intact.

In the battle you'd no horse on
Which to ride off when attacked
So I watched you fight with caution
Burning, and yet still intact.

Ruth Berlau asked me once whether the final strophe should not rather be:

In the battle you'd *a* horse on
Which to ride off when attacked

276

Yet I watched you fight with caution
Burning, and yet still intact.

I could not deny it.

It was Ruth Berlau's wish to tell the story of her love for Brecht and their work together. Several times, during Brecht's lifetime and afterward, she set out to give an account of their association of more than twenty years. But she did not have—or no longer had—the strong nerves and the staying power to describe so close, changeable, and complicated a relationship, neither from a subjective nor—least of all—from an objective point of view.

She was not the only one to face these difficulties. Elisabeth Hauptmann, too, was defeated by the same self-imposed task. She took refuge in her labor on the collected edition of Brecht's works. Once it became clear that she would never write her reminiscences, I made frequent attempts to persuade Elisabeth Hauptmann to describe her time with Brecht in a connected series of conversations. Unfortunately, I had no success, and just as unfortunately, nobody committed to paper the many anecdotes she would tell from time to time.

With Ruth Berlau I had more luck. My demand for her memoirs met with success. Once she had listened to my taped interviews with Hanns Eisler, she was interested in attempting a similar experiment. In the period from mid-September to mid-October 1959 we had a total of seven sessions together, starting in Prieros an der Dahme, where Ruth Berlau was recuperating in Hanns Eisler's summer dwelling, and ending in her Berlin apartment, Charitéstrasse 3. Our conversation took the form of interviews. No documents were used, with the exception of Brecht's own texts: Ruth Berlau relied solely on her memory. The frankness with which she replied to my questions was founded on years of friendship between us. Despite that, she did not tell the whole truth. Ruth Berlau, three years after Brecht's death, thought of future readers and kept silent about certain of her sufferings. Thus, perhaps even unintentionally, there remains a gap between things as they really happened and as they are described.

Ruth Berlau did not imagine that our conversations could be put to use or published at an early date, if indeed at all. She always assumed that the possibility would arise only after her own and Helene Weigel's death. She saw the transcriptions of our talks and gave me a free hand with their editing, which she not only considered necessary but on which in fact she insisted. Ruth Berlau trusted me, for since 1953 I had been editing practically everything she wrote in German, at her request and always to her complete satisfaction. Revision was necessary, since she spoke a curious, heavily accented, Danish type of German. A certain amount of experience was necessary in order, while listening, to understand everything correctly. Reading what she wrote presented even more difficulties. Ruth Berlau always freely admitted that her knowledge of German grammar was incomplete, and there was her very idiosyncratic handwriting to contend with as well, possibly interspersed with typing errors into the bargain. All that taken together could render a sentence utterly unintelligible. Untroubled by such considerations, she wrote it all down as fast as it came into her mind and left the corrections to others. It took a lot of practice before I got used to her peculiarities, ironed out the mistakes, and discovered the correct meaning.

In this edition I have cut out my questions, since their

function was exhausted in conversation and a continuous narrative seemed to me more attractive. What was said during several conversations on one particular subject I have brought together, and I have eliminated repetitions, except where they impart new aspects. In the opposite direction, I have interpolated certain passages written down during other conversations between us, when I considered they had something to add. However, I have used a light hand and have remained faithful to the manuscript Ruth Berlau knew, as far as it was possible. I have made no attempt to amend factual errors, neither by altering the text nor by supplying footnotes. Authors of memoirs must be granted the right to tell their story as it exists in their own memory. Every story is a mixture of fact and fiction, and it invariably provides an entirely personal view of the events described. Which of us can claim proprietary rights to the truth? But to avoid misunderstandings: Ruth Berlau had a great regard for the truth; there is evidence enough of that. And this book will have shown how little she spared herself. The sovereign manner in which she depicts herself is something I find particularly endearing.

This book is neither a work of science, nor is it literature in the true sense of the word. It is a spontaneously uttered account of the experiences of a lifetime, coupled with a number of reflections. Thus must its contents be read, and each component be left to speak for itself. For the form in which these are here presented in print I must accept my share of the responsibility.

For the section entitled "Occasional Writings" I have chosen pieces by Ruth Berlau preserved in my own archives. They are intended as a corrective to the memoirs. The aim is to balance the one-sidedness of the former against the one-sidedness of the latter, for in effect they represent the two sides of a single coin. My hope is that the reader will not seek to evade the issue by picking out only the parts he finds pleasing.

Hans Bunge
May 1985

Chronology ✒

1929 Bertolt Brecht (1898–1956) married Helene Weigel (1900–1971). Their children: Stefan (b.1924) and Barbara (b.1930).

1930 Ruth Berlau joined the communist party.

1932 Ruth Berlau founded workers' theater in Copenhagen.

1933 Brecht and Weigel arrived at Thurø in June, moving to Skovsbostrand, Denmark, in December. Margarete Steffin joined Brecht in Denmark (Dec.).

1934 Brecht worked with Hanns Eisler on *Round Heads and Pointed Heads* (Mar.); wrote the *Dreigroschenroman* (summer); started *Fear and Misery of the Third Reich*; visited England (Oct.–Dec.). Berlau produced *The Mother* in Copenhagen (Oct.).

1935 Brecht started work on the "Me-ti" stories. Berlau played scenes from *Saint Joan of the Stockyards* in Copenhagen. Her novel *Videre* published. Brecht in New York for production of *The Mother* (Nov.).

1936 Brecht and Berlau worked on *Jedes Tier kann es.* Berlau separated from Robert Lund. Brecht in London for work on *I Pagliacci* film; Berlau in Wales (Jul.). *Round Heads and Pointed Heads* and *The Seven Deadly Sins* produced in Copenhagen (Nov.).

1937 Brecht and Berlau in Paris for Writers' Congress; Berlau went on to Spain. Brecht wrote *Señora Carrar's Rifles* (Paris premiere Oct.); Berlau produced *Carrar* in Danish in Copenhagen (Dec.).

1938 Brecht and Berlau wrote *Alle wissen alles*; Brecht wrote his first "Lai-tu" story. Premiere of *Fear and Misery* in Paris (May). Brecht completed first version of *Life of Galileo* (Nov.). Berlau's first meeting with Hella Wuolijoki while acting in her play.

1939 Brecht and family left Denmark for Sweden (Apr.); Steffin followed later. Berlau published the *Svendborg Poems* in Copenhagen (spring). Brecht wrote *What's the Price of Iron?*; completed *Mother Courage* (Nov.).

1940 Brecht, with family and Steffin, left Sweden for Finland (Apr.); Berlau joined them shortly after. Brecht completed *The Good Person of Szechwan* (Jun.); began work on *Puntila* with Wuolijoki (completed Sept.). *Flüchtlingsgespräche* begun in Oct.

1941 Brecht wrote *Arturo Ui* (Mar.–Apr.). Brecht and family, Steffin, and Berlau left Finland for Moscow (May 13), where Steffin died (June 4). The Brechts and Berlau sailed from Vladivostok on June 13, arrived in California on July 21, and rented houses in Santa Monica. Brecht started work on film scripts in Dec.

1942 Berlau moved to New York (May). Brecht started work on film script of *Hangmen Also Die* (completed Dec.); wrote *The Visions of Simone Machard* with Lion Feuchtwanger (Nov.–Jan. 1944).

1943 Brecht's first visit to New York (Feb.–May); wrote *Schweyk in the Second World War* upon return to Santa Monica (completed Oct.). Brecht's second visit to New York (Nov.–Mar. 1944); worked with W. H. Auden on *The Duchess of Malfi* and began *The Caucasian Chalk Circle* (completed summer 1944).

1944 Brecht met Charles Laughton (Apr.) and started revising *Galileo* (completed Dec. 1945). Berlau lost her New York job and returned temporarily to Hollywood (summer). Her son Michel born Sept. 3 in Los Angeles and died a few days later. Brecht met Charles Chaplin. Berlau began photographic archive of Brecht's works (Dec.).

1945 Brecht began work on versification of Communist Manifesto (Feb.). Berlau returned to New York (Mar.). Brecht in New York for premiere of *The Private Life of the Master Race* (Jun.); visited Elisabeth Bergner in Vermont and finished work on *The Duchess of Malfi* (Jul.). Returned to Santa Monica; completed *Galileo* with Laughton.

1946 *The Duchess of Malfi* opened in Boston (Sept.) and then New York (Oct.). Brecht in New York at this time.

1947 Brecht worked on various film projects in Hollywood. *Galileo* premiered in Beverly Hills (Jul.).

Brecht in New York with Berlau (Oct.). Hanns Eisler appeared before House Committee on Un-American Activities (Sept.); Brecht testified (Oct.). Brecht flew to Switzerland (Nov. 1). *Galileo* opened in New York (Dec.). Brecht and Weigel settled in Feldmeilen, near Zurich (Nov.); Brecht completed *Antigone* (Dec.).

1948 Berlau arrived in Zurich (Jan.). *Antigone* premiere in Chur (Feb.). Berlau went to Germany to look after Brecht's affairs. Brecht wrote *Little Organon for the Theater* before leaving for Berlin with Weigel (Oct.).

1949 First performance of *Mother Courage* in Berlin (Jan.). Weigel set up Berliner Ensemble office in Die Möwe (Feb.) and home in Weissensee. Brecht returned to Switzerland with Berlau to write *The Days of the Commune* (Feb.–May). On return to Berlin, Berlau set up home in Charitéstrasse. Berliner Ensemble opened with *Mr. Puntila and His Man Matti* (Nov.).

1950 Berlau directed *The Mother* in Leipzig (Jan.); hospitalized after nervous breakdown (Mar.). Brecht adapted *The Tutor* (Berlin premiere Apr.). Berlau directed *Mother Courage* in Rotterdam (Dec.).

1951 *The Mother* produced in Berlin (Jan.). Brecht and Berlau worked on *Mother Courage* model book and *Theaterarbeit*. Berlau in Greiz at end of year to supervise *Antigone* production.

1952 *Urfaust* produced in Potsdam (Apr.); *Señora Carrar's Rifles* in Berlin (Nov.). Brecht acquired summer villa in Buckow.

1953 Brecht spent summer in Buckow, wrote *Buckower Elegien* and *Turandot.* He and Weigel sold their house in Weissensee and, after a short separation, set up new home in Chausseestrasse, Berlin (Oct.). Rehearsals began on *The Caucasian Chalk Circle* (Nov.).

1954 Berliner Ensemble opened at Theater am Schiff-bauerdamm with *Don Juan* (Mar.). Berliner Ensemble in Paris with *Mother Courage* (Jun.–Jul.). *The Caucasian Chalk Circle* opened in Berlin (Oct.).

1955 Becher's *Winterschlacht* opened in Berlin (Jan.). Berliner Ensemble in Paris with *Chalk Circle* (Jun.). Brecht and Berlau revised the *Antigone* model book for the Henschelverlag. Brecht started *Galileo* rehearsals in Berlin (Dec.). Berlau in Copenhagen.

1956 Brecht in Rostock for Besson's production of *The Good Person of Szechwan* (Jan.) and in Milan with Hauptmann for *The Threepenny Opera.* Rehearsed *Galileo* in Berlin. Brecht died on Aug. 14.

1974 Berlau died on Jan. 15.

Index

287

Braunbock, Carola, 187
Brecht, Barbara, 23, 83, 101,
102, 103, 108, 146
Brecht, Bertolt, *passim*. Plays:
see *Alle wissen alles*; *Antigone*;
Caucasian Chalk Circle, The;
Dansen; *Days of the Com-
mune, The*; *Drums in the
Night*; *Duchess of Malfi, The*;
Edward the Second; *Fear and
Misery of the Third Reich*;
*Good Person of Szechwan,
The*; *Happy End*; *Life of Gali-
leo*; *Mother, The*; *Mother
Courage and Her Children*;
*Mr. Puntila and His Man
Matti*; *Pauken und Trompe-
ten*; *Report from Herrnburg*;
*Resistible Rise of Arturo Ui,
The*; *Round Heads and
Pointed Heads*; *Saint Joan of
the Stockyards*; *Schweyk in
the Second World War*; *Señ-
ora Carrar's Rifles*; *Seven
Deadly Sins, The*; *Step, The*;
Threepenny Opera, The; *Tur-
andot*; *Tutor, The*; *Visions of
Simone Machard, The*; *What's
the Price of Iron?* Poems, 27,
28, 30, 42, 48, 49, 73, 109,
125, 129, 142, 185, 222, 224,
245, 257, 264, 265, 267, 276;
see also: *Buckow Elegies*;
Communist Manifesto (versification of); *Kriegsfibel*;
Svendborg Poems. Prose
works, 84, 87, 104; see also:
Dreigroschenroman; *Flüchtlingsgespräche*; *Jedes Tier
kann es*; "Lai-tu" stories; *Little Organon for the Theater*;
Me-ti/Buch der Wendungen;
Modellbücher. Scripts for
films, 112–16. Working

methods as theater director,
55–56, 72, 122, 153–56,
166–70, 179, 180–81, 186–
88, 191–97. Working meth-
ods as writer, 63, 69–70, 72,
73–77, 88, 98–99, 177–78,
183–85, 253–58, 265–66
Brecht, Stefan, 23, 83, 101,
102, 103–04, 108, 182, 254
Bredel, Willi, 48
Buckow Elegies, 42
Buckwitz, Harry, 160, 242
Budzislawski, Hermann, 128,
146
Bunge, Hans, 190–91, 249–80
passim
Burg, Ursula, 180
Busch, Ernst, 48, 122, 276

*Caucasian Chalk Circle, The
(Der kaukasische Kreidekreis)*,
157–58, 159–60, 162, 189,
208–13, 257
Chaplin, Charles, 141–43, 149,
156
Christoffersen, Gerda, 43, 44
Communist Manifesto (versifi-
cation of), 129, 152–53, 182,
184, 254
Curjel, Hans, 168, 169–70
Czinner, Paul, 136

Dansen, 257
*Days of the Commune, The (Die
Tage der Commune)*, 18, 86,
175–79, 180, 257
Dessau, Paul, 162, 164, 173,
185
Donath, Ludwig, 96
Dreigroschenroman, 62–63,
171, 257
*Drums in the Night (Trommeln
in der Nacht)*, 14, 21, 64

288